Wages Prices Profits and Productivity

Final Edition

Background papers and the Final Report of the Fifteenth American Assembly, Arden House, Harriman Campus of Columbia University, Harriman, New York April 30-May 3, 1959

The American Assembly
Columbia University
June 1959

PRINTED IN U.S.A.

Library of Congress Catalog Card No. 59-12574

Preface

Wages, Prices, Profits and Productivity was the subject of the Fifteenth American Assembly at Arden House, Harriman, New York, April 30-May 3, 1959. About sixty Americans from business, labor, government, agriculture, education, communications and the clerical, legal and military professions engaged in three days of round table discussions, ending with a final report approved in plenary session on the fourth day. That report appears in this volume beginning on page 181.

Formal addresses were given at the Assembly by Secretary of Labor James P. Mitchell, and Sumner Slichter of Harvard University.

As with previous American Assemblies, so with the Fifteenth: the national meeting at Arden House will be followed by at least three regional assemblies.

The papers which follow, prepared under the editorial supervision of Dr. Charles Myers of Massachusetts Institute of Technology, served as background for the Fifteenth Assembly and will be used at the regional meetings. The essays reflect the thought and experience of the individual authors. The American Assembly itself takes no official stand on the subjects of its sessions.

Basic research amounting to one-tenth of the cost of the Fifteenth Assembly program was paid for by a grant from the Rockefeller Foundation. Other costs are to be met by a grant from the Maurice and Laura Falk Foundation of Pittsburgh. The Assembly expresses its thanks and warm appreciation.

THE AMERICAN ASSEMBLY
Henry M. Wriston
President

Contents

Introduction:

Central issues in wage-price relationships

CHARLES A. MYERS *Editor*

Are prices being pushed up by wage increases, or are wages simply following prices upward in the spiral of creeping inflation caused by other factors? These are simple and controversial questions which mask a complexity of factual data and analysis. The facts—and the blame—are hotly debated in the public press, by labor and management at collective bargaining sessions and also publicly, and even by professional economists who do not always agree among themselves.

Furthermore, the issues involved in the controversy are important for public policy. Widespread concern for the maintenance of "a stable dollar"

CHARLES A. MYERS is Professor of Industrial Relations and Director of the Industrial Relations Section in the Department of Economics and Social Science, Massachusetts Institute of Technology.

He has been at M.I.T. since 1939, except for absences during the War when he served in the Labor Division of the War Production Board and subsequently as a Public Panel Member of the War Labor Board. He was a Public Member of the Regional Wage Stabilization Board in 1952-53, and has served as arbitrator in numerous labor disputes since 1944. Between 1949 and 1956 he was a member of the Committee on Labor Market Research of the Social Science Research Council and served as an elected member of the Executive Board of the Industrial Relations Research Association in 1952-55.

He is author or co-author of the following: *Movement of Factory Workers* (1943), *The Dynamics of a Labor Market* (1951), *Industrial Relations in Sweden* (1951), *Personnel Administration* (1956 3rd ed.), *Labor Problems in the Industrialization of India* (1958), as well as many other articles on wages, labor mobility, and labor-management relations.

and the avoidance of further inflation has emphasized not only the importance of government's monetary and fiscal policies (as the Fourteenth American Assembly considered), but also the need for examination of the relationships between wages, productivity, profits, and prices. In his State of the Union message to the Eighty-sixth Congress, President Eisenhower called attention to the importance of a balanced federal budget to maintain price stability and urged labor and management to exercise restraint in making wage and price increases in order "to curb the wage-price spiral." The President has also appointed a Cabinet Committee on Price Stability for Economic Growth, headed by Vice-President Nixon, and there are several other governmental committees working on various aspects of this problem. Congressional committees continue to hold hearings, so that wage-price issues are kept hot on the front burner. And if all this were not enough, collective bargaining negotiations in 1959, particularly in steel, promise front-page news and editorial comment on these issues.

We need to examine carefully, therefore, the facts on wages, prices, profits and productivity, to assess their interrelationships, and to try to unravel some of the causal connections among them. Those involved directly in the wage and price-setting mechanisms seem to find little difficulty in pointing to a particular "culprit." But sober examination of the facts and their patient analysis reveal much more complexity and suggest the need for public policies which are both realistic and workable, even though they will probably not be panaceas for the inflationary pressures confronting the American economy.

It is the purpose of the papers presented in this volume to examine both the facts and their significance for policy. Each of the authors has devoted a considerable portion of his professional life to the study of wage-price problems. Several have participated directly in earlier governmental efforts to stabilize wages and prices in periods of national emergency. Furthermore, some of them have studied at first-hand the experience of other countries in attempting to maintain stable prices through voluntary restraint or direct control of wage and price increases. Their combined study and judgment on these controversial issues provide the basis for a more informed discussion of appropriate public policies.

The problem of measurement

How much has productivity increased per year, and over different periods? What has been the increase in the "cost of living," in average hourly money earnings, in "real wages"? To answer these questions with reasonable accuracy, we must consider problems of definition and measurement. One of the very great difficulties is that most measures have a number of limitations, yet these are often lost sight of in the battleground of words about what has happened or will happen.

"Labor productivity" is used loosely in many discussions, but until recently the most common measurement was "output per man-hour" of production workers, published by the Bureau of Labor Statistics of the United States Department of Labor. One of the limitations of this measurement is that the proportion of non-production employees, such as white-collar workers, research and development staffs, etc., has been increasing. Consequently, the proportion of *production* workers to total output has been declining, and the index of output per man-hour of *production* workers has an upward bias; it does not accurately reflect the total *employee* productivity. Kendrick's paper brings out this point as well as many other difficulties in measuring productivity. Output per man-hour, he emphasizes, is only a partial productivity measurement, since it is necessary to include inputs of capital to get a measurement of real product per unit of total factor input. This will measure changes in productivity efficiency generally.

The BLS has recently released estimates of productivity which measure real product per employee man-hour paid for the private economy. These differ from its earlier index of physical output per production worker man-hour. Even this measure, as both Kendrick and the BLS have emphasized, does not measure "labor efficiency" in the sense of greater labor skill or effort in increasing output. The index will move upward for a variety of reasons: (1) increases in plant output resulting from technological change and the increased amount of capital required; (2) improvements in managerial as well as worker efficiency; (3) changes in methods, processes, and materials; (4) shifts from less efficient to more efficient plants and industries; and (5) shifts in the relative importance of industries with different levels of productivity.

While the productivity index may move upward because workers in a particular industry may work harder or have more responsibility and skill in their jobs, it can move also upward for the other reasons (principally the first). It will do so even though physical labor effort and job responsibility may be *lower* as a consequence of improved technology, processes and methods. It is important to emphasize that the measurement of productivity involves no ethical connotation of what workers or employees generally "contribute" to output and hence what they "should" receive in wages or salaries.

The limitations of existing productivity indexes have led some specialists to concentrate on the development of new and better productivity measurements. The recent work of the BLS has already been noted; the National Bureau of Economic Research has also been in the forefront of this effort. Kendrick's paper outlines some of the alternative concepts and measurements, as well as their limitations, and summarizes the available data for the period since 1889. Among other points he stresses the difference in the level of productivity when output per man-hour worked is used as compared with output per man-hour paid for. The latter more accurately reflects the fact that the increase in paid holidays and paid vacations should be included, especially if comparisons are made with total average hourly earnings (including such hours not worked but paid for). But existing data do not always permit such comparisons over a period of time, so that some productivity measurements are subject to an upward bias. Conversely, they underestimate real productivity to the extent that quality improvements cannot be measured accurately and taken into account in constructing the indexes.

Similar difficulties arise in measuring changes in "the cost of living" or, more accurately, the Consumer Price Index of the BLS. Improvements in quality are difficult to take into account, and may give the index an upward bias. On the other hand, if there has been quality deterioration, a downward bias results. Furthermore, changes in the "market basket" of goods and services, as a result of changes in family spending patterns, are reflected periodically in changes in the composition of the index. Some changes in the weights assigned to different items in 1947-49 were made in 1953 and minor ones in 1955. As a consequence, the importance of commodities in the index has declined while the importance of services has increased. If the composite index has risen, therefore, is it because the "cost of living" has risen or because the level of living ("the cost of better living") has risen? If better living is thus involved in the construction of the index, then it has an upward bias. Probably this bias is small, for the BLS has tried to construct an index which measures price changes only, and not a rise in the standard of living.

Computations of average hourly money earnings also involve debatable questions. Should they be based on hours worked, or hours paid for? To be comparable with productivity measurements using "hours paid for," the earnings index should be computed from total compensation (including paid holidays and vacations), divided by hours worked. But what about the other "wage supplements" which Rees's paper mentions? These include employer contributions for unemployment compensation and supplementary unemployment benefits, old-age and survivors' insurance, and private pension plans. If these are added, the index of total compensation rises in recent years. Finally, if the Consumer Price Index is not wholly satisfactory, then indexes of real earnings or real compensation are also partly inaccurate.

The need for better statistics and research

All of this points to the clear need for better statistical data on basic changes in the economic quantities which directly affect price and wage decisions. These are vital in each bargaining session as well as at the national level when public policies for dealing with such problems as the alleged "wage-cost push" are being hammered out. As Dr. Ewan Clague, United States Commissioner of Labor Statistics, has said, "The statistical tools which economists must use to analyze economic developments are not good enough to do the job which is needed." Will responsible representatives of labor and management, and of the Congress, demand better statistics, or will charges and counter-charges continue to be hurled with the support of inadequate or questionable data? The papers in this volume point to some of these difficulties, and illustrate how carefully couched and qualified our conclusions must be on the basis of all presently available information. Clearly, more study and research are needed on these important issues.

Trends in productivity, prices, profits and wages

With all the qualifications just mentioned, the available historical record is, nevertheless, instructive. In addition to the productivity indexes summarized in Kendrick's tables, Rees presents yearly data from 1889 through 1957 on average hourly money earnings in manufacturing, wage supplements per hour and total compensation per hour at work, together with the Consumer Price Index, total real compensation (computed in 1957 dollars per hour at work), and two productivity indexes. Some of these data for the earlier period are new, developed by Rees in a study for the National Bureau of Economic Research.

Average hourly earnings in manufacturing (including paid holidays and vacations) have increased nearly 14 times during the 69-year period, to an average of $2.08 in 1957. Other wage supplements, computed since 1929, add almost 16 cents an hour to this figure. Consumer prices have tripled since 1889, as measured by a linking of several indexes. Because money earnings rose so much faster than consumer prices, real average hourly earnings in manufacturing (total real compensation in 1957 dollars per hour at work) rose five times between 1889 and 1957.

During part of this period, output per man-hour in manufacturing rose more rapidly than real hourly earnings, as Rees points out, but after 1929, real earnings moved ahead of the productivity index. Taking Kendrick's productivity index of real product per unit of labor and capital combined (total factor input in the private economy), we find that real average hourly earnings rose at a faster rate than this measure of productivity after 1913, and much faster after 1929. During the same period there has been no upward trend in the return on capital per unit, because the total stock of capital has increased relative to labor.

None of these trends, it should be emphasized, explain the *causal* relations. The fact that real average hourly earnings outstripped total factor productivity after 1913 does not necessarily mean that wage increases made voluntarily by employers during the period or negotiated with unions were the primary *cause* of rising prices. Nothing in these data tells us what caused the greater increase in real average hourly earnings. Clearly, unions were not strong enough between 1913 and 1929 to exert an independent influence on general wage levels, whatever the merits of the argument that they have so influenced wage levels in a more recent period.

We need to look further and deeper, as does Rees in the last part of his paper and as do the other writers in the papers which follow. The picture then becomes more cloudy. Through the haze of complex interrelationships in the real world where "other things don't remain the same," we see that answers to our questions are not so clear cut, that the facts do not all point in one direction, and that informed judgment and evaluation are the best we can expect in the present state of our statistics and our knowledge.

An outline of the principal wage-price issues

Our purpose in this volume is to raise some of the most pressing issues for public discussion, and to present the best available evidence on them. The task of the introductory essay is to pose the questions and not to provide answers. Some answers are suggested by the authors of particular papers, and these authors do not always completely agree among themselves. Even informed judgment and analysis do not result in identical conclusions in this range of questions any more than they do in most other controversial and complex fields. Perhaps those who have all the answers do not start with all the relevant questions, or consider all the available evidence dispassionately. The first step toward more informed public discussion of the issues, therefore, is to ask the right series of questions. The following may contribute to this goal.

1. The measurements: their usefulness and limitations

Accurate and generally understood measurements of productivity, wages, prices, and profits are needed for the process of setting wages and prices in hundreds and thousands of centers of decision-making. Effective and equitable public policies designed to maintain price stability and economic growth depend upon reliable data on these economic dimensions. But, as we have noted and as the papers bring out more clearly, there are important limitations in the existing indexes, and they should be used with more caution than they have been in many public discussions. How can the adequacy and accuracy of these important indexes be improved? Should additional funds be appropriated to improve the collection of data, the construction of the indexes, and the widespread public dissemination of their meaning? To what extent can we rely on existing measurements without further improvement in their coverage or quality? Which of the available indexes of productivity and wages (or earnings) should be used in evaluating private decisions and in guiding public policies? Does a review of the long-term relationships between these indexes throw any light on the present controversy over "cost-push" or "wage-induced" inflation?

2. The role of wages and prices in the postwar inflation

The growth of a strong labor movement in the United States after 1933, the postwar wave of strikes and substantial wage settlements, and the tendency of unions and workers to expect periodic wage increases have all combined to focus public attention on rising wages as a cause of the postwar inflation. Union leaders and others have countered by pointing the finger at industrial price policies and profits as more basic explanations of rising prices. In most public discussions, some weight is also given to demand factors, particularly to government expenditures. But the tendency is to assess the blame rather than to analyze the causes of the postwar inflation.

What are the facts on the movements of wages and prices in the different sectors of the economy since 1947? How do the rates of change compare? Is there any significant distinction between parts of the 12-year period from the beginning of 1947 through 1958? How do movements in labor productivity compare with wage movements? To what extent does the "demand pull" explanation help us to understand the wage and price behavior of this period as compared to the "cost push" or "wage induced" explanation? What has been the role of profit margins in relation to price changes during this period? Can we say anything about the causal relationship? What significance has the condition of the postwar labor market in general and in particular occupations or industries had in explaining wage movements? Were government monetary and fiscal policies responsible for the "demand pull" on costs during this period, or any part of it, and to what extent? Considering all of the evidence, what is the most generally valid explanation of the postwar inflation in the United States?

3. Labor movements and their impact on wages and prices

Unions in the United States are strongly organized in certain manufacturing industries such as steel and autos, as well as in mining and heavy construction; but union membership is a much smaller proportion of the labor force in cotton textiles and chemicals, for example, and in the service industries generally, such as banking, insurance, finance, and trade. Moreover, wage bargaining is seldom on a national or centralized basis, even though the phenomenon of "pattern bargaining" has evolved in the postwar period of full employment. But the labor movements of other countries are often different from ours; there is more centralized wage bargaining in Sweden and in the Netherlands, for example. Deliberate policies of "wage restraint" have been followed by these labor movements in some postwar years, as a part of a governmental program (often a labor government) for economic recovery or stability. Even within the American labor movement there have been different approaches to wage-price relations. Some unions appear unconcerned about the impact of wage demands on prices; others relate or profess to relate wage bargaining to the prosperity of the firm or industry, and its ability to remain competitive or to avoid price increases.

What is the relationship of different types or classifications of unions and labor movements to wage-price policies? What has been their impact on wage changes and price-level changes? Are there significant differences between the types of labor movements and the changes in wages and prices? Does the available evidence point to the superiority of any one type of labor movement over the others in helping to maintain price stability? What implications does this have for general economic policies directed toward avoiding inflation?

4. Conditions leading to a cost-push or wage-induced inflation

A cost-push inflation may develop because some important cost component, such as the price of imported raw materials, rises as a result of external influences which may be caused by a demand pull (as during the Korean War). This example illustrates the interrelationships between demand and costs, and the great difficulty in attributing all of the influence to one factor. The cost-push influence may also result, as Reynolds points out in his paper, when some strong interest group in the economy strives to improve its relative position, as in the case of the farm bloc, certain manufacturers and retailers' organizations, as well as some trade unions.

Is a cost push possible in these cases only when demand conditions are favorable, or made permissive by monetary and fiscal policy? If the monetary authorities act vigorously enough, can't they damp down demand sufficiently to discourage the cost push from separate interest groups? Or are there certain built-in structural causes of the cost push, particularly in wages? Is it realistic to expect that average hourly money earnings will go up just as fast as the average national rise in output per man-hour? If labor productivity is increasing faster in some industries, and if wages there are increased more than the *national* average increase in productivity for the economy as a whole, are wages likely to rise considerably less in the industries with slower increases in productivity? How do worker expectations of further wage increases, and the structure of unionism and collective bargaining, affect this possibility? What about the impact of long-term agreements for future wage increases, related either to changes in the Consumer Price Index, or to expected increases in productivity (as in the case of the "annual improvement factor" in the automobile collective agreements), or to fixed automatic increases at specified future dates regardless of economic conditions at a later time? Have all these developments made wage costs more rigid in an economic downturn, and less likely to lag behind price increases during the upturn? These questions are central to an evaluation of the significance of so-called "wage-induced inflation," but do they cover the whole problem? Are wage increases the basis for even greater price increases in the industries characterized by so-called "administered prices"? To what extent are industrial price policies the real initiating factors in the cost push?

5. Alternative policy proposals for dealing with "wage-induced inflation"

Public discussions of the postwar inflation and its causes have been filled with proposals for dealing with that part of the cost push which is attributable by the critics to wage pressures from unions. These range from greater reliance on monetary and fiscal policies to damp down demand (including the demand for labor) to suggestions that the power of unions be curbed by a variety of methods. Sometimes, policy proposals contain a mixture of both.

What is the likelihood that monetary and fiscal policies can be effective in reducing demand enough to discourage continued wage and price increases? Do we know what rate of unemployment is sufficient to accomplish this objective? What are the *specific* proposals for legislative restriction of union power over wages, and to what extent are these likely to be effective in achieving the objective of discouraging "wage-induced inflation"? Will other forms of union regulation (such as those designed to prevent corruption or encourage greater democracy) have any impact on union wage demands, and if so, in what direction? Alternatively, would unions be more "responsible" in their wage demands if collective bargaining were centralized on an economy-wide basis or industry-wide basis? Or, would the power of trade unions be more effectively offset if employers combined on a regional or industry-wide basis for collective bargaining, and resisted wage demands with more vigor—including willingness to take strikes? Would the public be willing to pay the cost in labor strife and inconvenience?

Should government impose wage controls, as it did during World War II and the Korean War? If this is done, will price and profit controls also be necessary? Finally, are governmental pleas for "restraint" and "responsibility" in wage and price decisions likely to have much effect on unions and employers? Can some procedure be devised for bringing key union and management officials together periodically with responsible government officials for discussions of the impact of price and wage policies on price stability? What are the prospects that such a procedure would be successful? Are there alternativc procedures for dealing with the cost push in key sectors of the economy?

6. *Conflicting national goals and policy choices*

In our national policy since the war we have emphasized full employment. But the postwar inflation has increased our concern for price stability, and proposals have been made to write this into the Full Employment Act of 1946 as a twin and equally important objective. More recently, the growing threat of Soviet economic supremacy has emphasized the necessity for the United States to achieve a higher rate of economic growth.

To what extent are these three goals fully compatible? Or are we as a nation forced to make some hard and unpleasant choices? If we want price stability above all, will this require some greater percentage of unemployment than the March, 1959, 5.8 per cent rate (seasonally adjusted), which means nearly 4.4 million unemployed workers? Can we even countenance this much unemployment for very long? If productivity has been lagging behind wages recently, as some contend, is this partly a consequence of a slower rate of economic growth? Would economic expansion and a higher rate of investment mean another demand-pull inflation bringing wages and prices along on an upward course? How much do we value the American system of trade unions and collective bargaining? In short, what price are the American people willing to pay to achieve price stability, or full employment, or economic growth, or free collective bargaining and industrial peace—or some measure of each?

1. Patterns of wages, prices and productivity

ALBERT REES

Learning from history

In the period since World War II, there has been intense interest in the pattern of behavior of wages, prices, and productivity—interest with which is mixed more than a little anxiety. It will help us to see whether there is now special cause for concern if we examine the recent past against the background of the long-term record. Are wages rising more rapidly now than in earlier times? Has the relation of wages to productivity changed? If so, why? This paper will look into these questions to see whether the answers, in so far as we know them, shed light on our present position.

We shall see that there has in fact been a marked acceleration in the rate of growth of both real wages and productivity, but that since 1929 real wages have been growing faster than productivity. This pattern can be reasonably well explained in terms of fundamental economic forces—

ALBERT REES is Associate Professor of Economics at the University of Chicago and editor of the *Journal of Political Economy*. He has served on the staff of the Council of Economic Advisers and as research associate of the National Bureau of Economic Research.

In preparing this paper Dr. Rees benefited from discussion with C. F. Christ, H. G. Lewis, and G. P. Shultz of the University of Chicago.

chiefly changes in the supplies of labor and capital—though part of the pattern may also be due to institutional changes in wage determination.

The historical record: earnings

Money earnings

The figures on money earnings presented here are confined to manufacturing wage earners. This is one of the largest groups of workers in the economy, one that has been heavily affected by the growth of unionism in the past twenty-five years, and one of the very few groups for which we have reasonably consistent earnings figures covering a long period. Even for this group, the record has gaps and defects, so that it has been necessary to construct a new wage series for this paper.[1]

The first column of Table 1 shows average hourly earnings of manufacturing wage earners annually since 1889. The same definition of manufacturing is used throughout. Thus railroad repair shops, which were considered a part of manufacturing before 1937, are excluded from all the data.

Earnings have been measured per hour at work, so that increases in paid holidays, paid vacations, or paid sick leave increase average hourly earnings. In this respect, the figures presented are unlike the familiar ones of the Bureau of Labor Statistics, which measures earnings per hour paid for. In the BLS series, increases in paid vacations, holidays, or sick leave do not raise hourly earnings.

Other forms of time paid for but not worked are not accounted for in the series shown here. Thus the figures understate the rise in earnings per hour of actual work to the extent that there has been an increase in pay for such things as lunch periods, coffee breaks, wash-up time, call-in time, and jury duty. According to a survey by the Chamber of Commerce of the United States, such items amounted to 2.5 per cent of payroll for manufacturing firms in 1957. However, the firms surveyed may have made more generous payments for such time than did all manufacturing firms.

The series on earnings per hour at work is based largely on data from the Census of Manufactures. In 1956, hours at work as measured by the Census Bureau were 5.4 per cent lower than hours paid for as reported by the BLS. This by itself should cause earnings per hour at work to be 5.4 per cent higher than earnings per hour paid for. In addition to this conceptual difference, however, there is a difference in the sample of

[1] For the period 1890-1914, the wage series is taken from my larger study "Real Wages in Manufacturing, 1890-1914," done with the assistance of Donald P. Jacobs for the National Bureau of Economic Research. I am grateful to the National Bureau for permission to draw on this study and other unpublished studies.

establishments covered. In recent years, the sampling difference and the difference in the hours concept roughly offset one another. In the 1930's, only the sampling difference is important because few manufacturing wage earners received paid holidays or paid vacations. The result of this is that the new series rises more than the BLS series between 1939 and 1956.

From 1889 to 1957 the money earnings of manufacturing wage earners increased from 15.1 cents per hour at work to $2.08, almost a fourteen-fold increase. However, this is not the whole story. We must take account of employer payments for pensions and insurance, which were unknown for wage earners in 1889 and are almost universal today.

Wage supplements

The second column of Table 1 presents new estimates of wage supplements per hour of work, beginning with 1929. Estimates of wage supplements have previously been available for this whole period only for wage earners and salaried workers together, and these were not expressed per man-hour. Wage supplements consist of employer contributions to old age and survivors insurance, unemployment insurance, workmen's compensation, and private pension, welfare, and insurance plans. The figures do not include other items sometimes considered fringe benefits, such as Christmas bonuses, subsidies to company cafeterias, or discounts on goods bought from the company.

Including wage supplements along with wages in figuring worker compensation implicitly assumes that the benefits provided by both public and private insurance and welfare plans are worth what they cost. Of course, this will not seem true to each worker individually. There are always some workers, or groups of workers, who would prefer to have cash. But unless most workers feel that wage supplements are worth what they cost, it is hard to account for their rapid growth in both union and non-union plants. Many forms of insurance can be bought at less cost for groups of workers than for individuals, and are in this sense "worth" more than they cost.

Later I shall divide wage supplements, together with wages, by the Consumer Price Index to put them in dollars of constant purchasing power. It may be objected that this is incorrect to the extent that pensions or other benefits are not received at the time the contributions are made, and thus their real value depends on the price level when they are received. This does present a problem, but one for which there is no perfect solution. Moreover, the same objection applies to adjusting money earnings by a price index, to the extent that individual workers use money earnings to add to their savings.

Data on wage supplements are not available before 1929. The 1929 figure was only 0.4 cents per hour at work, most of which probably represented the cost of workmen's compensation. The amount in earlier years must have been smaller still, and the error caused by its omission is negligible.

From 1929 to 1957, the estimated cost of wage supplements per hour at work rose from 0.4 cents to 16.2 cents. The first big jump comes in the late 1930's, following the enactment of the Social Security law. After 1943, private pensions, insurance, and welfare plans became increasingly important.

Total compensation

By adding money earnings and wage supplements, we get total compensation per hour at work, shown in the third column of Table 1 and in Chart 1. Total compensation increased from 15.1 cents per hour in 1889 to $2.24 in 1957, almost 15 times the initial level. For the first nine years of the period the trend was slightly downward; the low point was 13.8 cents in 1898. Thereafter the course of total compensation can be broken into five main segments: (1) a gradual rise from 1898 to 1915; (2) a very rapid rise from 1915 to 1920 in which money wages more than doubled; (3) a drop in 1921 followed by a slow rise to 1930 in which the 1920 level was not regained; (4) a short, rather sharp drop from 1930 to 1933; and (5) an almost unbroken rise since 1933, most rapid during World War II. Total compensation per hour in 1957 was four times the 1933 level.

It seems clear that the pattern of compensation just described is strongly influenced by changes in consumer prices, and can be better analyzed if we translate it into dollars of constant purchasing power.

Consumer prices

The fourth column of Table 1 is an index of consumers prices. For the years 1914-1957, it is the familiar Consumer Price Index of the Bureau of Labor Statistics, converted to the base 1957=100. To this have been linked two similar indexes for earlier periods: my index for the years 1890-1914, and one year from the index by Professor Clarence D. Long which covers the decade of the 1880's. As measured by these indexes, the level of consumer prices has tripled since 1889. The cautious wording of the last sentence is necessary because the indexes are subject to error.

There are many reasons why it is hard to measure price changes accurately over long periods. For example, the indexes do not follow the prices of the same bundle of commodities. Many items included in the early indexes have disappeared from the present index—such items as coal cooking stoves, celluloid collars, or corset covers. And of course, many

TABLE 1. *Manufacturing Wages, Consumer Prices, and Productivity, 1889-1957*

Year	(1) Average Money Earnings	(2) Wage Supplements	(3) Total Compensation	(4) Consumer Price Index	(5) Total Real Compensation (1957 dollars per hour at work)	(6) Output per Man-hour, Manufacturing	(7) Output per Unit of Labor and Capital, Private Economy
	(Dollars per hr. at work)			(1957=100)		Indexes: 1929=100	
1957	2.08	.162	2.24	100 0	2.24	213	179
1956	1.99	.155	2.15	96.7	2.22	204	177
1955	1.90	.148	2.05	95.3	2.15	200	177
1954	1.83	.138	1.97	95.5	2.06	193	168
1953	1.81	.127	1.94	95.2	2.04	186	166
1952	1.71	.121	1.83	94.4	1.94	180	162
1951	1.61	.115	1.73	92.3	1.87	177	160
1950	1.46	.094	1.55	85.5	1.81	176	159
1949	1.39	.073	1.46	84.7	1.72	165	149
1948	1.35	.061	1.41	85.5	1.65	157	146
1947	1.24	.059	1.30	79.5	1.64	152	143
1946	1.08	.051	1.13	69.4	1.63	144	144
1945	1.01	.052	1.06	64.0	1.66	153	153
1944	1.00	.047	1.05	62.6	1.68	152	148
1943	.934	.041	.975	61.6	1.58	151	137
1942	.827	.037	.864	58.0	1.49	152	133
1941	.701	.036	.737	52.3	1.41	152	131
1940	.634	.036	.670	49.8	1.35	149	122
1939	.603	.035	.638	49.4	1.29	140	120
1938	.603	.036	.639	50.2	1.27	128	115
1937	.606	.027	.633	51.1	1.24	127	114
1936	.542	.011	.553	49.3	1.12	128	111
1935	.537	.005	.542	48.8	1.11	126	106
1934	.523	.004	.527	47.6	1.11	119	101
1933	.437	.004	.441	46.0	.959	114	91
1932	.441	.005	.446	48.6	.918	108	92
1931	.499	.004	.503	54.1	.930	112	96
1930	.522	.004	.526	59.4	.886	106	96
1929	.522	.004	.526	61.0	.862	100	100
1928	.513	not	.513	61.0	.841	95	96
1927	.510	available	.510	61.7	.827	92	96
1926	.503		.503	62.9	.800	88	96
1925	.497		.497	62.4	.796	85	94
1924	.498		.498	60.8	.819	82	94
1923	.479		.479	60.6	.790	76	90
1922	.435		.435	59.6	.730	77	85
1921	.464		.464	63.6	.730	70	85
1920	.537		.537	71.3	.753	62	81
1919	.477		.477	61.6	.774	63	82
1918	.417		.417	53.5	.779	64	78
1917	.316		.316	45.6	.693	65	73
1916	.262		.262	38.8	.675	69	77
1915	.226		.226	36.1	.626	69	72
1914	.220		.220	35.7	.616	62	70
1913	.221		.221	35.3	.626	62	76
1912	.207		.207	34.7	.597	58	74
1911	.202		.202	34.0	.594	51	73
1910	.198		.198	33.8	.586	53	72
1909	.186		.186	32.6	.571	52	73
1908	.184		.184	32.7	.563	48	68

TABLE 1—*Continued*

Year	*(1)*	*(2)*	*(3)*	*(4)*	*(5)*	*(6)*	*(7)*
1907	.191		.191	33.5	.570	49	73
1906	.184		.184	32.2	.571	50	74
1905	.172		.172	31.6	.544	50	69
1904	.169		.169	31.7	.533	49	67
1903	.170		.170	31.4	.541	48	68
1902	.165		.165	30.8	.536	48	67
1901	.158		.158	30.5	.518	46	70
1900	.151		.151	30.1	.502	43	66
1899	.146		.146	29.5	.495	44	65
1898	.138		.138	29.5	.468	—	64
1897	.141		.141	29.7	.475	—	64
1896	.145		.145	29.8	.487	—	60
1895	.139		.139	30.0	.463	—	62
1894	.141		.141	30.7	.459	—	58
1893	.153		.153	32.2	.475	—	59
1892	.147		.147	32.5	.452	—	62
1891	.146		.146	32.6	.448	—	59
1890	.146		.146	32.6	.448	—	59
1889	.151		.151	33.0	.458	36	56

A full description of the sources and methods for the new estimates in this table will be published separately at a later date. Estimates for 1953-57 are less accurate than for earlier years.

Column 1: Based primarily on data from the Census of Manufactures and the Annual Surveys of Manufactures. Interpolating data for 1932-49 are from the Bureau of Labor Statistics; 1920-31, from the National Industrial Conference Board; 1890-1919, from the bureaus of statistics of Massachusetts, New Jersey, and Pennsylvania; 1889 from Clarence D. Long, *Wages and Earnings in the United States, 1860-1890* (in press).

Column 2: Based on published and unpublished data on supplements to wages and salaries in manufacturing from the National Income Division, U. S. Department of Commerce, allocated between production and non-production workers on the basis of data from BLS Bulletin 1186.

Column 3: The sum of columns 1 and 2.

Column 4: 1914-1957, Bureau of Labor Statistics. 1890-1914 from Albert Rees and Donald P. Jacobs, *Real Wages in Manufacturing, 1890-1914* (typescript, 1958) 1889-1890 from Clarence D. Long, *op. cit.*

Column 5: Index of production from John W. Kendrick, *Productivity Trends in the United States* (in preparation), divided by index of production-worker man-hours at work. Hours per man are from the sources of column 1. Production worker employment is from these sources and Solomon Fabricant, *Employment in Manufacturing, 1889-1939*, (New York, 1942).

Column 6: From Solomon Fabricant, *Basic Facts on Productivity Change* (New York, 1959) based on Kendrick, *op. cit.* Output per weighted unit of labor and capital combined, private domestic economy.

important items in the present index did not exist in 1890—television sets, radios, and automobiles, for example. Even electricity was too unimportant to include before World War I.

Another difficulty is that as we go back in time, price records become less adequate. And today it is still hard to measure the true price for constant qualities of things whose quality is improving. For example, if the price of tires is unchanged, but the number of miles of use in each tire is

Total Money Compensation and Total Real Compensation Per Hour At Work, Manufacturing Wage Earners, 1889-1957

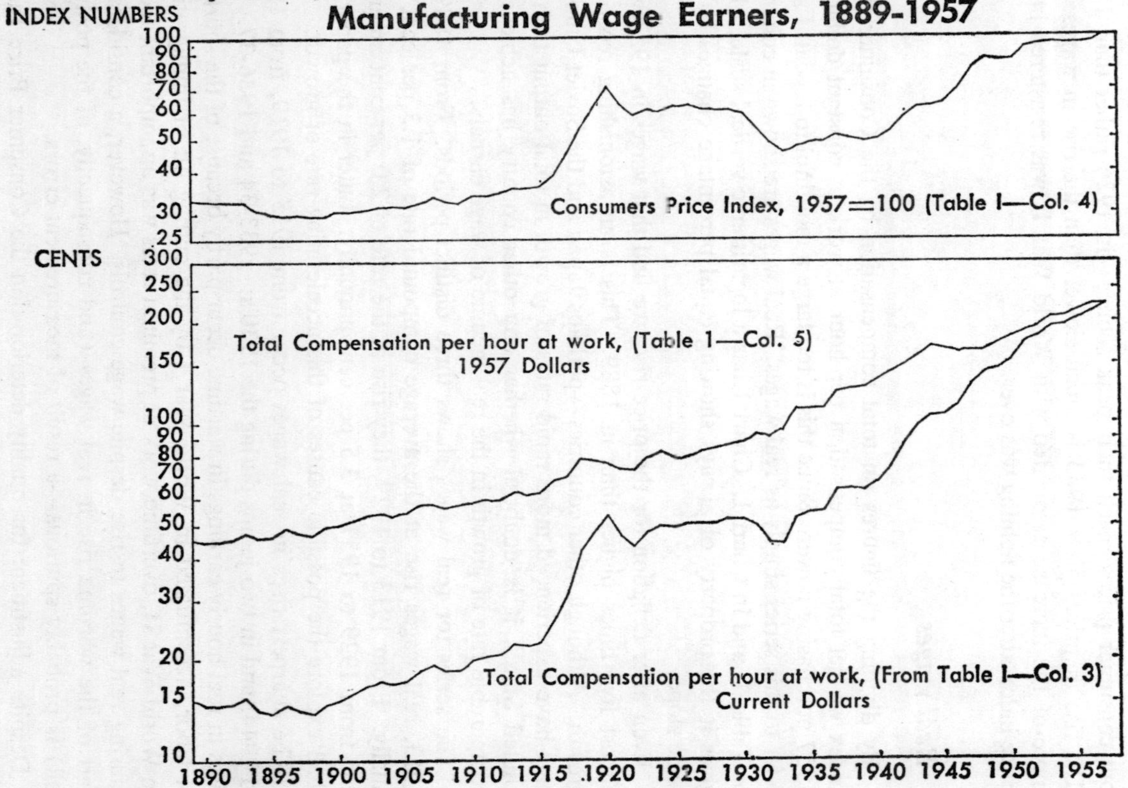

Chart 1

increasing, there is a disguised fall in the "price" of tires that may be overlooked in the price index. Thus failure to take the improvement in quality fully into account will cause us to overstate the rise in the price level. To the extent that this is true, we will understate the rise in real wages.

The general pattern of consumer prices is much like that of money wages, but less steep. Both fall until 1898, rise gradually until 1915, and rise sharply in World War I. Both drop after the war and then rise again, but consumer prices reach their peak sooner—in 1926 rather than 1931. The rise in prices after 1933 is much slower than the rise in wages, and more of the increase associated with World War II was registered in the price index after the fighting was over.

Real wages

By dividing the figures on total compensation by the Consumer Price Index we get total compensation per hour at work in constant dollars of 1957 purchasing power. Since this is too large a mouthful to repeat, I shall refer to this series simply as real wages. Real wages are shown in column 5 of Table 1, and in Chart 1. Chart 1 has a logarithmic vertical scale, which gives it the property of always showing equal percentage changes by the same slope.

Even after deflation for the price rise, we find that wages in 1957 were almost five times higher than in 1889. This is an astonishing record of growth. Although other countries—perhaps Japan and the Soviet Union—may have experienced more rapid rates of growth in total output than the United States, it is doubtful whether any other country has achieved a comparable rate of growth in the real income of wage earners.

The series for real wages shows three distinct periods. From 1889 to 1913, real wages rise at the average compound rate of 1.3 per cent annually. From 1913 to 1929, they rise at the rate of 2.0 per cent annually and from 1929 to 1957 at 3.5 per cent annually. Later in the paper we shall explore the possible causes of this accelerating rate of growth.

The sharpest rises in real wages occur from 1915 to 1919, from 1939 to 1944, and in two jumps during the 1930's: 1933-34 and 1936-37. The rises in real hourly earnings in wartime occur partly because of the shortage of labor, accentuated in World War I by the cutting off of immigration. In World War II, overtime work at premium rates was an important factor causing real wages to rise despite wage controls. However, a considerable part of the wartime rise in real wages (and consequently, of the postwar fall) is probably spurious—a result of measurement errors.

Despite adjustment for quality deterioration the Consumer Price Index probably fails to account for all of the quality deterioration in consumer goods during wartime, or for all of the transactions during World War II made at black market prices. Thus the index rises too little during the wars and too much in the immediate postwar years. More important, the use of the Consumer Price Index to measure real wages in wartime assumes that workers could spend their whole incomes at the prices given by the index. This, however, is not true. There was abnormally high saving during World War II (more than one-fourth of disposable personal income in some years). In part, people were helping the war effort by buying bonds; in part they were saving to buy homes, cars, or other durable goods when these again became available; in part they were using some of their abnormally high incomes as a cushion against future hard knocks. On a smaller scale, something similar must have happened in World War I. Had people attempted to spend all their income currently, prices would have risen much faster still, and measured real wages would have risen much more slowly.

The first of the two sharp rises in real wages in the 1930's coincides with the adoption of the NRA codes, which generally reduced full-time hours of work from 48 to 40 per week with no cut in weekly pay. This means a rise in hourly earnings of one-sixth. Our money-wage series rises a little more than this from 1933 to 1934, while the real-wage series rises a little less. The second sharp rise in real wages of the 1930's coincides with the recovery of 1937 and with the first major victories of the new industrial unions.

Apart from the two postwar declines, which as has been noted may be spurious, the rise in real wages has been remarkably steady. No other decline lasted longer than two years; indeed, none since 1908 lasted longer than one year. Real wages generally rise in periods when prices are falling, such as 1889-90 or 1926-31, as well as when prices are rising. However, before 1929 real wages fell rather consistently during the more important contractions in general business activity. Such falls occurred in 1894, 1904, 1908, 1914, and 1921. It is therefore somewhat surprising that in the great depression of the 1930's real wages fell in only a single year, 1932, and did not fall in any subsequent year except for the doubtful decline of 1944-46.

How can one explain this change in the cyclical behavior of real wages? It is possible that the change has been brought about by the spread of unions, which protect workers from wage cuts in recessions or even win them further advances. However, this leaves unexplained the rise of real wages from 1929 to 1931, when the fall in employment was precipitous and unions in manufacturing were very weak apart from the printing trades and the garment trades.

A simpler and perhaps better explanation is that the change in the cyclical behavior of real wages is itself a result of their sharper upward trend. The best way of measuring the losses suffered in a recession is to measure them relative to the growth that would normally have occurred. On this basis, we can as an example compare the recession of 1953-54 with that of 1907-08. Judged by the year-to-year percentage fall in manufacturing employment, the recession of 1907-08 was the more severe. Real wages fell 0.7 per cent from 1907 to 1908, while according to the trend for 1889-1913, they should have risen 1.3 per cent. The total gap is thus 2.0 per cent. From 1953 to 1954, real wages rose 1.0 per cent, when according to the trend for 1929-57, they should have risen 3.5 per cent. The gap is thus 2.5 per cent—larger than in 1907-08.

From 1889 to 1957 the average actual workweek in manufacturing fell from about 54 hours to about 38 hours, allowing for vacations and holidays. Thus a large part of the gain in real hourly earnings—about 37 per cent—has been used to buy leisure during the working years rather than to buy goods and services. Since the drop in working hours has been quite steady, there is every reason to expect it to continue, though it may take the form of longer vacations rather than shorter workweeks as such.

The historical record: productivity

Choosing a productivity index

It has become a commonplace of economic discussion, both professional and popular, to say that gains in real wages depend on gains in productivity, and that if money wages outrun productivity, prices will rise. There is a sense in which these statements are true. Gains in the real income per unit of input of any group furnishing inputs to the production process must come either at the expense of another such group or as a result of getting more useful output per unit of input—from gains in efficiency. Since it is difficult for any group to increase its share of income and since productivity has been rising rapidly, the second source of gain is generally much the more promising. This does *not* mean, however, that in all cases the redistribution of income from existing output is impossible, or wrong, or both.

Similarly, it is true that if money wages rise faster than productivity and if shares are constant, prices must be rising. This statement is somewhat like the statement that in a set of double-entry books the debits equal the credits; it is true by virtue of the way we define the terms, but it is rather empty. If money wages rise faster than productivity, they may be pushing up prices, or they may have been pulled up by independently rising prices. There is no sure or simple way to tell from wage, price, or productivity statistics.

There is a well-established body of economic theory relating wages to productivity, but the productivity concept used takes into account both the skill of the kind of labor in question and its scarcity or abundance relative to other production inputs. Neither of these crucial factors can be controlled directly in the productivity we measure by economic time series.

These cautions should be kept in mind in considering the last two columns of Table 1, which show two different measures of productivity with some relevance to real wages in manufacturing. Neither is an ideal productivity index for our purposes; each has some strengths and some weaknesses. Several other possible productivity indexes might be relevant, but perhaps confusing as well.

Output per man-hour at work

Column 6 of Table 1 shows manufacturing output divided by the number of production-worker man-hours worked in manufacturing. This is the familiar index of output per man-hour which most people have in mind when they speak of "productivity," except that the man-hours are man-hours at work rather than man-hours paid for.

The earnings series of columns 1, 2, and 3 have implicit in them a man-hours series. Column 1 is in effect production-worker payrolls divided by production-worker man-hours at work. Column 6 is manufacturing production divided by the identical man-hours series. This correspondence in coverage and concept with the wage series is the virtue of this particular productivity series. In fact, when we compare output per man-hour with earnings per man-hour, the man-hour terms cancel, and we are actually comparing the movement of manufacturing output with the movement of production-worker payrolls.

It is now generally well realized that output per man-hour does not necessarily reflect the contribution of production workers to changes in efficiency. It can rise because production workers work harder or are more skilled. However, it can also rise because more capital or more non-production workers are used per production worker. It can rise because of the improved quality of purchased materials or because of an increase in the ratio of purchased materials to final output. And, most likely of all, it can rise because of technological change.

Depending on its source, a gain in output per man-hour may or may not imply that real wages should rise. In general, we expect that in the sectors of the economy where output per man-hour rises least rapidly, wages will outstrip this measure of productivity, so that they will stay roughly in line with wages for workers of equal skill elsewhere in the economy. Where output per man-hour rises most rapidly, we expect wages to lag behind it. Some of the productivity gain will go into lower relative prices, and thus be shared with the consumers of the product. It is for this reason that an index of productivity for the whole economy may be more relevant to real

Real Compensation Per Hour At Work, Manufacturing, and Two Measures of Productivity

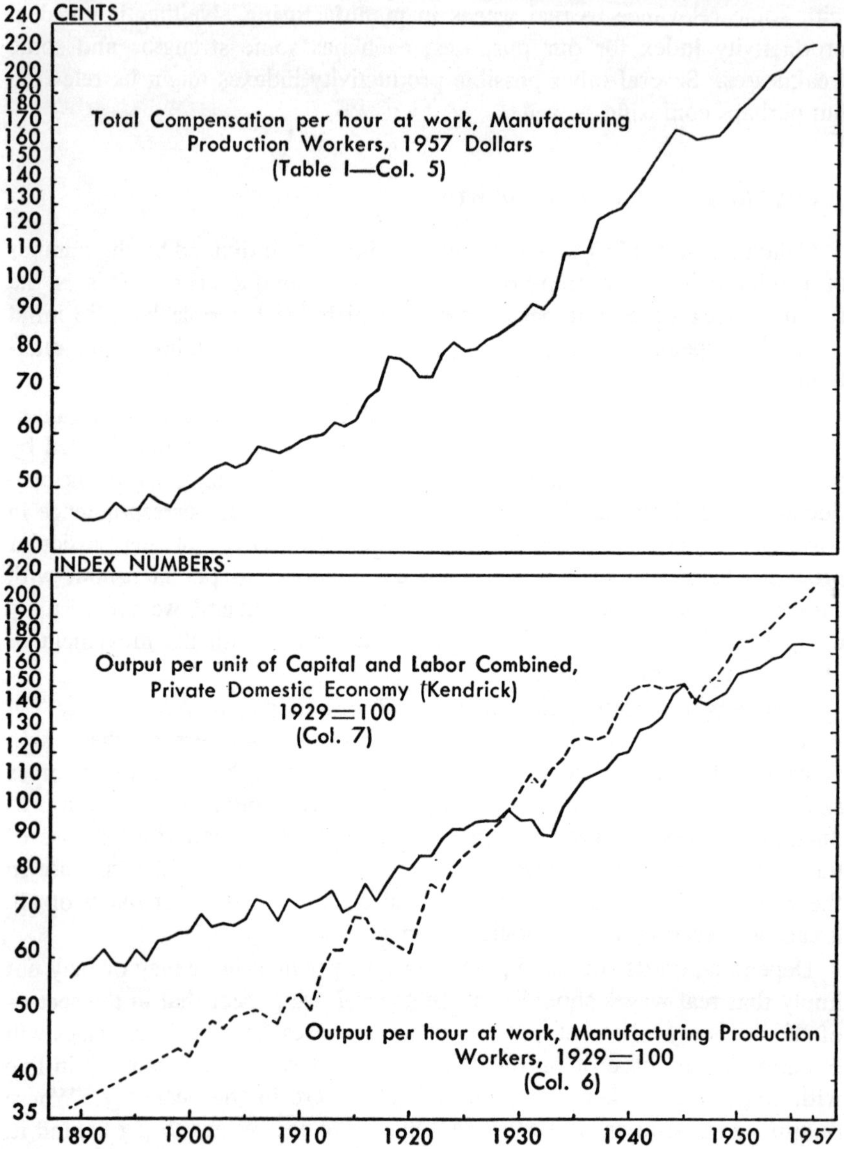

Chart 2

wages in manufacturing than an index for manufacturing alone—for we have computed real wages using a price index broad enough to reflect the performance of the whole economy.

Table 1 and Chart 2 show that from 1889 to 1929, output per man-hour in manufacturing rose faster than real wages. Since 1929, real wages have risen faster, though the changes are almost parallel after World War II. If it causes problems for real wages to outstrip output per man-hour, the problem period would seem to be 1929 to 1944. Over the whole period 1889-1957, the increase in output per man-hour is slightly greater than that in real wages.

Table 2 summarizes some of these comparisons in the form of annual percentage rates of change. We shall return to Table 2 after discussing the remaining measure of productivity.

It may be interesting to note that the cyclical fluctuation of output per man-hour is somewhat more pronounced than that of real wages, especially in the early period. The drop in output per man-hour in recessions occurs in part because employers retain more labor than they currently need in order not to lose skilled personnel, or they use labor to do maintenance work that is not reflected in current output. Then too, the labor force cannot be reduced in proportion to output, for certain minimum crews are needed as long as there is any production at all. The fall of productivity relative to wages in recessions is an important source of the sharp falls in profits.

The index of output per man-hour behaves in a rather peculiar fashion in both World Wars. In World War I it falls after 1915, while in World War II it is virtually unchanged from 1942 to 1945. These movements do not seem entirely plausible. They may reflect in part the difficulty of measuring output when its composition is changing rapidly.

Output per unit of labor and capital

The last column of Table 1 shows John W. Kendrick's index of output per unit of labor and capital combined for the entire private domestic economy. As we have seen, a productivity index for the whole economy is relevant to real wages in manufacturing for two reasons. First, productivity gains will often be diffused through price reductions and thus reflected in the Consumer Price Index. Second, the labor market will maintain a rough balance among money-wage rates for work of equal skill in different sectors of the economy. It is also meaningful to include the input of capital in a productivity index to be compared with real wages. If output per man-hour rises because more capital is used, the added output is not available for raising real wages until the costs of using the additional capital have been met. Output per unit of capital and labor combined is a measure of the gains available for distribution.

Kendrick's productivity index does not use exactly the same measure of man-hours that is used in the real-wage series. It is based to a considerable extent on man-hours paid for rather than man-hours worked because data on man-hours worked were often not available. This causes it to diverge further from the real-wage series in recent years than would otherwise be the case.

From 1889 to 1913, real wages rise at the same rate as output per unit of labor and capital combined in the private economy, as can be seen most easily in Table 2. From 1913 to 1929, real wages rise slightly faster than this productivity index, while after 1929 they rise very much faster. Our task in the rest of this paper is to interpret these divergent movements in the real wage and productivity series.

TABLE 2. *Annual Compound Rates of Growth of Real Wages and of Productivity, 1889-1957**

	1889-1913	*1913-1929*	*1929-1957*	*1889-1957*
Total real compensation per hour at work	1.3	2.0	3.5	2.4
Output per production worker man-hour at work, manufacturing	2.3	3.0	2.7	2.6
Output per unit of capital, manufacturing	−1.1	1.9	1.9	0.7
Output per unit of capital and labor combined, private domestic economy	1.3	1.8	2.1	1.7

* Computed from Table 1, except output per unit of capital, which is from Kendrick, *op. cit.* The 1913 data in this series are interpolated and the last date is 1953 rather than 1957. The dates have been chosen so as to separate the periods of differing growth rates in real earnings and so that each period ends with a prosperous year.

It may be mentioned in passing that most of the other possible productivity indexes that seem relevant to real wages in manufacturing probably lie close to or between the two presented here. At any rate, this is true of two more of Kendrick's indexes: (a) output per man-hour, all employees and proprietors for manufacturing; and (b) output per man-hour, all employees and proprietors for the private domestic economy.

Unit labor cost

If the hourly compensation of production workers in current dollars is rising faster than output per man-hour, the cost of production-worker labor per unit of output must be rising. Omitting the man-hours terms, which cancel, we can express unit labor cost simply as aggregate production-worker compensation divided by output, where compensation is payrolls plus the cost of wage supplements. This measure of unit labor cost for the

Indexes of Unit Costs of Production-Worker Compensation and Wholesale Prices of Finished Goods, 1919-57 (1929=100)

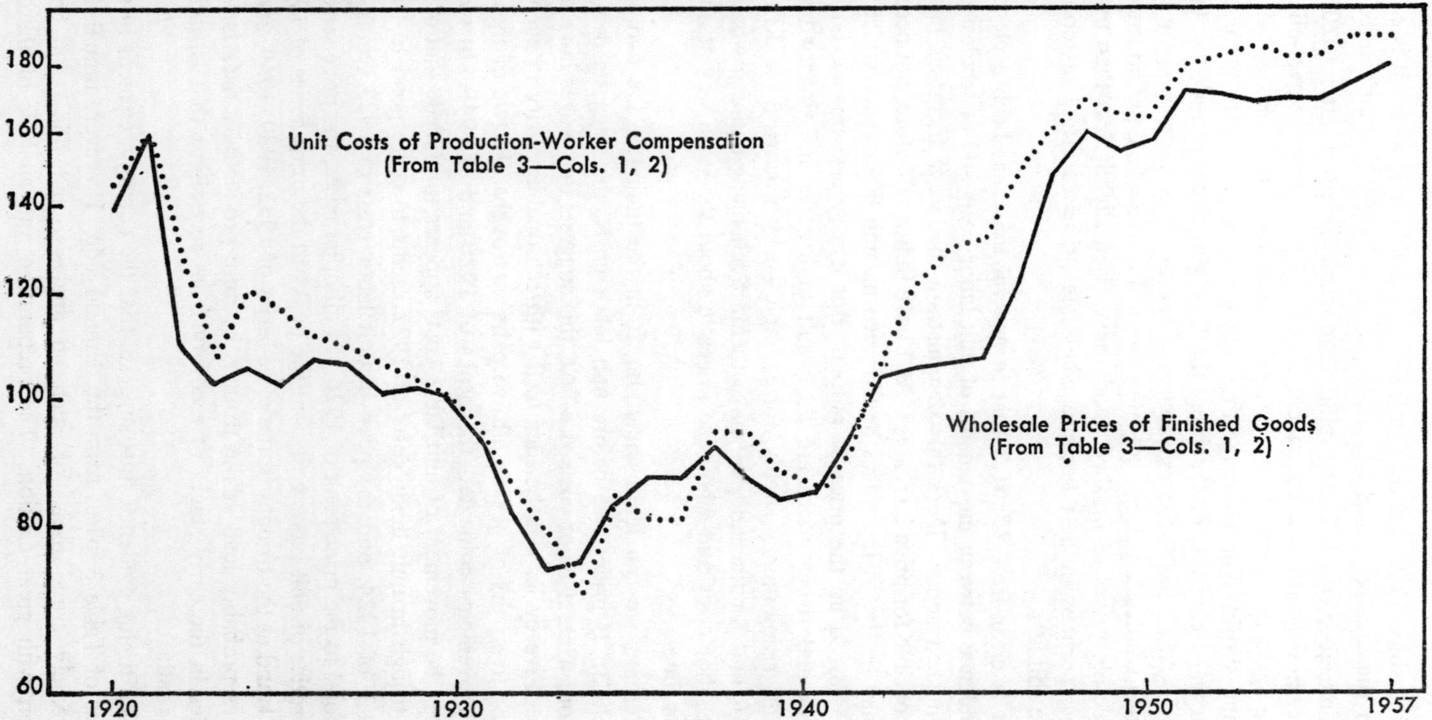

Chart 3

period since 1919 is shown in Table 3 and Chart 3, where it is compared with the change in the wholesale prices of finished manufactured goods.

Unit labor cost fell less rapidly than wholesale prices after 1920, though by 1929 they had fallen as much. From 1929 to 1940, the over-all changes were again the same. Wholesale prices then rose less than unit labor costs during World War II, suggesting that price controls were more effective than wage controls, or that only the legal prices got included in the price index. After 1948, the movement of the two series was roughly parallel, though wholesale prices fluctuated more. For the whole period since 1929, wholesale prices of finished goods have risen slightly less than unit labor costs, perhaps in part because wholesale prices of crude materials have risen still less.

It is clear from Chart 3 that in general there has been a close correspondence between movements of unit labor costs and of wholesale prices of finished goods. Does this demonstrate that wage increases have been responsible for price increases? As I have indicated before, not necessarily. It may be that rising wages have forced up unit labor costs, which in turn have forced up the price of output. But it may also be that both rising wages and rising prices are the result of broader inflationary forces—a rapidly rising money supply, for example—which increase the demand for goods and for the labor to make them. Such rising demand would affect unit labor costs and wholesale prices in about the same way at about the same time.

Perhaps we can learn something from the timing of the two series in Table 3. If prices rise before unit labor costs, this suggests demand inflation, while if labor costs rise first, this suggests that wages have a causal role. Five cycles can be identified with reasonable clarity in each series, giving five pairs of peaks and five pairs of troughs. In two of these pairs, the movements coincide: the peaks of 1920 and of 1948. In two early cases, the movement of unit labor costs appears to precede that of prices: the trough in unit labor costs of 1922 seems to correspond to the price trough of 1924, and the peak in unit labor costs of 1923 seems to correspond to the price peak of 1926. In all other cases, the price series leads the series of unit labor costs—at the peaks in the price series of 1937 and 1951 and at the troughs in the price series of 1932, 1939, 1949, and 1953. Prices probably lead at the troughs because productivity rises faster than wages in the early stages of recovery from recessions; that is, unit labor costs fall.

The timing evidence thus suggests that the common element in the two series of Table 3 arises from the demand side. However, annual data are extremely crude tools for such an analysis, and this result must be taken with great caution. The preparation and analysis of these series on a monthly or quarterly basis is beyond the scope of this paper; though such series might be helpful, they would not necessarily provide conclusive evidence.

TABLE 3. *Indexes of Unit Cost of Production-Worker Labor and Wholesale Prices of Finished Goods, Manufacturing 1919-1957*

(1929 = 100)

Year	*Unit Labor Cost*[1]	*Wholesale Prices of Finished Goods*[2]	*Year*	*Unit Labor Cost*[1]	*Wholesale Prices of Finished Goods*[2]
1957	193	184	1937	94	92 P
1956	193	178	1936	81	87
1955	187	173	1935	81	87
1954	186 T	173	1934	84	83
1953	190 P	172 T	1933	72 T	75
1952	186	174	1932	79	74 T
1951	183	175 P	1931	85	81
1950	167 T	160	1930	94	93
1949	168	157 T	1929	100	100
1948	170 P	162 P	1928	103	101
1947	163	150	1927	106	100
1946	150	123	1926	109	106 P
1945	133	108	1925	111	106
1944	131	107	1924	117	102 T
1943	123	106	1923	120 P	105
1942	108	104	1922	107 T	102
1941	93	94	1921	127	109
1940	86 T	86	1920	159 P	158 P
1939	88	85 T	1919	145	138
1938	94 P	87			

[1] Based on the BLS index of production-worker payrolls, wage supplements from Table 1, Column 2, and Kendrick's index of output in manufacturing, extended to 1957 by the Federal Reserve Board index. The letter P identifies a peak in the series, and the letter T a trough.

[2] BLS index of wholesale prices of finished goods converted to a 1929 base.

Interpreting the record

The problem restated

Two measures of productivity have been put forth here as having some relevance to the movement of real wages. We find that before 1913, real wages closely followed one of these—output per unit of labor and capital combined for the private domestic economy. From 1913 to 1929, the correspondence was not perfect, but was still very close. However, from 1929 to 1944 real wages rose appreciably faster than either productivity measure. Since World War II, real wages have closely followed output per man-hour of work of manufacturing production workers, and have risen much faster than the broader productivity measure. These facts seem to deny that there is any simple correspondence between real wages and the kind of productivity we have measured. What forces might explain the complex pattern that emerges?

Errors in concept and measurement

Some sources of measurement error have already been discussed, especially in connection with the Consumer Price Index. We should recognize that similar errors occur in the production indexes. When the quality of output is improving we may fail to account fully for this improvement and thus we may understate the rise in output. If the quality bias in the production index is greater than that in the Consumer Price Index, real wages will appear to outrun productivity though in fact they do not. But it would be extremely difficult to demonstrate the presence, much less the size, of this effect.

On the conceptual side, one of the main problems is the handling of taxes in the real-wage figures. The money-wage data include wages used to pay income taxes, either by payroll deduction or otherwise. The Consumer Price Index includes some excise taxes. Net of taxes, money wages and consumer prices would both rise less, but the effect on money wages would be much larger. Do we want to argue from this that the rise in real wages has been overstated? To the extent that workers' taxes have on balance been used to subsidize other groups, such as farmers, the rise in real wages has been overstated. But to the extent that workers receive government services for their taxes, we don't want to deduct taxes in figuring real wages. Any allocation of government benefits to particular groups of citizens must be very tenuous. It seems clear, however, that most of workers' taxes are spent in their own interests broadly conceived, and that to a first approximation our treatment of taxes has been correct.

Capital inputs and the return to capital

Table 2 shows a productivity index that so far has not been mentioned: output per unit of capital input in manufacturing. This is also taken from Kendrick's work, adapted to fit our purposes. Before 1913 (and until 1919) output per unit of capital in manufacturing was falling. Output per man-hour increased as rapidly as it did only because large additions to capital were made. To call forth this additional capital on a sustained basis, the costs of using the capital had to be covered before any of the added output was available for raising real wages. The increased use of capital per unit of output is taken into account when productivity is measured as output per unit of labor and capital combined rather than as output per man-hour. This thus helps to explain why before 1913 real wages tended to follow the first of these productivity measures rather than the second.

After 1919, output per unit of capital in manufacturing rose, though more slowly than output per man-hour. Since a smaller portion of output was needed to cover the costs of additions to capital, more was available for raising real returns per unit of labor.

The gains shown by the index of output per unit of capital and labor combined are available for increasing the real wages of labor and the real earnings of capital. But since the earnings of capital are measured as interest rates or yields, they are already stated in real terms. The rise in the price level is reflected in the smaller quantity of physical capital that can be bought with a dollar of money capital. But despite rises in the average productivity of labor and capital, separately and in combination, there has been no upward trend in the return on capital. Indeed, in recent years the yields on high-grade corporate bonds have been consistently below those prevailing in the period 1913-1929.[2] The suppliers of debt capital, at least, have thus not shared the fruits of the rise in productivity, and the trend for tangible equity capital may well be similar. Does this represent the use of power by labor to increase its share at the expense of capital? Not necessarily. For the economy as a whole, the rising average productivity of capital as measured by the ratio of output to capital inputs has apparently been offset by the increase in the stock of tangible capital relative to labor input. The contribution of an *additional* unit of capital to output may be no higher today than it was in 1913, or it may even be lower. If this is so, there is nothing in economic theory to suggest that the return on capital should have risen. The full gain in productivity under these circumstances could be distributed as higher wages or lower product prices, and could thus show up in a real-wage index. The real-wage index would then rise faster than output per unit of labor and capital combined, as it has done since 1913.

Immigration

The period 1889-1913, in which real wages rose least rapidly, was a period of heavy immigration, especially after 1899. There were several years in this period in which more than a million aliens arrived in the

[2] For data on the yields to maturity of high-grade corporate bonds for 1913-29, see David Durand, *Basic Yields of Corporate Bonds* (New York, 1942). For more recent data, see *Moody's Industrial Manual.*

United States. Moreover, most of the immigrants of this period were from Southern and Eastern Europe where levels of skill and education were low, not only relative to those of the United States, but to those of Britain, Germany, and Scandinavia, which had furnished most of the immigrants of earlier periods.

It is thus not surprising that real wages rose slowly in this period, both because immigration kept the average skill-level of the work force from rising at its recent rate and simply because labor was plentiful relative to other resources. Indeed, until recently it has been thought that real wages in manufacturing did not rise at all in the two decades 1894-1914. It is only the construction of the new and broader cost-of-living index for this period which has been used here that reverses this conclusion and produces a modest rise in real wages.

The flow of immigrants was curtailed first by World War I and then by restrictive legislation early in the 1920's. This timing coincides well with the movements of the real-wage series. It should be noted that the curtailment in immigration helps to explain not only the change in the rate of growth of real wages, but also the change in the rate of growth of productivity. The low average skill of the immigrants in the period just before World War I and the problems of absorbing them into the work force tended to check the rise in output per man-hour.

The skill and training of labor

Apart from the cutting off of immigration, broader forces have changed the skill composition of labor. New technology has tended to displace unskilled laborers and to require a larger proportion of skilled wage earners. This trend is clearly shown in Table 4. Although the table applies to the whole labor force and not to manufacturing alone, there is every reason to believe that trends within manufacturing have been similar.

TABLE 4. *Male Workers in Selected Major Occupation Groups as a Percent of All Male Workers, 1900-1950*

	Gainful Workers				*Labor Force*	
	1900	*1910*	*1920*	*1930*	*1940*	*1950*
Craftsmen, foremen, and kindred workers	12.6	14.1	16.0	16.2	15.5	19.0
Operatives and kindred workers	10.3	12.5	14.4	15.3	18.1	20.6
Laborers except farm and mine	14.7	14.7	14.0	13.7	12.1	8.8
Total	37.6	41.3	44.4	45.2	45.7	48.4

Source: Gertrude Bancroft, *The American Labor Force: Its Growth and Changing Composition,* (New York, 1958). Based on data from the decennial censuses of population.

An increasing proportion of skilled workers among wage earners will tend to raise the average hourly earnings of all wage earners quite apart from any improvements in technology. Of course, this would not be true of an index of wage rates with constant weights for the various skills. The effects of the changes in skill-mix on average hourly earnings are considerably smaller than they would otherwise be because skill differentials in wages have narrowed markedly since the beginning of the century. This narrowing of skill differentials may itself be an additional cause of the increased use of skilled labor.

The improving skill-mix does not represent an improvement in the efficiency with which inputs are used, but represents instead an improvement in the quality of these inputs. Nevertheless, it is fully reflected in the index of output per man-hour, since man-hours are a simple measure of labor time unadjusted for skill. Thus the reflection of the improving skill-mix in both real wages and output per man-hour may be another reason for these series to move closely together in recent years. On the other hand, Kendrick's index of output per unit of labor and capital combined will reflect little of the change in wage-earner skill-mix for two reasons. First, it includes other inputs—capital and the labor of salaried employees and proprietors. Second, the labor input component has been weighted to remove some of the effects of changes in skill-mix, so as to get an index that more nearly measures improvement in efficiency alone. Thus the skill-mix factor helps to explain why this index rises less than real wages after 1919, and especially after 1940, when the proportion of laborers among wage earners fell fastest.

Apart from the change in skill-mix, there has been within each of the broad skill categories an improvement in the training of workers, especially in their formal education. This factor will also tend to raise both real wages and output per man-hour, and will be diluted in its effect on the broader productivity index.

The relative earnings of production and non-production workers

If production-worker wages in real terms have risen more than output since 1929, as our measures indicate, then the returns of some other input must have risen less. I have already suggested that this is true of capital. It is probably also true of non-production workers. Some statistics from the Census of Manufactures will illustrate the point. In 1899 the average annual earnings of production workers were 40 per cent of those of non-production workers. By 1929, they had risen slightly to 49 per cent. After 1929, the rise was sharper; by 1956 the average earnings of production workers were 64 per cent of those of non-production workers. These figures are not strictly comparable because the Census of Manufactures has considerably broadened its coverage of non-production workers in recent years. But the narrowing of earnings differentials is so pronounced that it seems most unlikely that changes in coverage can account for all of it.

Again we may ask whether the gains of wage earners relative to salaried workers are the result of economic forces, or are entirely the result of changes in power positions. Again there is much to support the former view. The rapid spread of public secondary and higher education in this century has vastly increased the supply of people qualified to hold white collar jobs, at the same time that the principal sources of unskilled manual labor were being cut off. These developments tend to raise the relative earnings of blue collar workers quite apart from any action by government or unions. A contributing factor, in my view, has been the tendency in recent years for popular culture to idealize the white collar worker and to abase the blue collar worker, thus making blue collar careers less attractive.

The wage earner's share of income

It is often considered an established proposition in economics that "labor's share" of income is constant through time. This proposition does not rest on any theoretical base—it is simply a generalization made from observing statistics. For the particular income stream we have been considering (the output of manufacturing industry), and for the class of labor we have been considering (wage earners), the proposition is not strictly true. The first two lines of Table 2 imply that from 1889 to 1929 the wage earner's share of output was falling. From 1929 to 1957 it was rising again, though by 1929 it had not quite regained the level of 1889.

The pattern of the wage earner's share implied by our statistics of real wages and productivity is the same as that discovered in a direct investigation of the wage earner's share in manufacturing. Professor R. M. Solow of M.I.T. has examined the wage earner's share of value added in selected manufacturing industries since 1899, and finds a fall from 1899 to 1929 and a rise from 1929 to 1951, with the 1951 share slightly below that of 1899.[3]

Collective bargaining

I have left until last the force in which there is the most interest, the spread of unionism and collective bargaining. In general, it is very difficult to tell from the kind of record we have been reviewing just what the effect of bargaining has been. To do so would require a more precise estimate

[3] See "The Constancy of Relative Shares," *American Economic Review,* September, 1958, p. 627.

than I can make of the size of the effects of other forces discussed previously. One episode, at least, seems clearly to be the result of unions—the sharp rise in real wages from 1936 to 1937. It is true that 1937 was a year of rapid recovery, but despite this recovery there were still about eight million unemployed. It thus seems most unlikely that real wages jumped upward because of the tightness of labor markets. The wage rise was, of course, not primarily the result of bargaining by established unions. Much of it was a reaction to the threat of unionization—an unsuccessful attempt to head off the CIO.

Several statistical studies of the influence of unions on wages suggest strongly that unionized workers lost ground during the years 1939-1948.[4] In this period the forces of demand inflation pulled up non-union wages faster than unions could raise wages in collective bargaining. Since 1948, unions may again have been a factor in raising real wages in manufacturing. I know of no thorough study of their effect in this recent period, though work now in progress may give us further insights.

In any event, it is important not to take the results of collective bargaining simply at face value. Unions generally take credit for the whole of bargained wage gains, and management often blames them for the whole rise in wage costs. The historical record makes clear that real wages in manufacturing were rising long before unions were important. Unions may have contributed to the acceleration of the rise, but we cannot be certain. Most of the rise, however, must be due to technological progress, to the growing supply of capital per worker, and to the rising skill and education of the work force.

There is perhaps one other change in the wage-price pattern to which unions have contributed. From 1889 to 1898 and from 1926 to 1931, gains in real wages come largely from falling consumer prices rather than from rising money wages. There have been no such periods since 1931. The main reasons for this have been expansionary monetary and fiscal policy and the commitment to full employment. However, collective bargaining creates a strong bias toward taking real wage gains in the form of higher money wages.

In my opinion, this is not an adverse development. It is highly desirable for people to have correct expectations of the future price level. Inflation or deflation would cause little difficulty if everyone could anticipate them perfectly. But it will never be possible for everyone to anticipate a changing price level perfectly. Some decisions to lend or borrow, to be a land-

---

[4] See for example, Harold M. Levinson, *Unionism, Wage Trends, and Income Distribution* (Ann Arbor, 1951), especially pp. 66-79; Albert Rees, "Postwar Wage Determination in the Basic Steel Industry," *American Economic Review,* XLI (June, 1951), 389-404, and Stephen P. Sobotka "Union Influence on Wages: The Construction Industry," *Journal of Political Economy,* LXI (April, 1953), 127-143.

lord or a tenant under a lease, or to enter into other fixed money contracts will be made on the expectation (for want of a better one) that the price level will be stable. If the price level is in fact stable, fewer such decisions will prove to be unwise.

Many people believe that unions do more than make it necessary for real wage increases to come in the form of higher money earnings. They believe that unions push up money earnings fast enough to force the price level to rise. This would be unfortunate if true, but the evidence of this paper is not sufficient to test it. In my own opinion, it is not true in any direct sense. Perhaps it contains some truth in the indirect sense that unions help to create a political atmosphere conducive to inflation. But these are matters that I must leave to other contributors to this volume.

Conclusions

We have examined the dramatic increases in real wages and in productivity of the past seventy years. It is a record that gives us every reason to expect continued large gains in real income in the foreseeable future. At the same time we have seen that the interrelations between wages and productivity have been more varied and complex than is generally believed.

The advice is frequently given that wage increases should be based on gains in output per man-hour for the economy as a whole. For example, the Economic Report of the President of January, 1959 states, "Increases in money wages and other compensation not justified by the productivity performance of the economy are inevitably inflationary."

The advice that wage increases should be based on gains in productivity for the whole economy, like much sage-sounding advice, is far easier to give than to take. The difficulties in applying it to any particular situation must be as apparent to those who have tried to follow it in wage determination as they are to those who have tried to construct accurate measures of productivity and wages. One trouble with the advice is that it concerns broad averages, and there may be sound reasons why any particular situation should deviate from the average in one direction or another. An important class of such reasons is shortages or surpluses of labor in particular industries or occupations.

A second difficulty with the statement that wage increases in excess of productivity increases are inflationary is that it is true only if there are no shifts favorable to wage earners in the distribution of real income. But, as we have seen, there have been important shifts in this direction in the past, and there may be other shifts in either direction in the future. Sudden and temporary shifts in the distribution of income often represent nothing more than the use of economic power by an organized group. Gradual and persistent shifts, however, are likely to represent the operation of real economic forces. They will probably result in a new income distribution that contributes more to economic efficiency than would the continuation of the old one under changed circumstances, whatever we may think of the two distributions in terms of some non-economic standard of justice. It is for this reason that it seems unwise to tie wages or any other set of payments for inputs to a productivity index. To do so is to freeze the distribution of income among groups in the name of checking inflation.

We must devise methods of checking inflation that give more room than this for the apportionment of rewards to changes in the skill and effort of different kinds of workers, to changes in the nature of the labor supply, and to changes in our needs for labor services. We must devise means of checking the use of excessive economic power by labor or business that are both more selective and more effective than advice to unions and management in general about the just way to set wages and prices.

In general, the best way of checking monopoly power in product markets is to strengthen the anti-trust laws. The problem of checking excessive power of labor unions is an even more complex one. It will take creative thinking to reach workable solutions. All of the simple solutions, such as "putting labor under the anti-trust laws" seem to me as yet to be vague, unfair, or inadequate.

2. Productivity, costs and prices:

Concepts and measures

JOHN W. KENDRICK

Productivity, wages and other costs, and prices are closely related economic variables. If consistently defined and measured, the general price level will always rise less than the prices of the factors of production (labor and capital) in proportion to the increase in total productivity. These terms may at first cause difficulties for the non-economist, but their precise definition and meaning will be brought out in subsequent sections of this paper.

A statement about related changes in the variables does not reveal the causal forces at work. For example, if productivity has advanced, wage rates and capital return necessarily rise in relation to the general product-price level, since this is the means whereby the market mechanism distributes the fruits of productivity gains to workers and investors. But this statement is neutral with respect to the question as to whether product prices are pushed up by forces that are able to raise factor prices faster than increases in productivity; or whether factor prices are pulled up by

---

JOHN W. KENDRICK is Associate Professor of Economics at George Washington University. Since 1953 he has been a staff member of the Bureau of Economic Research; since 1956, Consultant to the Bureau of the Budget. In addition he has served with the National Resources Planning Board and in 1946-53 was Acting Chief, National Economics Division of the Department of Commerce. Dr. Kendrick is author of *Productivity Trends: Capital and Labor* and *National Productivity and Its Long-Term Projection.*

forces that inflate monetary demand faster than the physical volume of production can be increased by expansion of factor supplies and productivity; or whether both sets of forces interact.

It is not my assignment to analyze the underlying forces which have affected changes in product prices, factor prices, and productivity in recent economic history.[1] Rather, it is the more pedestrian task of defining the concepts and terms, and explaining briefly the nature of the statistical measures available to implement the concepts for purposes of analysis. It is important that we be clear about the basic concepts we are using in our discussions, and understand the meaning and limitations of the statistical measures to which we may refer to support or refute explanations of inflating forces.

Despite general awareness of the importance of changes in productivity, there is probably more confusion as to the concept, definition, and measurement of productivity than is the case with respect to wages and prices. A major part of this paper is devoted to these matters, since movements of productivity index numbers will differ—depending on concept and sources and methods used in preparing the estimates of both output and input.

Labor compensation, or "wages," is a more straightforward concept, but here, too, it is necessary to define just what is included, and to indicate the sources of data and their reliability. The same is true of nonlabor costs. Price indexes are important because (a) they have impact on purchasing power of money incomes, and (b) they are necessary for "deflating" the current dollar value of national and industry output in order to measure changes in physical production and productivity.

It is essential for analysis that the estimates of the several variables be statistically consistent. This matter will be covered when we describe the available measures.

Productivity concepts

General definition

The term "productivity" may be defined as the ratio of output to any or all of the inputs employed in production.[2] Output and input are measured in *physical volume* terms, since the purpose of productivity analysis is to get at the efficiency with which resources are utilized. The outputs, inputs,

[1] See John W. Kendrick, "Trends in Product Prices, Factor Prices, and Productivity," Joint Economic Committee Compendium, *The Relationship of Prices to Economic Stability and Growth* (March 31, 1958), pp. 225-236. See also Table 4 below.

[2] For fuller discussion of concept and meaning, see John W. Kendrick, *Productivity Trends: Capital and Labor,* Occasional Paper 53 (National Bureau of Economic Research, 1956) and Solomon Fabricant, *Basic Facts on Productivity Change,* Occasional Paper 63 (N.B.E.R., 1959).

and productivity ratios are generally expressed as *index numbers,* since the chief interest is in their proportionate movements over time.

The most commonly used productivity measure is "output per man-hour." This is a "partial productivity" measure since it is a ratio of output to only one class of input, although labor is the most important input. The partial productivity ratios are useful in showing economies achieved over time in the use of particular inputs. To measure the *net* saving of all cost elements, or inputs, however, and thus the change in overall productive efficiency, output should be related to *all* associated inputs. For example, output per man-hour may rise as a result of using more equipment. Only if the increase in capital cost is subtracted from the saving in labor cost can it be determined if there was a net reduction of costs, and if so, how much.

Before looking further at the "partial" and "total" productivity measures, we must first define output and the associated inputs at both the economy and industry levels.

Output and associated inputs

The broadest measure of the physical volume of final output of the economy as a whole is the *real gross national product.* It is "real" in the sense that the current dollar magnitudes have been deflated by appropriate price indexes in order to eliminate the influence of price changes and reveal the changes in physical volume of production of the various types of goods and services. Because of serious difficulties in measuring the output of government which is neither priced nor reported in physical units, the broadest measure appropriate for productivity measurement is the real gross *private product.* The values of "intermediate products" (materials and services purchased by one industry from another) are included in the value of *final* product (consumer goods, capital goods, and goods sold to government), and are not separately counted.

The inputs corresponding to the national product are the services of the basic *factors of production, labor and capital* (including natural resources). Factor services are measured in terms of hours available for productive use: (a) man-hours worked in the case of labor, and (b) the hours in which machinery and other types of real capital are available if the capital factor is included. When man-hours alone are related to output, they are generally *not* differentiated by type of industry or occupation and multiplied (weighted) by the average hourly earnings of a "base" period in each. However, they *may* be, and *must* be if they are to be combined with other inputs, since constant dollars then become the common denominator of input as well as of a diverse output.

At the level of the *industry or firm,* output may be measured *gross,* i.e. in terms of the physical volume of total output; or it may be measured *net* of intermediate products, i.e. as the constant dollar value of gross output, less the constant dollar value of purchased materials, etc. The net approach is the one consistent with the national product estimates, although in practice net and gross output measures show much the same movement in nonfarm industries. The inputs associated with industry net output are the services of labor and capital employed in the industry.

The meaning of the productivity ratios

Ratios of the physical volume of output to any particular input or class of inputs such as labor, capital, or materials are useful in showing changes over time in requirements for the particular input. This interpretation is more clearly indicated when the productivity ratio is inverted; its downward movement implies progressive savings or economies in the use of the input. For example, an increase in an index of output per man-hour from 100 to 200 could be expressed as a decline in man-hours per unit of output from 100 to 50, implying that "unit labor requirements" have been cut in half. The partial productivity ratio does *not* indicate changes in the efficiency of the particular input nor of the productive process generally.

Economies in the use of an input may result from increasing efficiency of production generally, or it may reflect changing proportions of inputs (resulting from changes in technology or in the relative prices of the inputs). In the latter case, the use of one input per unit of output may be reduced merely because the use of another input is increased. For example, installation of new automated equipment may reduce the need for machine tenders and other production workers per unit of output, but the requirements for maintenance workers may go up as does the value of equipment used in constant prices. In other words, maintenance workers and capital have been substituted for production workers.

In order to measure changes in productive efficiency generally, output must be related to *all* associated inputs. The *total productivity* ratio reveals the *net* savings achieved in the use of inputs as a whole, and thus the degree of advance in efficiency of the productive process. Measures of this sort, including capital as well as labor inputs, have been made primarily by the National Bureau of Economic Research. Index numbers published by the Bureau of Labor Statistics relate to output per man-hour.

Increases in total productivity reflect primarily

(1) technological progress resulting from innovations in plant and equipment and in the processes or organization of production

(2) economies of scale, as overhead-type expenses are reduced per unit of output and greater specialization of production is made possible as output grows, and

(3) more efficient rates of utilization of capacity.

Point (3) is primarily a cyclical factor and if productivity comparisons are made between years of high-level economic activity (1948-53, or 1953-57, for example), average rates of utilization of capacity probably do not differ markedly. As already noted, changes in the partial productivity ratios reflect factor substitutions in addition to the three variables listed.

The main element in productivity advance—technological innovation—is in part a function of the quantity and quality of resources devoted to the discovery and commercial development of improved ways and means of production. Research and development outlays have increased steadily in relation to sales for some decades, and so have the numbers of scientists and engineers as a proportion of the labor force. Behind the emphasis on research and development lie basic social values, such as the desire for material progress, willingness of the American people to adapt to technological change, economic freedom, and the spur of the profit motive in a relatively competitive setting.

Investment in research and development activity results in an increase in the real stock of intangible capital represented in peoples' technical knowledge, or know-how. Technological advance has also been accompanied by increasing average education and training of the labor force required to operate the more and more complex technology. This also adds to the stock of intangible capital. In some sense, rising total productivity reflects the cumulative result of investments designed to improve the quality of tangible inputs, as illustrated by the greater efficiency of a better educated labor force.

Labor productivity measures

The most usual measures of productivity relate output to part or all of the associated man-hours worked. The man-hours are usually a simple total, or sometimes each type is weighted by average hourly earnings in a base period. Unfortunately, these measures are popularly called indexes of "labor productivity." But despite the connotation, they do *not* measure the efficiency of labor in the sense of the effort or skill of this factor alone. In fact, changes in labor efficiency as such have probably had a minor influence on changes in productivity.

These indexes also do not measure changes in productive efficiency generally, since they are influenced by substitution of capital for labor and by savings in materials as well as by technological change. They do show savings in labor input achieved over time, better indicated by inverting the ratio to read "unit man-hour requirements." Since labor is the major factor input, real product per unit of labor input will not diverge greatly from total factor productivity measures, especially if the labor measure is comprehensive and weighted by major types of labor input. But it is not as good a substitute for total productivity when related to gross output at the industry level, since capital and materials inputs may overshadow the labor element altogether—as in the petroleum refining industry, for example. Several different versions of "labor productivity" measures should be noted.

Output per Man-hour — This measure is merely the quotient of an index of output and an index of unweighted man-hours. We will note several variants, but first the use of unweighted man-hours deserves comment. Insofar as there is a relative shift of man-hours toward industries or occupations with relatively higher rates of pay in the base-period, this really means an increase in the quantity of labor input if it is agreed that higher-paid man-hours contribute more than lower-paid man-hours to production. Since there has been this type of shift, man-hours have a downward bias as a measure of "real labor input," and output per man-hour an upward bias. Also, from the viewpoint of collective bargaining, increases in output per man-hour do not give a measure of the extent to which wage rates of various occupational categories can be increased without inflationary implications, since some increase in average hourly earnings in the industry or economy is realized merely as a result of upgrading.

Certain measures of output per man-hour, including some of those published by the Bureau of Labor Statistics, relate output to *production worker man-hours* only, rather than all employee man-hours or the still broader concept of man-hours of all persons engaged including proprietors and unpaid family workers. Since World War II there has been a distinct decline in production workers as a proportion of all employees or persons engaged in manufacturing (where the distinction is particularly relevant). Since output results from the efforts of all persons engaged, output per production-worker has an upward bias as an efficiency measure. It can be argued that some non-production workers, such as those engaged in research and development, are not contributing to *current* output, and that insofar as such workers are an increasing proportion, this imparts a downward bias to output per man-hour measures that include all man-hours. Separate data on employment in investment-type activity are not generally available, but the defect of the ratio here would seem to be to indicate the desirability of including in output an allowance for the real value of the capital created by this activity.

A second problem in man-hour measurement relates to the choice between using "man-hours worked" and "man-hours paid for" data. Since the number of paid vacations, holidays, sick leave, etc., per employee has gradually increased, particularly since 1940, output per man-hour worked tends to rise somewhat faster than output per man-hour paid for. The divergence is indicated by the alternative BLS estimates for the private economy shown in Table 1. Industry hours data are usually collected only on a paid-for basis, but the Census Bureau's Current Population Survey data can be used to estimate hours worked—although a portion of the difference between the two series presented by BLS may be due to some conceptual differences other than the one noted. The consensus is that man-hours worked is the proper statistic for purposes of productivity analysis. In this case, however, to be consistent with output per man-hour worked, average hourly earnings should represent total compensation (including pay for time not worked) divided by man-hours worked. Thus, the increasing proportion of time paid for but not worked shows up as an increase in average earnings per man-hour worked over and above increases in wage-rates as such.

TABLE 1. *Productivity Ratios, Private Economy*[1]

Average Annual Percentage Rates of Change

	1889-1957	*1919-1957*	*1948-1957*
National Bureau of Economic Research			
Real product per unit of:			
Total factor input	1.7	2.1	2.1
Capital input	1.0	1.3	−0.2
Weighted man-hours[2]	2.0	2.4	3.1
Unweighted man-hours[2]	2.3	2.6	3.4
Bureau of Labor Statistics			
Real product per:			
Man-hours worked (Census)[3]			3.6
Man-hours paid for (BLS)[3]			3.1

1 The N.B.E.R. estimates relate to the private domestic economy, but real net income from abroad, which is deducted from private product to put it on a "domestic" basis, is a relatively minor item.

2 The man-hours used in these estimates are primarily man-hours worked, but in some industries only man-hours paid-for data were available.

3 There are other differences between the man-hour estimates based on Census as compared with BLS data.

Source: Computed by the compound interest formula from the estimates contained in Tables 2 and 3.

Output per Unit of Labor Input (Weighted Man-hours)— When man-hours worked are weighted by base-period average hourly earnings in about 40 industry groups of the private economy, the weighted aggregate rises significantly more than straight man-hours, and real product per unit of "labor input" (weighted man-hours) rises correspondingly less (see Table 1 and Chart 1). The weighted measure is economically more meaningful, as noted above, since it does not make sense to count an hour worked by a highly-trained engineer the same as an hour worked by an unskilled laborer. Note, however, that the measure shown does not reflect intra-industry shifts among smaller industry classes and among occupational groupings. If the effect of these shifts could be measured, weighted labor

Indexes of Productivity in the United States, 1889-1957
Estimates for the Private Domestic Economy

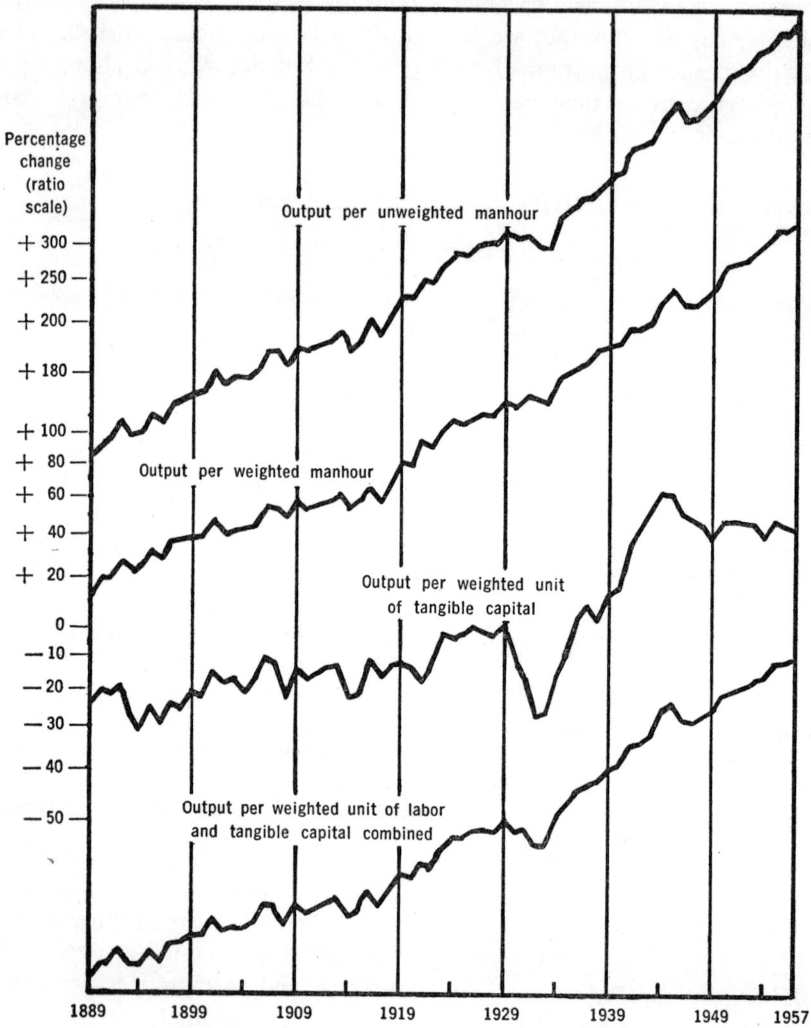

Source: S. Fabricant, *Basic Facts on Productivity Change,* Occasional Paper 63 (National Bureau of Economic Research, 1959).

CHART 1

input would probably rise significantly more than the available measure, and output per man-hour would be subject to even more of an upward bias than is indicated by the table. In other words, part of technological advance is caused by, or at least accompanied by, an upgrading of the labor force which is not fully measured by existing labor input measures. To this extent, productivity advance is less than available measures indicate. Output per unit of labor input also has an upward bias as an efficiency measure due to failure to take account of capital, as noted earlier.

Output per unit of capital input

This index, while referred to less than output per man-hour, is of interest in its own right as well as a component of the total factor productivity ratio. Like the "labor productivity" measures, "capital productivity" does not indicate changes in the efficiency of capital as such, nor in productive efficiency generally. It does indicate economies achieved over time in the use of capital per unit of output. The fact that the output-capital ratio has generally risen less than the output-labor ratio (Table 1) means that capital per unit of labor input has risen, and that the effect of rising overall productive efficiency on the output-capital ratio has been offset to some extent by the substitution of capital for labor. Conversely, factor substitution explains the fact that output per unit of labor input rises *more* than total productivity.

It is assumed that the input or "services" of capital are proportional to the deflated stock of capital goods—land, plant, equipment and inventories (net of depreciation in the case of plant and equipment). No adjustment is made for hours used as contrasted with hours available, since private capital carries an implicit charge, whether in use or not, as opposed to the labor factor, which is a direct private cost only when employed. The degree of utilization of capital is one aspect of productive efficiency from the private enterprise viewpoint; the degree of employment of the labor force is an aspect of *social* efficiency, but most productivity measures are constructed from the private economy standpoint.

Total factor productivity

Based on capital as well as labor input, this measure has risen less than the "labor productivity" measures since total input rose more than weighted man-hours due to the growth of capital per unit of labor input (Table 1 and Chart 1). Although the best measure of changing productive efficiency, total productivity measures are not yet published by government agencies (except for agriculture). This is due partly to theoretical and statistical problems connected with the measurement of real capital stocks and services. But interesting exploratory work along these lines has been done at the National Bureau of Economic Research and elsewhere. The total productivity studies reveal that output per man-hour indexes for the economy and most industries have an upward bias as measures of changing productive efficiency. We have already noted that both the labor and total productivity measures would probably show still smaller increases if man-hours (and capital) could be weighted in detail, and if the services of intangible capital were included in the inputs.

In the absence of total factor productivity measures, and particularly as supplements to these measures, indexes of output per man-hour can be useful if the limitations on their meaning are kept in mind. Even as indicators of productive efficiency, the bias is generally not very large, since labor input is the preponderent component of value added. Industries with the largest increases in output per man-hour generally show the largest increases in total productivity as well.

But it is important to observe that the bias of labor productivity indexes as measures of changes in productive efficiency differs from one period to another. For example, in the postwar period 1948-57, output per man-hour rose somewhat more than over the long period 1919-57. But this did *not* mean that the rate of advance in total factor productivity had accelerated. It merely reflected a higher rate of substitution of capital for labor due to the relatively high rate of investment in the postwar period. The rate of advance in total productivity was exactly the same in the postwar decade as it was over the longer period 1919-1957 (Table 1).

Concepts of factor cost or income

It is useful in analyzing price changes to be able to break down price per unit of output into the various types of costs per unit of output. Total costs of each type depend on the physical volume of input of the cost element, and its price. Thus, changes in labor cost per unit of output, for example, depend on changes in output per man-hour and on changes in average hourly earnings. If average hourly earnings rise faster than output per man-hour, unit labor cost will rise.

We are also interested in factor cost in its obverse role as factor income, and the factor income per unit of input as the price or wage of the factor. Wages in current dollars may be deflated by appropriate general price index numbers in order to estimate changes in real wages.

The national income and product accounts provide a consistent framework for this type of analysis. Corresponding to the notion of the national product is the concept of the national income, or "factor cost" of production. The alternative designations merely mean that the employment of factor services represents a cost from the viewpoint of the producer, but compensation or income to the owners of the factors. For example, wages and salaries are the cost of labor to the employer, but income to the employees.

The national income is sometimes called the net national product at factor cost. It is net of indirect business taxes and depreciation. It is estimated by summing the compensation of employees, net income of proprietors, net rents, royalties, and interest, and corporate profits. Functionally, it may be broken down into the compensations of the two major factor classes, labor and capital (including natural resources).

Labor compensation

Estimates of employee compensation should include all types of pay—not only wages and salaries as such, but also the "fringe benefits" or supplements, such as employer contributions to pension funds. The value of services to employees, such as the use of health and recreational facilities furnished without charge, could be included by imputation, but is generally not. Wages and salaries, plus the usual supplements as estimated in the national accounts and by Albert Rees for manufacturing, account for most of employee compensation.

To get an average employee compensation per hour, which is the "price" of labor services, total compensation should be divided by hours *worked.* This is consistent with the productivity measures, and makes sense in that firms are paying for hours of work. A relative increase in hours of paid vacation time, sick leave, holidays and other time paid for but not worked really represents an increase of labor cost per hour of productive work. Divergence between hours worked and paid for has been important only since about 1940. In the economy man-hour estimates, I was not able to get estimates of average hours worked for all industries, and my series include some hours paid for which impart a slight downward bias to the productivity and average hourly earnings estimates (but the two series are consistent in this regard). The Bureau of Labor Statistics has tried to estimate real product per man-hour on both bases (Table 2).

In studying changes in the functional distribution of income, imputed compensation for the labor of proprietors (and their unpaid family members) should be included with employee compensation. The same amount should properly be deducted from the total net income of proprietors in order to isolate the return to the proprietor's capital and enterprise. Since a conventional basis of imputation for the labor compensation of proprietors is the average earnings of employees in the same industry, the average earnings estimates based on employee compensation alone must be used in studying movements of the "price" of labor.

TABLE 2. *Indexes of Real Product per Man-Hour for the Private Economy, 1947-58*

(1947-49 = 100)

	Man-hour estimates based primarily on data from:							
	Bureau of Labor Statistics					*Bureau of Census*		
			Nonagricultural industries					
Year	*Total*	*Agri-culture*	*Total*	*Manu-facturing*	*Nonmanu-facturing*	*Total*	*Agri-culture*	*Nonagri-cultural industries*
1947	96.7	90.5	97.5	97.6	97.3	97.4	90.6	98.4
1948	100.2	107.1	99.4	100.1	98.9	100.3	107.5	99.4
1949	103.1	102.2	103.3	102.6	103.9	102.2	101.6	102.4
1950	110.4	116.2	108.8	109.5	108.4	110.3	116.1	108.5
1951	113.2	114.6	110.6	111.2	110.0	115.2	114.1	112.8
1952	115.7	124.5	112.0	113.0	111.3	118.9	124.0	115.5
1953	120.4	138.6	115.1	118.3	112.8	123.9	138.0	119.0
1954	122.6	148.3	116.9	117.4	116.7	127.0	147.9	121.8
1955	128.0	153.3	121.9	125.6	120.0	133.1	152.9	127.5
1956	128.8	160.7	121.8	127.1	119.1	134.2	160.2	127.7
1957	132.3	168.6	124.4	127.7	122.9	137.8	168.6	130.0
1958[1]	133.4	190.1	124.3	[2]	[2]	137.6	190.1	128.6

Source: "Recent Changes in Output per Man-hour, Total Private Economy and Major Sectors."
Material submitted by Ewan Clague, Commissioner of Labor Statistics, to Joint Economic Committee of Congress. (Bureau of Labor Statistics, processed release, 1959)

[1] Preliminary, subject to revision.

[2] Not available.

Note: The indexes in this table were computed by the Department of Labor, Bureau of Labor Statistics, from estimates of real product and man-hours. The real product estimates, referring to 1954 prices, are based primarily on national product statistics of the Department of Commerce, Office of Business Economics, except for the manufacturing real product estimates which were developed by the Bureau of Labor Statistics.

Output per man-hour estimates based primarily on Bureau of Labor Statistics man-hour data relate, in concept, to man-hours paid whereas estimates based primarily on Bureau of the Census labor force data relate, in concept, to hours worked. The difference between the two measures may, however, be due in part to statistical as well as conceptual differences. Both sets of man-hour estimates cover the man-hours of wage and salary workers, self-employed and unpaid family workers.

Concepts, methods, and sources are described in forthcoming BLS report, "Postwar Trends in Output Per Man-Hour, Total Private Economy and Major Sectors."

Capital compensation

When labor compensation is deducted from total national income (factor cost) for the economy or component industries, the remainder may be called the compensation of capital. It consists of net interest, rents and royalties, corporate profits, and the nonlabor portion of proprietors' net income. This total is useful (a) in surveying the changing distribution of national income between the two broad factor classes, (b) for computing capital charges (including profit) per unit of output as a companion series to unit labor cost, and (c) in estimating "price" of capital which is analogous to average hourly earnings.

Although estimates of real capital stocks and input are in little more than an exploratory stage, when capital compensation is divided by an index of real capital the quotient may be called an index of the "price of capital," that is, compensation per unit of real capital input. During years of relatively high-level production, it may be assumed that the real capital stock is utilized at comparable rates, so the index reflects compensation per real capital hour employed. But in other years, the index would tend to reflect cyclical variations in rates of utilization.

The compensation per unit of real capital input so computed reflects changes in two elements: (1) the average price of capital goods, and (2) the rate of return on net capital assets. Each of these components, which are important for inflation analysis along with average hourly labor earnings statistics, can be estimated separately. The average rate of return can be calculated as the percentage that capital compensation is of the value of the associated net capital assets in current prices. Price indexes are available for various major types of capital goods. If capital goods prices rise, the absolute return to capital must rise proportionately just in order to preserve a constant rate of return on capital values at replacement cost. But if the rate of return on capital rises, there is ground for suspicion that price inflation may be the result of demand inflation.

Concept of the price level

The most comprehensive available index of final prices is the index used to deflate the gross national product. We shall call this the "national price index." It represents a weighted average of price indexes for all the final goods and services purchased in the nation's economy from one period to another—consumption goods and services, capital goods, and government purchases. Actually, the individual price indexes used for deflating the national product are drawn largely from the consumers price indexes (for personal consumption expenditures) and the wholesale price indexes (for capital goods, including inventory change, and government purchases), supplemented by indexes from several other sources, such as the composite construction cost index compiled by the Commerce Department and the Department of Agriculture's indexes of prices paid by farmers for family living. Coverage is comprehensive, but not complete.

The meaning of the national price index may be expressed by saying that it measures changes in the average prices of the changing collection of goods and services that make up the national product. This concept may be contrasted with that of the Consumer Price Index (CPI), which reflects changes in the average prices of the contents of a market basket of goods which is held constant over intermediate time periods reflecting the buying patterns of urban wage earners in the base period. That is, the national price index has quantity weights that change in each time period as expenditure patterns change; the weights for CPI are changed only occasionally. The different weighting procedures, as well as the differences in coverage, would tend to cause the indexes to move somewhat differently.

Now, what index should be used for deflating factor income in order to estimate real wages, or real nonlabor compensation? Actually, we do not have information as to the distribution of each type of factor compensation among alternative uses, and so we cannot construct an ideal deflator. The compromise that I have adopted is to deflate the compensation of each factor class by the national price index. This has the advantage that real factor compensation will thereby equal real national product, although the deflator does not perfectly reflect the patterns of spending or saving out of each type of income. Rees has adopted the more conventional compromise of deflating wages (plus supplements) by the Consumer Price Index. This is also not perfectly satisfactory, since some wage income is subject to the personal income tax and some is saved, although the proportion is probably minor. Further, while the CPI is designed to measure the prices paid for family living of industrial wage-earners in cities above a certain size, some wage income is spent in smaller places, or in types of stores not covered.

As a practical matter, the CPI and the national price index do not differ widely in trend. Thus, the movements of real labor income whether obtained through deflation by the CPI or the national price index show the same general trends. Both are, of course, subject to the shortcomings of all available price indexes, which will be discussed further in the next section.

Sources and methods of measurement

Not only must movements of productivity, cost and price index numbers be viewed in the context of the concepts underlying the measures, but we must also remember that the movements are influenced by the adequacy of the basic data and the methods of preparing the measures. In general, it may be said that all the measures are at best approximations because of lack of perfect data, and that their movements are to some extent a function of the methods used in their preparation. Here, we can do no more than mention a few of the major methodological problems, and give a general appraisal of the reliability of the estimates in the light of the nature of the basic data sources.

Prices

It is convenient to start with the price indexes, since these are not only our "dependent variable," but they are used to deflate value of output to get real product used in the productivity estimates, and to convert current dollar factor compensation to dollars of constant purchasing power.

All price indexes are based on sample data. It would obviously be impractical and far too costly to collect data on the prices established in all transactions in the economy, or even certain major classes of transactions such as retail or wholesale sales. The Labor Department collects data for certain dates in each month or quarter, from selected distributive outlets in selected cities or regions for specified types of goods or services whose price movements are believed to be representative of price movements for other qualities or price lines of the product type and other types in the general product family. In recent years the reasonableness of the "imputations" involved has been periodically tested, and pricing procedures adjusted as necessary. The large number of items priced for both the consumer and wholesale price indexes suggests that the indexes reflect quite well the broad movement of the general price level that is covered, but this cannot be proved since there are not even occasional comprehensive estimates.

The degree of coverage of the broad price indexes has gradually increased over the years, and the methods employed have improved. Although the indexes for earlier years are of somewhat poorer quality than those for more recent years, Albert Rees has improved on earlier consumer price indexes for the years from 1890 to 1914 (when the Labor Department index begins) by significantly expanding the coverage of relevant items.

In the overall national product price deflator, there are more imputations of price movement of covered to uncovered items than is true of the CPI. More importantly, some of the "price" indexes used for deflating certain components of the gross private product, and all of the government product, are little more than input price indexes—wage rates, sometimes combined with materials prices. This type of pseudo-price index is used for products that are custom built and therefore cannot be consistently priced over time, such as ships, aircraft, and new construction, and also for services of households and nonprofit institutions which are obviously not priced. Since these input price indexes contain no allowance for productivity advance, they are subject to an upward bias to the degree that productivity has advanced in the sectors involved.

It is well known that price indexes are biased upward to the degree that the quality of the same products has improved over time, on net balance. Also, since new products are not introduced into price indexes until their production is commercially significant, this introduces a slight further upward bias into price indexes since usually the relative price of a new good declines significantly during the phase of rapid output expansion.

Finally, there is the weighting problem posed by the fact that the composition of market baskets changes over time, whether it is the market basket of the nation or of the families of urban wage-earners. Since there is a tendency for purchasers to shift to items which are falling relatively in price, recent quantity weights generally result in a slower rise in a composite price index than is the case when weights from an earlier period are used. The weights of the consumer and wholesale price indexes are changed only occasionally, and then the new weights are not used to re-weight earlier years but only the time segment from the year of the shift onward. The national price index involves annually changing weights in respect to the several hundred expenditure categories of the national product that are separately deflated, so that it tends to rise less than other composite indexes.

A system of variable weights is required for a price deflator designed to convert a value series to constant prices. But even in a consumer price index, there are good arguments in favor of frequently changing weights in order to reflect the changing patterns of consumption. My own opinion is that the CPI contains some upward bias because of the infrequent changes in weights. Despite the several sources of upward bias in the available price indexes, however, I do not think they are great enough to call into serious question the basically inflationary tendencies of our times.

Productivity

Evaluation of the sources and methods used to calculate productivity indexes must be made in terms of output and input separately. It should not be thought, however, that the margins of error in the numerator and denominator are compounded in the productivity ratio. Since the data for both output and input tend to be drawn from the same or consistent sources, and consistent methods are used in estimating both series, it is reasonable to suppose that the margins of error attaching to productivity changes are less than those attaching to changes in the individual components.

Output — Estimates of the current dollar value of output in the economy or its industrial segments, and physical volume estimates that can be made for some industries, are tied into data obtained from periodic comprehensive economic censuses (now a quinquennial basis). Estimates for intervening years, and for years since the most recently available census, are based on sample or partial data. This makes it clear that estimates are more reliable in indicating trends over a number of years than annual changes; and they are less reliable for years since the most recent benchmark. At present, estimates are being tied into the 1954 censuses; results of the 1958 censuses will not be available until 1960. Monthly or quarterly estimates are based on still more partial data than the annual estimates. Certainly, significance should not be attached to small changes or differences in the order of tenths of percentage points.

Even the trend of the national product estimates prior to 1929 is not as accurate as that since 1929, since a number of important economic censuses were first taken in that year. Censuses for several industries, including manufacturing, go back to the 19th century, so early output estimates for these industries do have reliable benchmarks although the degree of product detail is often less in earlier censuses than in those for more recent years.

When physical volume estimates are obtained by deflating the value of product, the real output estimates are subject to the same shortcomings as are the price indexes. That is, since the price indexes are based on samples, their margins of error carry over into the output figures. The use of input prices as deflators for some segments of national product creates a downward bias in real product that I have estimated to be around 10 per cent (or 0.2 percentage point) of the average annual secular growth rate. Inability to measure net quality improvements also creates a downward bias in real output and productivity corresponding to the upward bias of the price indexes. Finally, failure of price data to catch special discounts tends to dampen their cyclical amplitude which accentuates the fluctuations of real product and productivity estimates. To illustrate, equipment installation costs may be absorbed by the seller in recessions but added as an extra charge in boom times. Our price indexes do not catch such changes in terms of sale.

Two qualifications with respect to quality bias should be noted. Insofar as quality improvement is associated with a larger volume of factor and material inputs required by a new model of a product, the associated increase in unit cost is deducted from the price change by the Labor Department, so real product increases to the extent that quality changes are accompanied by increased real cost of a commodity. Second, real product increases as a result of *shifts* of expenditures from lower to higher price-lines (qualities) of the same product.

Output is sometimes estimated as a weighted aggregate of physical units of various types of goods, such as tons of steel or numbers of tractors of various types, as is possible for manufacturing. Theoretically, this would give the same result as deflating output values if data were perfect. Since data are not perfect, a few possible shortcomings of physical production series should be noted.

Physical unit data are not available for all goods produced. In manufacturing, the proportion of value added covered by items for which units were reported increased from about one-half to more than two-thirds between 1899 and 1954. The physical volume indexes are usually adjusted for changing coverage by a procedure that involves the assumption that the average price (or unit value added) of the uncovered items moves with that of the covered items. So price imputations, with attendant possible margins of error, are involved in "physical" production as well as in deflated value estimates.

Physical units are often reported for more or less gross categories, and not for the various qualities of a product separately. For example, numbers of pairs of shoes produced are reported separately for the categories "children's," "ladies'," and "men's," but not for the many price lines of each. To the extent that there has been a secular shift toward higher quality types of a product group, the physical production indexes tend to have a downward bias which is not present in deflated value series. But since the amount and degree of detail of physical unit data have increased in recent censuses, the possible biases have grown less.

A final point involves the relationship of gross and net output. Most industry output measures are available on a gross basis only. In farming, for which both measures are available, net output has increased significantly less than gross because of the increasing relative purchases by farmers of intermediate products from other industries. In the case of manufacturing, for which estimates of net output have been prepared by the Labor Department commencing in 1947, there has been little difference between movements of the net and gross output measures. Other evidence suggests that this may have been typical of most non-extractive industries.

Weighting is a technical matter, but it should be noted that recent price weights produce somewhat smaller increases in physical output series than do earlier weights. The important thing in productivity analysis is that a consistent weighting system should be applied to outputs, inputs, and related series.

Inputs — Man-hours worked are usually obtained as the product of employment and average-hours-worked estimates. Employment estimates have been quite good even on an annual basis since 1939, when Social Security data became available. In earlier periods, employment estimates are tied into the periodic industry censuses or reports of regulatory agencies, and in the trade, finance and service areas are tied into industry groupings of the occupational data gathered in the decennial Census of Population. The estimates give a good picture of trends, but annual estimates up to 1939 are less accurate since they are based on partial data, as are current monthly estimates. It is important that the economy employment estimates since 1929, underlying the productivity estimates in Table 1, are estimated by the Commerce Department on a consistent basis with the national product (and employee compensation) estimates. Likewise, Albert Rees' estimates for manufacturing are consistent with his output and wage estimates, since all are based on the Census of Manufactures.

The estimates of average hours worked are not as high in quality as the employment estimates. Until the postwar period, man-hour data were not included in the censuses. For earlier years, and for interpolation between censuses, estimates are based on sample or partial data, or adjustments of standard workweek data to an actual average weekly hours basis. Much of the average-hours data relate only to production workers, in which case it is usually assumed that the trend of average hours worked by non-production workers applies to all employees, and to proprietors if they are included. Once again, it is apparent that average-hours and man-hours estimates are better indicators of trend than of short-period changes.

Even for trend indications, the tendency toward an increasing proportion of time paid for but not worked since 1939 or so has created problems. Manufacturing *Census* and *Annual Survey* data are on an hours-worked basis since 1947, but Rees had to rely on fragmentary data to adjust the BLS estimates of average hours paid for to an hours worked basis back to the 1930's. The economy man-hour estimates are primarily hours worked, but unavailability of necessary information necessitated use of hours-paid-for data in some instances, which imparts a slight upward bias to the series over the last two decades.

Estimates of real capital stocks are generally obtained by deflating the book value of assets, or depreciating real purchases of new fixed assets over their lifetimes and cumulating the net additions. The latter "perpetual inventory" method was used by Raymond Goldsmith in his *Study of Savings in the United States*. Goldsmith's estimates largely underlie the real capital input series implied in Table 3. These estimates are not as reliable

TABLE 3. *Productivity Ratios, Private Domestic Economy*

National Bureau of Economic Research Estimates

(Index Numbers, 1929 = 100)

Year	*Real product per unit of* Total Factor Input	Capital Input	Weighted Man-hours	Unweighted Man-hours
1889	56.0	74.8	50.0	43.6
1919	82.1	86.8	80.4	79.0
1929	100.0	100.0	100.0	100.0
1937	113.6	107.7	115.6	114.0
1948	145.9	144.6	146.4	156.7
1953	166.4	145.3	173.1	190.9
1957	179.4	142.4	192.6	211.7

Note: Annual estimates, plotted in the chart, may be found in Solomon Fabricant, *Basic Facts on Productivity Change*, Occasional Paper 63, National Bureau of Economic Research, 1959.

as the labor input estimates due in part to inadequacies in the capital-goods price deflators, and possibly unrealistic assumptions as to economic lengths of life of capital goods, not to mention margins of error attaching to the current dollar capital outlay or asset estimates. The trends of real capital stocks gotten by alternative methods are relatively parallel over long periods, but there may be common errors in both methods.

The same system of occasionally changing weights was used to combine individual labor and capital input estimates by industry, and to aggregate the two types of input, as was used for the output estimates. As is true of consumers, producers tend to shift to inputs that are becoming relatively cheaper, which helps account for the increase in real capital relative to labor input. Since differences in weight-base make a similar difference in the movements of output and of input indexes, the differences between total productivity indexes on alternative bases are minimized.

Factor compensation

Employee compensation estimates generally come from the same sources as the employment estimates, and are of comparable quality. It is important that the average earnings and productivity estimates are consistent as in the economy estimates and Rees' estimates for manufacturing.

The economy capital compensation estimates are subject to a somewhat larger margin of error. Interest and net rent are estimated by a somewhat roundabout procedure. But it is the corporate profit estimates that are subject to the greatest margins of error as far as the national accounts are concerned. Profits are calculated after deduction of depreciation allowances at original costs, in line with corporate accounting procedure. When prices are rising, depreciation reserves are inadequate to cover replacements at current prices, the level of profits is overstated, and the movements may be distorted. The Commerce Department is experimenting with the estimation of depreciation in constant dollars and current replacement cost as well as in original cost, which will make possible adjustment of the profit estimates, but these are not yet published.

When compensation is divided by the same output and input indexes used in the productivity ratios, the resulting unit-factor-cost and factor-price measures are, of course, consistent with the productivity estimates and may be used together in price analysis. An example of this use is contained in Table 4, which illustrates the basic relationship set forth at the beginning of the paper.

Need for statistical improvements

Although annual estimates of productivity, prices and wages are available going back to the late nineteenth century, this review has indicated that they are far from perfect. The estimates probably give a fairly good notion of the general order of magnitude of trend rates of change, but even these should be interpreted in terms of the known biases in the series—par-

TABLE 4. *Productivity, Product Prices and Factor Prices Private-Domestic Economy*

(Average annual percentage rates of change for selected periods)

	(1)	*(2)*	*(3)*	*(4)*	*(5)*
				Factor Prices	
Period	*Product Prices*[1]	*Total Factor Productivity*	*Total*[2]	*Labor*	*Capital*
1919–1953	1.2	2.1	3.3	3.8	1.9
1948–1957[3]	1.6	2.1	3.7	5.2	−1.0

Source: As published in J. W. Kendrick, "Productivity: Contributions of Capital and Labor," *The Conference Board Business Record,* June, 1958. Based on estimates by Kendrick for the National Bureau of Economic Research. See also the Joint Economic Committee, Compendium, "The Relationship of Prices to Economic Stability and Growth" (G.P.O., March 31, 1958), pp. 225-236.

[1] At factor cost. If 100% is added to the average annual percentage rates of change, column (1) = column (3) ÷ column (2).

[2] Column (3) is the weighted average of columns (4) and (5). Column (4) is based on estimates of average hourly labor compensation, and column (5) on the quotient of current value capital compensation and the constant dollar stock of real capital goods. In effect, column (5) is based on the product of a composite capital goods price index and the rate of return on capital.

[3] Preliminary.

ticularly the downward bias in the real product and productivity estimates and the upward bias in the price index numbers. Significance should definitely not be attached to small annual changes in the variables. Monthly or quarterly productivity estimates, needed for detailed analysis of price-cost relationships particularly in current periods, are not available at all on a regular basis.

There can be little question but what further expansion and improvement in the relevant statistics would improve the quality of our analysis and understanding of the inflationary process. A program to improve federal statistics was outlined in the *1958 Economic Report of the President (Appendix C).* We shall mention here only a few of the major improvements needed in the estimates of the variables with which we have been concerned.

In the first place, the coverage of the price indexes needs to be expanded. There are major gaps in the areas of consumer and business services, producers goods, new construction, and government procurement items, particularly munitions. Further attempts to collect realistic net realized prices rather than list prices should be made. Improvement in price series not only increases our knowledge of price change, but also of changes in production when deflated values are resorted to as in the case of the real national product.

Relatively good estimates of payrolls, employment, average hours and average hourly earnings exist for many industries, but even here industry coverage needs to be expanded, particularly in the noncommodity-producing sectors. The samples underlying the BLS monthly estimates would need to be strengthened in this area. Information about average hours worked by nonproduction workers is also needed. Equally important, industry data on hours paid for as well as hours worked should be collected; these would be useful both for productivity estimates and for estimates of average earnings per hour worked. In addition to direct payroll costs, data on supplements to wages and salaries are needed so that total labor compensation per hour worked can be calculated.

With respect to estimates of capital compensation, current quarterly estimates of corporate profits and net income of proprietors need to be strengthened. Further work in the national accounts is needed to estimate depreciation in terms of replacement costs as well as original cost, and to adjust the profit estimates accordingly.

On the output side of the productivity estimates, it will be a major contribution when the real private national product can be broken down by major segments in addition to the present farm-nonfarm division. Such a breakdown within the national accounting framework will permit the consistent estimation and analysis of prices, productivity and costs by industry. Productivity estimates by smaller industry divisions, such as are currently estimated by BLS for several manufacturing and nonmanufacturing industries, should also be expanded.

Significant improvement in the quality and coverage of output estimates depends, of course, on improvements in basic data. The cornerstones of our statistical system are the periodic economic censuses, with annual sample surveys for intervening years. Yet even the censuses do not cover all areas of the economy, and annual surveys are made only for manufacturing and trade. Even within manufacturing, physical volume data should be collected in somewhat greater product detail to permit the compilation of more accurate output indexes. The coverage of the monthly or quarterly Census *Facts for Industry* reports is far less than that of the annual surveys, as indicated by the fact that more than half of the well known Federal Reserve Board Index of Manufacturing Production is based on adjusted man-hours rather than physical volume series. If we wish to know more about production and productivity on a monthly or quarterly basis, basic data collection will have to be expanded. There is a limit on the extent to which ingenuity can be substituted for data.

Annual employment data are in good shape, and we have already noted the areas in which monthly reporting of employment and average hours need to be strengthened. There are, however, no continuing estimates at all of the real capital stock of the nation or its industry division. Even if we were content to work in terms of output per man-hour rather than estimates of total factor productivity, knowledge of changes in real capital per worker or per man-hour is important for explaining changes in labor productivity.

Capital estimates are also necessary to explain changes in capital costs per unit of output. It is true that labor represents the major factor cost of production, but in analyzing the sequence of price-cost change, labor cost must be looked at in conjunction with the cost of capital.

At best, the analysis of dynamic economic processes is not simple. But there can be no doubt that a better analytical job could be done if our basic economic statistics were further improved.

3. Underlying factors in the postwar inflation

JAMES S. DUESENBERRY

Introduction

Whenever we suffer from any evil, we have a natural tendency to seek a devil on which to blame it. The inflation of the last twelve years is no exception. Some blame government spending, some blame the trade unions, some blame the price policies of industry. In fact, the inflation of the postwar period is a very complex phenomenon with many causes. The rise in the general price level is the resultant of diverse movements of half a dozen different groups of prices. Moreover, the forces at work on those groups of prices have operated differently in different time periods.

The complexity of the inflation can be shown by even a very brief examination of the movements of different groups of prices. Rents and the prices of other services have risen steadily ever since the war. The prices of durable manufactures have moved upward in step fashion, periods of rapid increase being followed by periods of relative stability. The wholesale prices of non-durable manufactures on the other hand have moved erratically. They rose rapidly after World War II, declined moderately

---

JAMES S. DUESENBERRY is Professor of Economics at Harvard University. His books include *Income Saving Theory of Consumer Behavior* and *Business Cycles and Economic Growth.*

from mid-1948 to the beginning of the Korean War, rose rapidly during that war, fell from 1951 to 1956, and rose slowly until the end of 1957. Food prices also moved erratically but with even more violent fluctuations. Finally retail margins in the durable goods field fell significantly for some years after the Korean War.

The movements of general price indices such as the Consumer Price Index (CPI) and the Bureau of Labor Statistics (BLS) wholesale price index are weighted averages of the diverse movements of the components. The periods of most rapid increase in these general indices are naturally those in which all the components were rising. On the other hand, periods of stability were those in which increases in some components were offset by decreases in others. In particular during the period from mid-1951 to mid-1956, increases in rents, other service prices and wholesale prices of durable manufactures were offset by reductions in food prices, prices of non-durable manufactures and retail margins on durable goods. The general indices conceal as much as they reveal, and we cannot understand the nature of the inflation until we understand the causes of the divergent movements of the component prices indices underlying the general ones.

This complex pattern of movements (and I have drastically understated the real complexity in the interest of brevity) should make one suspicious of any simple general explanation of the postwar movement of the price level.

In this paper I have attempted to sort out the various factors responsible for the rise in prices since the end of World War II. To that end I shall begin with a brief review of the classical or "demand-pull" explanation of inflation and its newer competitor the "cost-push" theory. Before attempting to evaluate those explanations, we must examine in some detail the movements of different types of prices. Later, the movements of several different types of prices since the start of the Korean War are examined in some detail. It is argued that the major factor responsible for the general rise in prices since 1951 is the high rate of increase in wages generally. The effects of rising labor costs were offset for a time by the downward adjustment in profit margins, and raw material prices from the high levels reached during the Korean War. Rising wage costs were also offset for a time by falling retail margins on durable goods. From the beginning of 1956 the effects of rising wage costs were reinforced by the cyclical upturn in profit margins and by rising raw material prices. Throughout the postwar period, prices of consumer services, particularly transportation and medical services, have been rising more rapidly than other prices. This was largely due to their slow rise during the war.

Some temporary factors like lagged adjustment of service prices have reinforced the effects of rising wage costs, and others like retail margins for durables have offset them.

Similarly, profit margins and raw material prices have moved erratically —sometimes reinforcing, sometimes offsetting rising wage costs. Those factors obscure our understanding of the picture, but it seems safe to say that over the whole period since the Korean War their effects on the general price level roughly cancel out. We are left with the conclusion that rising wages are primarily responsible for the rise in prices since 1951.

That does not tell us what caused the inflation, it only shows that the causes worked through wages. In another section we turn to the causes of the wage inflation. It is argued first that neither the "trade union pressure" explanation nor the "demand-pull" explanation is by itself adequate to explain what has happened to wages. It is then argued that demand-pull has been a major factor in the rise in wages in the trade and service sectors, that trade union pressure is the more important factor in manufacturing, construction utilities and transport. Finally, it is argued that trade union pressure and the balance of supply and demand in labor markets interact with one another in determining both the extent of wage increases in unionized industries and the secondary effects of those increases on wage movements in other sectors.

Trade union pressure played a major role in the inflation of the past few years, but that pressure would have been much less effective and wages of unorganized workers would have risen still less had demand for labor not been so strong. We turn later to the explanation of demand and argue there that the special buoyancy of postwar demand has been due to

(1) the very favorable situation in which the economy found itself at the end of the war,

(2) the high marriage and birth rates of the postwar years, and

(3) the rise in government expenditures.

Many other factors of course influence the movement of income, but those are the ones which account for the strength and duration of the postwar boom.

There is, of course, no particular reason for picking out any one of those factors as responsible for the demand component in this inflation. If any one of them had been removed, we would have had no problem of excess demand for labor.

Finally, it must be noted that the supply of labor (excluding women over 45) grew at a very low rate in the postwar years. To some extent our problem was not an abnormally high rate of growth of demand but a low rate of growth of labor supply.

I shall conclude with a few remarks on the policy problems posed by this analysis of the causes of inflation.

Theories of inflation

The classical theory

Inflation is not a new phenomenon, and economists have long had explanations which seemed to give a satisfactory account of the observed periods of inflation. Most of those incidents, it should be noted, took place during wars or immediately after wars. The classical analysis of inflation can be summarized in the following way.

Suppose that for any reason the aggregate amount of goods and services (measured by their value at current prices) which households, business and governments wish to buy increases from one year to the next. Suppose that the increase exceeds the increase in industrial capacity. But also suppose that additional labor can be recruited without an increase in wage rates. As a result, prices and profit margins will tend to increase because additional output can only be obtained at higher cost, through overtime work, use of obsolete plants, or badly located plants, etc. That tendency may be offset by the increase in labor productivity which takes place with the passage of time. In that case the increase in demand has forestalled a decline in prices instead of causing an increase. How much of a price increase will result will depend on competitive conditions and pricing policies of firms and on the speed with which the increase in demand takes place.

In industries dominated by a few large firms following long-run price policies, the increase may be confined to the elimination of price shading of various kinds because those firms expect capacity to catch up with demand and do not wish to first increase prices and then reduce them. In sectors with larger numbers of firms, prices will have to rise enough to make it currently profitable to produce the additional output.[1] In agriculture, prices will have to rise enough to bring demand into line with available supplies because of the time lag involved in increasing output. The amount of price increase will be much influenced by the expectations of speculative holders of existing stocks. In any case, it is clear that any increase in demand in excess of the increase in capacity will tend to produce price increases.

Let us now revise our assumptions and suppose that industrial capacity increases as much as the amount of goods demanded at the initial price level. Suppose, however, that there was no more than the frictional minimum amount of unemployment at the start and that the increase in output

---

[1] In some cases it may be physically impossible to increase output to meet demand. In competitive industries prices will then have to rise enough to reduce the amount demanded to the amount available. In industries dominated by a few firms there may be informal rationing or a build up of unfilled orders.

potential of the labor supply (resulting from increased labor supply and increased productivity) falls short of the increase in demand. In those circumstances wages will tend to rise as employers bid against one another for labor (if the increase in demand is regarded as permanent). Prices will also be increased. In industries with a small number of firms, prices are likely to rise by the full amount of the increase in costs (including the increase in raw material or component costs due to rising wages in other industries). That is so because prices in those industries are limited by such factors as fear of attracting entry or fear that customers will decide to make rather than buy.[2] If production costs rise for old firms they will rise for new ones as well.

In other industries there may be some squeeze on profit margins, but most of the increase in wage costs (plus increases in materials costs) will be reflected in prices.

We have considered separately the cases in which demand increases faster than industrial capacity or faster than the output potential of the labor supply. Of course, both limits on output may be effective at once.

Thus far we have considered a one-shot increase in demand. What happens next. The mere fact that prices have risen will not stop the inflationary process.[3] The increase in prices would reduce the amount of goods and services demanded if money incomes did not rise, but it is in the nature of the case that money incomes and expected future incomes will rise with prices. If wages and prices rise, consumer expenditures will increase. On the other hand, when there is a price increase but no wage increase (i.e. when demand increases faster than capacity) profits are increased and businesses are likely to expand investment expenditures by at least as much as the increase in profits. After the first round of price and/or wage increases, real demand (i.e. expenditures adjusted for price change) is likely to be just as high as before the price increase.[4] However, if the initial force behind the first increase in demand was a single shot, real demand will not increase and, after some further price and/or wage increases, capacity and labor supply will eventually catch up and stop the price increase. According to classical theory, a continuing inflation will take place only if demand

---

[2] This is, of course, a crude and inadequate statement of the many factors determining prices in oligopolistic enterprises. The important point is that firms in these industries have not usually charged the prices which would maximize their profits in the short run. They are therefore able to raise prices when costs rise.

[3] In the discussion which follows it is assumed that the terms on which credit is available are not changed by the rise in prices. Monetary factors are discussed in a later section.

[4] For purposes of this discussion, I have assumed that the government's budget for purchases of goods and services is fixed in real terms in that money expenditures for goods and services will rise with the price level. With fixed legislation some types of tax revenue will rise by a greater percentage than the price level. Other types of tax revenue and transfer payments will rise less than proportionately. Some rough calculations indicate that the two factors will just about cancel each other.

at constant prices tends to grow faster than industrial capacity or labor supply, adjusted for productivity increase.

The cost-push theory

The so-called cost-push theory is not strictly speaking an entirely independent theory of the causes of inflation. It is rather a major amendment of, or addition to, the excess-demand theory outlined above. No one who supports the cost-push theory denies the essential correctness of the argument given above. Those who support the cost-push approach deny the applicability of the classical theory to the inflation in the American economy in the last few years. Essentially, they argue that trade union pressure can cause prices to rise in circumstances in which the classical theory tells us they ought not to rise.

Suppose for example that there is moderate unemployment so that there is no shortage of labor at existing wage rates but no great surplus either. Similarly suppose that industrial capacity is fairly well utilized but not excessively so. In those circumstances employers have no incentive to raise wages or prices. If, over a period of time, demand increases at about the same rate as labor supply (adjusted for productivity) and industrial capacity, prices will be constant or perhaps fall as productivity increases.

On this peaceful scene the villain now appears—the trade union. Trade unions, by threatening to strike, slow down, and raise hell generally, force employers to grant wage increases which they would not otherwise give. The employers then raise prices by the corresponding amount or proportion. If we can assume either (a) that trade unions have organized the whole labor force or (b) that they exercise an indirect influence on the wages of unorganized workers, so that their wages also increase, the general rise in wages does not cause unemployment. Everything is essentially as it was before, except that prices and wages are higher.

Assumption (a) is obviously untrue for the American economy and assumption (b) is extremely doubtful. Alternatively, suppose that demand for the commodities produced by trade unionists is either inelastic (sales do not fall much as prices increase) or growing. Then it can be argued, though I shall not go into details, that the wage and price increases are likely to generate roughly as large a percentage increase in money expenditures as in the average price level. The process is not *per se* self-limiting in the short run.

Over long periods there must be some limits to the power of trade unions to push up wages relative to the wages in the unorganized sections. Presumably, as union non-union differentials increase, the danger that non-union firms will grow at the expense of unionized ones will increase and so will the danger that new non-union firms will appear. Similarly, the effect of competition from substitute products produced by non-union workers will become greater. The effectiveness of these factors in limiting wage increases will vary with the competitive structure of the industry, ease of entry, and the ability of the trade union to restrict the activities of non-union workers and employers.

The effectiveness of those limiting factors may be reduced if increases in union wages have a significant influence on non-union wages. However, it does seem likely that unions whose membership covers only a fraction of the labor force cannot push up wages indefinitely unless there are other factors which tend to generate wage increases in other sectors.

The monetary factor

An inflationary spiral, whether originally due to excess demand or to trade union pressure, may in principle be choked off if the money supply does not increase. If prices increase and the volume of real production does not decrease, the amount of money balances which businesses and households wish to hold will increase. This will cause interest rates to rise and may also reduce the availability of credit (i.e. cause lenders to refuse to lend to some borrowers of marginal quality who were previously accommodated).

Prior to 1951 the monetary factor did not impede the inflation, because the Federal Reserve was committed to a policy of providing enough bank reserves to prevent a long-term rise in interest rates. But from the end of 1952 to the end of 1957 demand deposits and currency have grown by only 4%, while during the same period Gross National Product (in dollar terms) has grown by about 40%. Interest rates have accordingly risen. However, the extent of the rise required has been limited by the willingness of the public to hold money substitutes, i.e. time and savings deposits and savings and loan shares and treasury bills. The resulting rise in interest rates and the accompanying reduction in availability of funds to borrowers of moderate quality (and to those trying to obtain government guaranteed mortgages) have undoubtedly restricted demand to some extent but not enough to control the inflation.[5]

Price movement since 1950

As I have already indicated, the prices of different types of goods have followed different patterns in the postwar years. To gain an understanding of the movements of the general price level, we have to have some knowl-

[5] It is undoubtedly true, however, that if the Federal Reserve wished to adopt a sufficiently stringent policy, it could limit the growth of money expenditures to any extent that it wished.

edge of how its components moved. In this section I shall consider the movements of a number of different kinds of prices in the period since the beginning of the Korean War in June 1950. The movements of prices in the years from 1946 to 1950 were so dominated by the special circumstances connected with decontrol and reconversion that they throw little light on the long-term inflation problem. That is also true of price movements during the first year of the Korean War. But the latter movements left some important after-effects we must consider if we are to understand later price movements.

In this section we will first consider the reasons for the rapid rise in the prices of services in the years since World War II. There follows a brief outline of the movements of raw materials prices since the start of the Korean War and a very brief comment on the decline in retail margins for consumer durables. Next there are some observations on the changes in labor cost in manufacturing and a discussion of manufacturing profit margins. Finally, the results of the preceding section are brought together in a discussion of their influence on the prices of finished manufactures and on the Consumer Price Index.

Service prices

One of the outstanding features of the pattern of price movements since the end of World War II is the steady upward movement of the prices of services—gas and electricity, transportation services, medical services and personal and repair services. Other prices have had their ups and downs and periods of stability, but service prices have moved upward month after month and year after year. Moreover, since 1951 service prices as a whole have moved upward more rapidly than the general price index, or than any major category of prices. Indeed, since 1951 virtually the whole increase in the Consumer Price Index is due to the increase in the prices of services and rents. The BLS All Services Index rose from 114 in 1951 to 140 at the end of 1957. The commodities index rose from 110.3 to 114.7 (see chart: *Prices of Commodities and Services*).

Further examination of the price indices for services indicates that between 1939 and 1948 the prices of medical services, transportation services, and gas and electricity rose much less than the prices of most other things. Other services (consisting mainly of laundry, dry cleaning, barber and beauty shop services and various kinds of repair services) rose in price by about as much as most commodities. From 1939 to date, however, the prices of services as a whole have risen only a little less than the prices of commodities. (The rise was much smaller for gas and electricity, much larger for transportation, and somewhat larger for medical services and other services.)

Finally, wage increases in the service industries were not very different from those in manufacturing, though they were slightly smaller. We do not have adequate figures on productivity in the service field. However, estimates of productivity-change for the private non-agricultural sector as a whole show a somewhat smaller increase in productivity than the estimate for manufacturing. Wage costs for the service industries as a whole must therefore have changed in roughly the same way as for manufacturing.

Over the whole period since 1939, then, service prices have moved upward with wage costs. Electricity rates rose much less than other prices

Prices of Commodities and Services

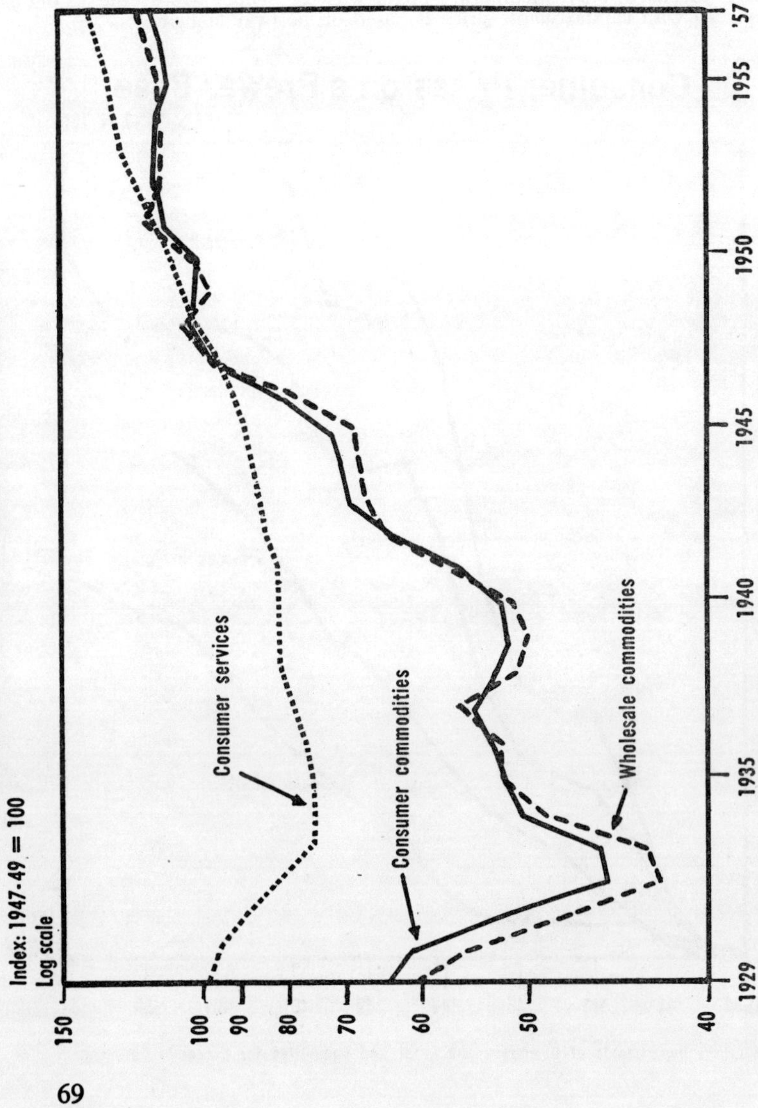

Sources: Departments of Commerce and Labor and Committee for Economic Development

partly because labor costs are less important than in other industries [6] and partly because of the great improvement in load factors. Public transportation prices have risen more than commodity prices because of the volume problems of the public transport services.

The relative rise in service prices since 1951 is due to two factors. First, the prices of public transportation, gas and electricity rose less than other prices during and immediately after the war and more afterward because the regulatory process works slowly. Prices of medical services followed the same pattern because of the delaying influence of custom on

[6] This is of course only a temporary factor whose influence will decline as old capital is replaced with capital whose price is based on postwar labor costs.

Consumer Prices on a Prewar Base

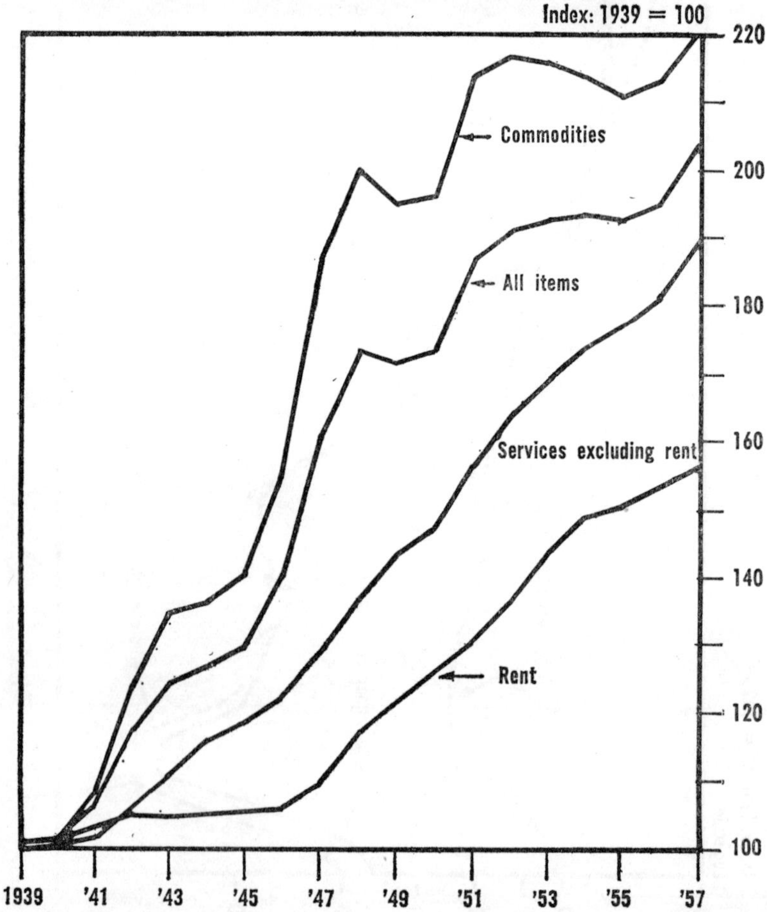

Sources: Departments of Commerce and Labor and Committee for Economic Development

changes in medical charges. Second, commodity prices have been held down since 1951 by the decline in agricultural and raw material prices which do not influence service prices.

Agricultural and other raw-material prices since 1951

In the period since 1951, price-level movements have been influenced to an important extent by the movement of the prices of agricultural products and other raw materials.

Between 1951 and 1956, the prices of farm products fell by 23 per cent and although there has been some recovery since 1956, the farm price level

Wholesale Prices of Producer and Consumer Goods and Construction Costs

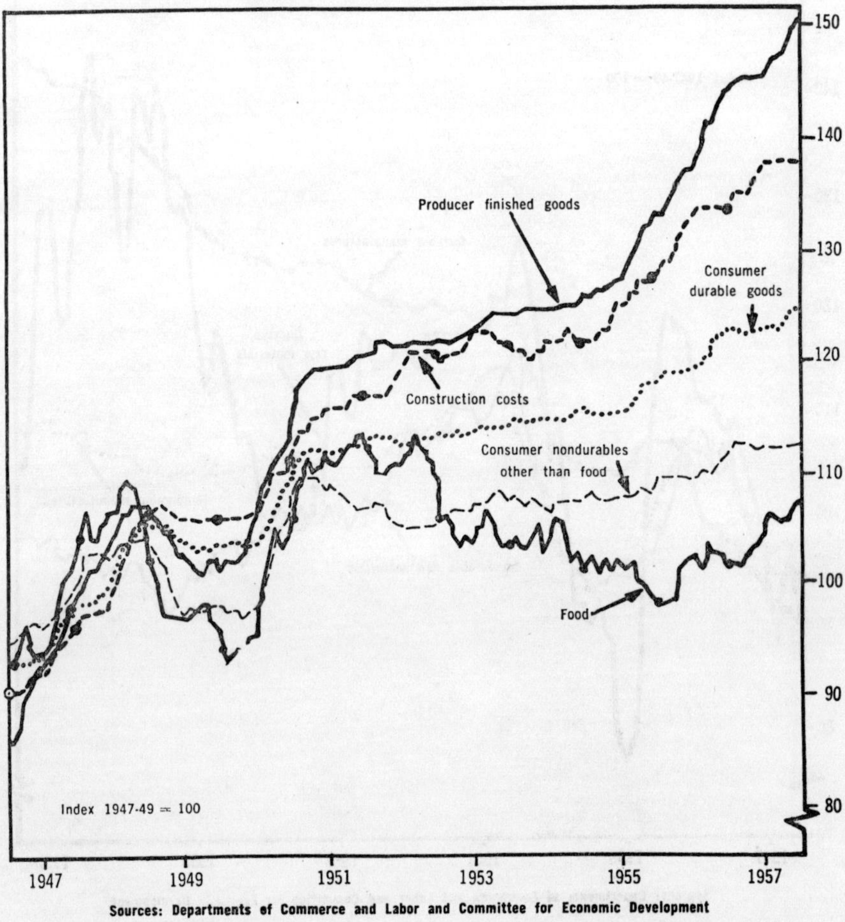

Sources: Departments of Commerce and Labor and Committee for Economic Development

at the end of 1957 was still 19 per cent below the level of 1951. The general downward movement is due to two major factors:

(1) The price increase during 1950 resulted from a very rapid increase in demand over a period so short that increased prices could not influence supplies (with some assist from speculative factors). As soon as farmers had time to respond to higher prices (and the rate of increase of demand was reduced) supplies increased and prices were forced down. At the same time the effect of speculative factors was reversed. It should be noted that in the case of meat animals, the effect of a change in prices on supplies is spread over several years because of the long period required to produce meat animals.

Wholesale Prices of Durable and Nondurable Manufactures and Raw Materials

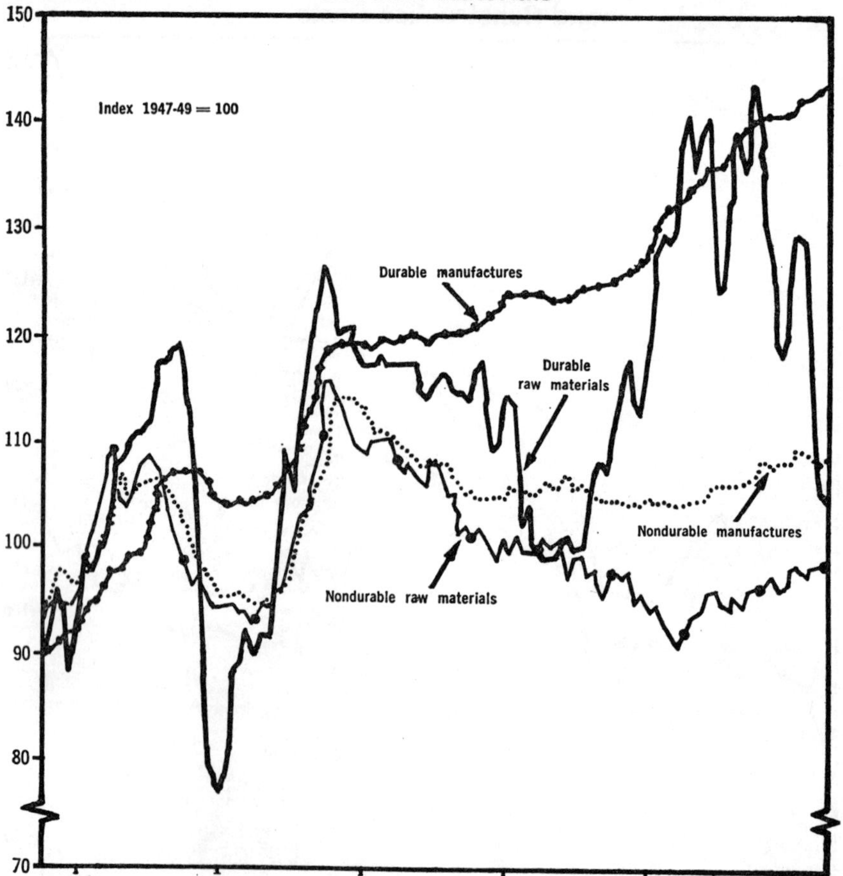

Sources: Departments of Commerce and Labor and Committee for Economic Development

(2) Since the war, agricultural productivity has been growing very rapidly, and farm output has generally tended to rise more rapidly than demand in spite of a substantial decline in the farm labor force. This longer-period force works to prolong the decline in agricultural prices initiated by the "kickback" from the Korean War boom.

The partial recovery of farm prices after early 1956 was due at least in part to the depressing effect of low prices on farm output. Because of the lag in the response of farm output to price changes, supplies of farm products began to decline just when consumer demand was rising rapidly.

The prices of crude non-agricultural materials followed a pattern similar to that of agricultural materials up to 1954. The price index for those materials rose by more than 30 per cent from 1949 to 1951, then fell almost to the pre-Korean level by 1954. Though they rose by 10 per cent from 1954 to 1956, they have since fallen slightly.

The prices of these materials responded to the Korean War in much the same way as agricultural materials. But after 1954 they moved differently because (a) there is no long-term force tending to depress their prices, (b) the fluctuation in durable-goods demand from the beginning of 1955 to date has been much more violent than the fluctuation in consumer demand for food and other consumer non-durables.

Retail margins on durable goods

From early 1951 until near the end of 1955 the wholesale prices of consumer durable goods rose by about 5 per cent. Meanwhile, retail prices of consumer durables fell by about 10 per cent. From the beginning of 1956 both price indices rose, but the retail index rose less than the wholesale index. During the whole period, then, the retail margins on durable goods declined to a marked extent. This was apparently due to the widespread development of discount houses selling at low margins in the household appliance field and to a general reduction in the margins on sales obtained by automobile dealers.

Wages and labor costs in manufacturing

The outstanding fact about wages and labor costs per unit of output in manufacturing is that they have risen throughout the whole postwar period. That is true by almost any measure of labor costs. But the extent of the rise depends a good deal on how labor costs are measured. Before any figures are cited, a few comments on measurement problems are in order.

The most commonly cited measure of wages is that for "average hourly earnings." Data for average hourly earnings are available by finely classified industries monthly. The figure measures pay received for hours worked, including premium payments for overtime. To exclude the effects of cyclical variations in the amount of overtime, the BLS also publishes a series for Straight Time Hourly Earnings, which is obtained by adjusting the Average Hourly Earnings Series. Neither of these series measures the full costs of labor to the employer. They do not include pay received for hours not worked, i.e. mainly paid holidays and vacations. Those costs are included in data for "payrolls." Payroll costs per hour worked can be computed by dividing the payroll indices by man-hours indices.

In addition to payments for hours not worked, employer labor costs include payments for "fringe benefits" such as pensions, social security taxes and supplementary unemployment benefits.

These latter items are included in the Commerce Department series on compensation of employees. Unfortunately, the BLS data on man-hours cover only "production or non-supervisory employees." One cannot therefore compute directly a series for total compensation of employees per man-hour.

These considerations are important because payments for paid vacations and holidays and fringe benefits have been increasing faster than regular wage payments and because "non-production" workers have increased as a percentage of total numbers employed in manufacturing.

The best measure of labor cost seems to be obtained by dividing compensation of employees in manufacturing by the index of manufacturing production. This measure is available only for all manufacturing and on an annual basis, and it does not permit us to consider the effects of changes in compensation rates and in productivity separately. For those purposes we must use other measures.

In manufacturing as a whole, compensation of employees per unit of output increased by 12 per cent from 1951 to 1957. The increase was erratic, but compensation per unit of output increased in every year except 1955. During the same period production worker payrolls per unit of output increased only 4 per cent. The difference was due to the relatively rapid growth in the number of non-production workers and fringe benefits.

Profit margins in manufacturing

In discussing the classical or demand-pull approach to the inflation problem we noted that an increased demand relative to industrial capacity will tend to raise profit margins and prices. Profit margins will tend to rise for two reasons: (1) because prices rise faster than wage costs at a given volume of output, and (2) because unit overhead costs (for depreciation, interest, property taxes and overhead labor) fall with rising volume when output grows relative to capacity.

The first cause of increase in profit margins is inflationary. The second is not. During the first few months of the Korean War, wholesale prices of manufactured products rose faster than production-worker payrolls per unit of output, but from June 1950 to March 1951, wholesale prices of manufactured goods and production-worker payrolls per unit output had both risen by about 12 per cent. Since raw-material prices had risen by more than 12 per cent it appears that wholesale prices of manufactured goods rose by a smaller percentage than the increase in direct costs of labor and materials per unit. Even in the first year of the Korean War, then, prices did not rise because of an increase in the margin between prices and direct costs.

However, manufacturing firms did benefit greatly from the improvement in volume. Between 1949 and 1951, unit value added in manufacturing (which measures the wholesale prices of manufacturing products adjusted for changes in the prices of raw-material inputs) rose by about 12 per cent while total compensation of employees rose by only 8.5 per cent. Since prices rose about as much percentagewise as direct costs, the difference represents the effect of spreading overhead over a larger volume.

Between 1949 and 1951, before-tax profits in durable manufacturing increased from 13.4 per cent of sales to 15.9 per cent. In non-durables, the increase was from 14.5 per cent to 18.2 per cent. Because of the increase in corporate income taxes, after-tax margins actually fell in both cases. How much influence the change in corporate income taxes had is problematical.

After 1951, profits of manufacturing corporations as percentages of sales began to decline. They reached their low, of course, in 1954 and recovered in 1955 and 1956. Even in 1956, however, they had not recovered to the 1949 level. Allowing for the rise in prices, profits in dollars per unit of physical output were just about the same in 1956 as in 1949. Over the period as a whole, then, prices were substantially unaffected by changes in profits.[7] But changes in profit margins did contribute appreciably to the upward movement of prices during 1950 and again in 1955 and 1956. On the other hand, declining margins offset other inflationary factors from 1951 to 1955.

It seems to me that the movements of profits correspond to those which would be expected from the classical model on the assumption that (a) over the period as a whole, real demand grew slightly less rapidly than industrial capacity and (b) it grew more rapidly during 1950 and again during 1955 and 1956, falling behind again in 1957.

---

[7] Over the period, however, depreciation allowances did rise relative to replacement costs. But even after allowance for that consideration, the net effect of profits on prices from 1949 onward was negligible.

Prices of manufactured products

Wholesale prices of all finished manufactured goods rose rapidly from 1949 to 1951 when raw-materials prices, profit margins and compensation of employees per unit of output were all rising. After 1951, wholesale prices of finished manufactured goods actually fell until 1955 by about one per cent. During that interval, compensation of employees per unit of output rose by about 8 per cent (as wages and fringe benefits rose faster than productivity). The decline in profit margins offset part of that increase so that unit value added rose only 3 per cent.[8] Declining raw-materials prices more than offset the rise in unit value added so that wholesale prices of finished manufactures fell by about one per cent.

From 1955 onward the rise in compensation of employees continued. From 1955 to 1956 compensation of employees per unit of output rose another 4.7 per cent. Unit value added rose 3 per cent (profit margins improved but this was due to reductions in unit overheads rather than to a rise in the margins of price over direct costs). Wholesale prices rose about 3 per cent as raw-materials prices rose in line with other costs.

During 1957 compensation of employees per unit of output rose by 2.5 per cent and unit value added by about 2 per cent.

Over the whole period from 1949 to 1957, compensation of employees rose by 26 per cent, while unit value added rose 21 per cent due to the reduction in profits as a percentage of value added. Wholesale prices of manufactured goods rose only 17 per cent due to the fact that raw-materials prices rose only slightly over the whole period.

In the period from 1949 to 1951 labor costs, profit margins and raw-material prices were all rising. From 1951 to the end of 1954 labor costs were rising but raw-materials prices were falling and so were profit margins. From 1954 to 1955 profit margins rose, labor costs fell slightly (primarily, because of the improvement in the utilization of overhead labor; production worker payroll costs per unit rose) and raw-materials prices fell. From 1955 to the beginning of 1957 raw-materials prices, wage costs and profit margins all rose.

It seems to me that a fair conclusion from all this is that over the last 10 years prices have risen primarily because labor costs have risen. The ups and downs of raw-material prices and profit margins sometimes reinforced, sometimes offset the trend in labor costs but did not contribute much to the upward trend of prices.

---

[8] The drop in profit margins per dollar of sales between 1951 and 1955 was much smaller in percentage points than the drop in profits as a percentage of value added, because sales are about twice as high as value added.

The movements of raw-materials prices and profit margins are very similar to those experienced in the past in response to similar movements in demand. If anything is unique about this inflation, it is the rapid upward movement in wages.

TABLE 1. *All Manufacturing Industries (except newspapers)*

PROFIT RATIOS, 1947–58

	Profits as Percent of Sales	
Period	*Before Tax*	*After Tax*
1947	11.0	6.7
1948	11.1	7.0
1949	9.3	5.8
1950	12.8	7.1
1951	12.2	5.4
1951 (new series)	11.2	4.8
1952	9.2	4.3
1953	9.2	4.3
1954	8.4	4.5
1955	10.3	5.4
1956	9.7	5.3
1953		
1st quarter	10.0	4.3
2nd quarter	10.4	4.4
3rd quarter	9.6	4.3
4th quarter	6.7	4.0
1954		
1st quarter	8.4	4.3
2nd quarter	8.9	4.7
3rd quarter	8.2	4.4
4th quarter	8.1	4.7
1955		
1st quarter	9.9	5.1
2nd quarter	10.6	5.5
3rd quarter	10.2	5.4
4th quarter	10.3	5.6
1956		
1st quarter	10.2	5.3
2nd quarter	10.3	5.5
3rd quarter	9.0	4.9
4th quarter	9.3	5.2
1957		
1st quarter	9.7	5.1
2nd quarter	9.4	5.0
3rd quarter	8.5	4.7
4th quarter	7.6	4.4
1958		
1st quarter	6.4	3.4

Source: FTC-SEC Quarterly Financial Report

Manufacturing prices by type of product

The prices of all manufactured goods were influenced by the factors described above. There were, however, important differences in the movements of prices of different types of manufactured products. These differences were due to differences in the relative importance of raw materials and to differences in changes in labor productivity.

From 1951 to 1956, the wholesale and retail prices of food declined as reductions in raw-material costs offset increases in labor costs of processing. After 1956, food prices turned up as the rise in farm prices reinforced the rise in labor costs.

The prices of other consumer non-durables also declined after 1951, but the decline was much smaller and came to an end in 1955. The decline in other non-durables was small because raw materials are less important than in the case of food.

Prices of consumer durables advanced very slightly from 1951 to 1955. Thereafter they advanced more rapidly. Once again declining raw-material prices were helpful in offsetting wage cost increases in the early stage and reinforced it later. There is also some reason to believe that productivity increase in the consumer durable field was larger than in other sectors, particularly in the years up to 1955.

The prices of producers durables rose steadily after 1951. The increases were particularly large from 1955 to 1957. At least a part of the price rise for producer non-durables is accounted for by the importance of steel in their products. Steel prices have risen more than those of most other products since 1951. This in turn has been due to (a) a greater-than-average increase in labor costs, and (b) a greater-than-average rise in profits per unit of output.

Average hourly earnings in all manufacturing increased 41 per cent from 1950 to 1957 while hourly earnings in Iron and Steel rose by 50 per cent. Profit margins on sales in all manufacturing fell from 12.8 per cent in 1950 to 9.5 per cent in the first half of 1957. Profit margins on sales in Iron and Steel fell from 15.5 per cent in 1950 to 14.3 per cent in the first half of 1957.

The causes of wage inflation

The movements of raw-material prices, the special factors influencing service prices and the cyclical variations in profit margins confuse the picture of postwar inflation. But when all those influences are sorted out, it seems clear enough that the primary factor underlying the general rise in price levels since 1951 has been the steady upward movement of labor costs. We cannot understand the inflation unless we can understand why wages have risen faster than productivity.

The most spectacular wage increases are those negotiated by the large trade unions in industries like steel and autos. Every two or three years we are treated to the spectacle of negotiations between the representatives of the Steelworkers Union and the steel companies, or the U.A.W. and the

TABLE 2. *Manufacturing by Primary Iron and Steel Industries*

PROFIT RATIOS, 1947–58
(per cent)

Year	*Profits as Percent of Sales* — *Before Tax*	*After Tax*
1947	10.9	6.6
1948	12.4	7.4
1949	11.1	6.5
1950	15.5	7.9
1951	15.9	5.7
1951 (new series)	16.0	5.8
1952	9.7	4.7
1953	12.6	5.3
1954	10.5	5.3
1955	14.5	7.2
1956	13.2	6.7
1953		
1st quarter	13.3	5.2
2nd quarter	14.8	5.2
3rd quarter	13.9	5.4
4th quarter	7.7	5.3
1954		
1st quarter	9.6	4.7
2nd quarter	10.8	5.2
3rd quarter	9.7	4.6
4th quarter	12.0	6.7
1955		
1st quarter	13.6	6.6
2nd quarter	15.1	7.3
3rd quarter	14.0	6.9
4th quarter	15.2	7.9
1956		
1st quarter	14.8	7.3
2nd quarter	14.5	7.2
3rd quarter	7.7	4.1
4th quarter	14.5	7.5
1957		
1st quarter	14.5	7.1
2nd quarter	14.2	7.0
3rd quarter	12.1	6.1
4th quarter	11.0	5.8
1958		
1st quarter	8.2	4.2

Source: FTC-SEC Quarterly Financial Report

auto companies gathering around the bargaining table. After much publicity, threats of a strike or an actual strike lasting a few weeks, a settlement is reached. In every contract since the war the steel workers, the auto workers and several other large unions have obtained very substantial wage increases.

It is hardly surprising that many observers of these proceedings have concluded that the power of trade unions is responsible for the rapid rate of increase in wages in the past few years. That type of observation has led to the widely prevalent notion that we have been suffering from an inflation due to "cost-push" rather than to the classical type of inflation in which wages are pulled up by demand.

But the situation is really much less clear than it appears when we consider only large-scale wage negotiations. Only about one-third of private non-agricultural wage and salary earners are trade union members. Allowance must be made for the fact that, when wage earners are organized, the wages of non-union employees (i.e. clerical and supervisory personnel) of companies are strongly influenced by union wage rates. On the other hand a substantial proportion of union membership is in unions much less powerful than the steel and auto workers.

Because of the problem created by fringe benefits and variations in overtime it is not easy to make precise comparisons of wage increases in different industries. But it is fairly clear that the wage increases obtained by the strongest unions in the period since the beginning of World War II have not exceeded the general average by any large percentage.

Average hourly earnings in the steel industry in 1956 were just about triple those of 1940. The average increase in wages for all manufacturing was just about the same. The increase for autos was actually below the average for all manufacturing. Wage increases in durable goods manufacturing, where unions appear to be strongest, have not exceeded those in the less well organized non-durables sector (in percentage terms). Data on wages in the service trades are far from adequate, but wages changes there appear to be about as large as in manufacturing.

Some years ago there was a good deal of statistical controversy over the question whether wage increases in organized industries were larger than those in other industries. Because different answers can be obtained by different methods of comparison, complete agreement has not yet been reached. But the important conclusion is that at best union wages (plus fringe benefits) have not increased *much* more than non-union wages.

In view of those considerations, one cannot attribute the rapid increase in wages in the last few years to trade union power by simply noting the large increases obtained by unions in large-scale negotiations. Those who wish to support the "cost-push" hypothesis must explain how it is that wage increases obtained by trade unions have been so fully reflected in unorganized industries.

On the other hand, those who wish to maintain that wages have risen because of demand-pull have their troubles also. During wars wages rise rapidly, and there is obviously a shortage of labor. It is then perfectly clear that wages are rising because employers find it profitable to bid more to get additional labor.

In the years since 1951 we have not had large labor shortages like those of the war years. Nonetheless, there is evidence that there have been shortages of the types of labor employers normally wish to obtain. The evidence for that statement is the very large increase in the employment of older married women, the willingness of employers to take on part-time workers, the prevalence of "moonlighting," and the ease with which migrants from farms and Puerto Rico have been absorbed into the urban labor force. Those classes of marginal workers can be drawn into employment only in conditions when there is excess demand for labor of the type usually employed. A shortage of "bodies" has been avoided by reducing the apparent quality of the labor force. (I say apparent because many "marginal" workers perform just as well as "normal" workers even though employers are reluctant to hire them until they have had some experience with them.)

In these circumstances one would expect that wages would rise to some extent. When there is a shortage of the types of labor normally hired, employers may be expected to compete for the normal labor force by raising wages before they fall back on the expedient of hiring marginal workers. (That is especially so when there is difficulty in making wage differentials correspond to employers' beliefs about quality differentials.)

The question is whether the labor shortage or demand-pull explanation of wage movements can account for wage increases as large as those which have occurred in the last few years. We have no absolute standards by which to judge how much wage increase should be associated with a given situation in the labor market. We can only ask whether wages are now responding to labor market conditions in the same way as in the past when trade unions were less important.

The only comparison worth making is that between the post-1951 period and the years 1923-1929, and that is not entirely satisfactory. The labor market in the 20's was roughly similar at least to the labor market since 1951. Average levels of unemployment were apparently about the same in the two periods.

In both periods workers from farms were absorbed into the labor force; there was an increase in labor market participation by women in both cases. However, both the last two movements have been on a greater scale in the more recent period than in the earlier one. Moreover, there is no evidence of moonlighting or of general increase in employment of part-time workers during the 1920's. Finally, it is probable that if unemployment were measured on the same basis in the 1920's as now, the unemployment figures for the twenties would be higher than those cited above. Unemployment compensation increases reported unemployment, since women who lose one job and do not actively seek another report themselves unemployed in order to draw compensation.

All things considered, then, it is probable that labor markets have been appreciably tighter on the average since 1951 than was the case during the 1920's.

The movements of wages in the two periods were very different. From 1923 to 1929 average hourly earnings in manufacturing increased from $.522 to $.566 or about 8 per cent. The average annual increase was therefore only about one per cent per year. From 1950 to 1957 average hourly earnings in manufacturing increased from $1.465 to $2.07 or by 41 per cent. The average annual increase was over 5 per cent per year. Allowance for fringe benefits would make the difference between the two periods even larger.

Admitting that labor markets have been somewhat tighter in recent years than they were in the 20's, it still seems very difficult to explain the difference in wage movements by the difference in the supply and demand position in the labor markets.

We have to conclude that neither the "trade union push" approach nor the "demand-pull" theory is really adequate to explain recent wage movements. But, after all, the two approaches are not mutually exclusive. There is no reason why both considerations cannot be given some weight in the explanation of wage movements. Moreover, as I shall argue below, there are strong interactions between the influence of trade unions and the influence of demand on wages.

As I have already indicated, the demand for labor has been expanding at a faster rate than the "normal" labor force. If labor markets were perfect, with uniform wages for similar workers in all sectors, there would have been (even without trade unions) a general competition for workers which would have raised wages generally. But labor markets are far from perfect. Wages in manufacturing, construction and public utilities and transportation are far above those in the trade and service sectors. In those circumstances, a shortage of labor causes much greater recruiting difficulty in the trade and service sectors than in manufacturing, construction, utilities and transportation. In the absence of strong trade unions, we should have expected wages to rise in the trade and service sectors. But because of the large initial differentials those wage increases would not have prevented the other sectors from absorbing the bulk of the net increase in the urban male labor force even if there were no wage increases in manufacturing, construction, utilities and transport. Wages in the trade and service sectors would have risen enough to make it profitable for employers in those sectors to recruit or accept marginal workers. Of course, a narrowing of differentials would have helped to hold workers in trade and service so that the other sectors would have had to raise wages somewhat. But relatively small increases would have been sufficient.

In fact, of course, the trade and service sectors have raised wages. Differentials for occupations in which women cannot readily be substituted for men have narrowed, and the trade and service sectors have avoided further wage increases by using older women, teen agers, moonlighters and so on. But in the other sectors, wage increases have been just as large as in the trade and service sectors. The large wage increases in those sectors were to a large extent due to the influence of trade unions. They would not have occurred as a result of competition for workers in the absence of trade unions.

Thus the first instance of the combined influence of excess demand for labor and trade unions is a simple one. Excess demand for labor pulled up wages in the sectors in which trade unions are weakest, and trade unions pushed up wages in sectors where excess demand was weakest.

But other interactions are also important.

First, the wage increases obtained by unions are not independent of the balance of supply and demand for labor. When labor markets are tight, employers have a number of incentives for raising wages even when they do not suffer from a general shortage of labor. When there is little unemployment, there are likely to be shortages of particular types of labor. Employers may be willing to raise the wages of those occupational groups in short supply and may find it necessary to extend the increases to other workers to maintain the internal wage structure.

When jobs are very easy to get, turnover rates tend to rise and employers may be prepared to give wage increases to reduce turnover. Similarly it pays employers to err on the side of generosity in disputes over piece-rate changes associated with changes in methods. Thus employers have a number of incentives to raise wages when labor markets are tight even in the absence of a trade union or an obvious labor shortage.

Moreover, the bargaining position of trade unions depends on conditions in the labor market. In the short run the bargaining position of a trade union is stronger when employment is high because the financial position of the union and its members will then be strong enough to permit an effective strike. Over longer periods, high employment makes things easier for trade unions because it reduces the possibility of competition by non-union employers.

To summarize, a very strong union may occasionally obtain a wage increase in the face of substantial unemployment, but in general the effectiveness of the pressure on wages exerted by trade unions will be much greater when there is little unemployment.

The wage increases obtained by trade unions will also have an influence on wages in unorganized sectors, but the extent of that influence will depend on the balance of supply and demand in the labor market. When the workers in unionized manufacturing firms obtain wage increases, workers in similar occupations, e.g. clerical workers and common laborers in the trade and service sector, will become dissatisfied if their wages are not increased. If jobs are easy to get, the result of such dissatisfaction will be an increase in turnover and a reduction of productivity. Employers in the trade and service sector will have an incentive to raise wages to improve morale and reduce turnover.

It was argued above that neither "demand-pull" nor "trade union pressure" taken alone gives an adequate explanation of the wage inflation of the past few years. When we take account of their joint effects and the fact that demand-pull works best in one sector and trade union pressure in another, we do have an explanation which seems to be reasonably consistent with the facts.

The sources of demand

In the last section we concluded that the inflation of wages was due to an interaction between the pressure on wages exerted by trade unions and a more or less chronic shortage of labor. Either of these forces would by itself have caused wages to rise, but the two together caused a substantially greater increase in wages than the sum of those two separate effects.

If we can explain why demand for labor was so large relative to labor supply and why trade unions were so effective, we shall have gone some distance in explaining the inflationary process. I shall not attempt to explain how trade unions have gotten where they are; but I shall attempt to outline briefly the factors responsible for the high level of demand which has prevailed in the postwar years.

I shall not give a play-by-play account of the movements of demand. I shall confine myself to a few of the special factors which have made aggregate demand particularly buoyant since World War II. Three such factors seem especially worthy of note: (1) the position of the economy at the end of the war, (2) the rapid growth of population, (3) the rise in government expenditures.

The situation at the end of the war

At the end of the war private demand was unusually strong for several reasons. Households had large stocks of liquid assets in relation to their income while the ratio of consumer debt to income was unusually low. At the same time, stocks of automobiles and other consumer durables were unusually low in relation to income. As a result, households spent an unusually high proportion of their income. Consumer saving during 1946, 1947 and 1948 was only about half its normal level.

Businesses found themselves in much the same position with a large amount of liquid assets, a low level of indebtedness and a deteriorated stock of physical capital. Demand for capital goods was therefore strong at the end of the war.

The rise in income during the war, the strong financial position of households and the large number of recent marriages provided the basis for a residential construction boom which was slowed down only by the limited availability of building materials and skilled manpower.

Finally, state and local governments were faced with demands for all sorts of public improvements and were in a strong financial position so that they were both willing and able to borrow.

Population growth

The large number of marriages and births in the years after the war had two important effects. First, it was a major factor in the postwar housing boom. This boom, though initially based on the backlog of demand resulting from low rates of construction during depression and war, could not have continued at so high a level for so long a period without the support provided by high marriage and birth rates. The rapid growth of housing construction in the years between the end of World War II and 1950 was one of the major forces behind the growth of demand during that period. In addition to its influence on housing, the growth of population has raised the level of consumption relative to income. It is not easy to measure this effect, but some rough estimates indicate that the growth of population has raised consumer expenditures by from $1 to $2 billion per year in each year since the war (over what they would have been with constant population).

Effect of government expenditures

The initial situation at the end of the war reinforced by the rapid growth of population was adequate to provide the basis for a strong postwar boom. The boom was interrupted by the recession of 1949, but it can reasonably be assumed that had the Korean War not intervened there would have been a strong recovery. By the end of 1949, recovery was already underway as residential construction increased; federal expenditures rose from the low levels (which had permitted large surpluses in 1947 and 1948) while tax rates had fallen, and business sentiment recovered from fears of a great postwar depression.

Without the Korean War and the subsequent expansion of federal expenditures, income would undoubtedly have expanded after 1949. The rate of growth of real demand would, however, have been substantially lower than was actually the case. We cannot calculate exactly the effect of the rise in government expenditures, but we can get a rough idea of its order of magnitude.

During the period from the beginning of 1950 when the federal budget was roughly balanced until the end of 1953, federal government purchases of goods and services expanded by about 40 billion dollars in 1958 prices, and the deficit increased by about 9 billion dollars. At a rough estimate, the net effect of those changes was to increase aggregate demand by 54 billion dollars in 1958 prices or by about one half of the total increase over the period. That figure was obtained by applying a multiplier of 2.6 to the increase in the deficit and a multiplier of 1 to the balance of 31 billion of increased expenditures financed through taxes and assuming that private investment was unaffected by the government's contribution to the rate of increase of income. Those figures are of course significant only in terms of their order of magnitude.

The actual difference in Gross National Product (GNP) would have been still greater. For had the rise in GNP been slower than it actually was, private investment would have been lower which would have further retarded the rise in GNP. That reduction in the growth rate would have had still further secondary effects and so on.[9]

Some of those secondary effects were not felt, however, until after 1953. Housing construction and state and local building were held down during the Korean War period, and at some points plant and equipment expenditures were retarded by shortages. During the period from 1950 to the end of 1953, then, it can be said that the federal government was responsible for at least half and probably substantially more than half of the increase in aggregate real demand.

After 1953, the federal government's fiscal policy worked in the opposite direction. Federal expenditures declined about 20 billions (in 1958 prices) between the end of 1953 and the end of 1957, while the deficit of 9 billion in 1953 was turned into a two billion dollar surplus. The effect of those changes was to reduce income (by comparison with what it would have been with constant expenditures and deficit) by about 37 billions.

---

[9] The conclusion reached above as to the magnitude of the effect of a balanced budget reduction in expenditures before taking account of the effect of the difference in GNP is probably conservative. Tax reductions for business instead of consumers would lead to a decline in consumption and some increase in investment by comparison with the case in which all the tax benefits go to households. It is hardly likely that the average propensity to invest out of profits after taxes can be as high as the average propensity to consume out of disposable income.

Any more realistic assumption about the distribution of tax benefits would imply an income redistribution in favor of high savers and increase the adverse effect of expenditure reduction.

The restrictive effects of federal policy were offset by the rise in private investment and the rise in state and local expenditures. The high volume of private investment and the rapid growth in state and local expenditures after 1953 were at least in part due to the rapid growth of income before 1953 and to the restriction of construction during the Korean period.

The restriction of federal expenditures after 1953 slowed down the rate of growth of income in drastic fashion. From the cyclical peak of 1953 to the peak in 1957, GNP in real terms increased by about 2.5 per cent per year which was less than half the growth rate achieved between early 1950 and the end of 1953.

Unfortunately, the rate of growth of productivity was also somewhat lower than in earlier years and the male labor force continued to grow at a very slow rate. The reduction in government expenditures therefore did little more than to keep the growth of demand for labor in line with the growth of supply without reducing the tightness in labor markets which had existed in 1953.

Over the whole period, the primary effects of federal fiscal policy were relatively small, but because of their timing the period since Korea reflects most of the secondary effects of the expansion of government expenditures prior to 1953 and only a part of the secondary effects of the restriction since 1953. Over the whole period since the Korean War, therefore, federal fiscal policy made a substantial net contribution to the generation of an excessively high rate of growth of demand for labor.

Can we control inflation by controlling demand?

Those people who believe that inflation is caused by trade union pressure on wages have frequently maintained that we cannot maintain a satisfactory level of employment and control inflation by controlling demand. They take the view that in order to prevent wage inflation it is necessary to have very large amounts of unemployment. They conclude that we must either let the inflation proceed or control wages and prices by some other method than by controlling demand, i.e. some kind of direct control of wages and prices or by some action to reduce the power of trade unions. Their position has been strengthened by the fact that the recessions of 1953-54 and 1958 slowed down but did not stop the rise in wages.

If it were true that all workers were organized in powerful trade unions and that all the inflation of wages were due to trade union pressure, their conclusion might well be correct. However, that is not the case. There has been a good deal of excess demand for labor in some sectors of our economy in the last few years and that has caused wage increases in those sectors directly and has reinforced the effects of wage increases negotiated by trade unions elsewhere. That conclusion suggests that the average rate of increase in wage rates might be considerably reduced if we could bring the average rate of growth of demand for labor into line with the average rate of growth of the normal labor force over a period of several years.

Suppose that were done. The consequence would be, I think, a substantial reduction in the rate of increase of wages in the unorganized sectors of the economy. There would still be wage increases in all sectors. Trade unions would still be able to negotiate wage increases, and those increases would still have some effect on wages of unorganized workers. Over a longer period a better balance between growth of demand for labor and growth of normal labor supply would tend to reduce the effectiveness of trade union demands for wage increases. For if wages rose slowly in the unorganized sector and rapidly in the strongly organized ones, the differentials between the two would widen. It does not seem likely to me that differentials between union and non-union wages can be widened indefinitely, particularly when labor markets are not too tight. A widening of differentials would encourage the entry of non-union employers and increase the effectiveness of the competition of products produced by unorganized workers. (Unfortunately, of course, there is the possibility that a widening of differentials would lead to extension of trade union organization into new areas of the labor market.)

A policy of holding down the rate of growth of demand would be costly in a number of ways. Many people believe that we need a high rate of growth of aggregate income (to compete with the Russians, to make possible an increase in public expenditures for defense, education, etc.).

Secondly, a high-pressure economy in which capacity and labor force are fully utilized may be likely to have a higher rate of growth of productivity than one in which there is less demand pressure. Full utilization of capacity increases the prospective profits from the installation of improved equipment and also raises the level of current profits which makes it easier to finance these improvements. The existence of tight labor markets increases the profitability of developing and installing labor saving devices. Against those effects must be set the reduction of efficiency on the part of both labor and management which results from high profit margins and tight labor markets.

Finally, a reduction in the rate of growth of demand for labor is likely to result in an increase in the level of unemployment. If the rate of growth of aggregate demand for labor is about in balance with the rate of growth of the normal labor supply, there are bound to be areas in which the rate of growth of demand for labor is less than the rate of growth of normal labor supply. In addition, there will be absolute reductions in employment in some industries. Since workers do not transfer instantly from one industry or area to another, there is bound to be greater unemployment in the normal labor force than there would be with a higher rate of growth of demand.

Conclusion

We have argued that the inflation is due to both demand-pull and trade union pressure on wages. A reduction in the rate of growth of the demand for labor would reduce the rate of increase of wages even in the face of the wage pressure exerted by trade unions. Some of the resulting gain might, however, be offset by a reduction in the rate of increase of productivity. In addition, a reduction in the rate of growth of demand would be costly in itself and would lead to higher levels of unemployment.

4. The impacts of unions on the level of wages

Clark Kerr

Inflation and industrialization have marched together for the past two centuries. Rising prices and growing industrial output have characterized much of the economic history of this period, with the notable exception of the second half of the nineteenth century. While they have marched together, they have not marched closely and evenly in step until the past few years. The alternations of war and peace and prosperity and depression have variously affected the course of both inflation and industrialization. The pace of both has been subject to great variations.

Clark Kerr is President of the University of California, Professor of Business Administration and Economics, and Research Associate in the Institute of Industrial Relations, Berkeley. He was Chancellor of the University's Berkeley campus from 1952 to 1958. Previously he had taught, and served as Director of the Institute of Industrial Relations at Berkeley (1945-52). Additionally, he has served as Consultant to the Departments of State (1950) and Labor (1954), as a member of the 6th and 12th Regional War Labor Boards during World War II, and on the National Wage Stabilization Board as public member and vice-chairman (1950-51). He has acted as arbitrator in numerous labor disputes, and presently is a Director of the Center for Advanced Study in the Behavioral Sciences of the Ford Foundation. Dr. Kerr is the author of articles in various scholarly and professional journals, and has contributed sections to numerous books on industrial relations and the social sciences.

Dr. Kerr acknowledges the assistance of Margery Galenson in the preparation of this paper.

The past few years, since World War II, on the other hand, have been marked in Western Europe and North America by more nearly constant, rather than sporadic, inflation and industrialization. And, while a little less than a decade and a half constitutes a great deal less than an everlasting trend, a spectre is haunting Western capitalism—the spectre of constant inflation. Many, although not all, of the powers of society have been allied to exorcise this spectre—government officials and editorial writers, monetary authorities and economists, financiers and ministers—but it still exists.

It is a real spectre though it is not new and it need not make society tremble. It is a real spectre because constant inflation could become constantly greater inflation; because it redistributes income often in an inequitable fashion; and because policies to combat it may also combat progress.

Constant inflation presumably should have a constant source. Several new or relatively new developments have accompanied constant inflation and are, consequently, the most likely causes. One of these is the growth of the trade union movement and of its power over the wage-setting process. But it is not the only companion. Other companions have been governmental commitments to full employment, policies and practices leading to unbalanced budgets and low interest rates, rapid industrial expansion, new supply conditions in labor markets and new patterns of mobility and immobility, and new mechanisms for price control by private agencies; and several of these companions are closely related to each other.

The question here is the responsibility of one of these companions—the trade union—for constant inflation. This is not an easy question to answer, partly because of the intermingling of ideology and group self-interest with analysis in so much of the discussion, but particularly because with so many things happening it is almost impossible to state precisely the force of any one development by itself. For example, what would be the effect of the trade union if there were no industrial growth or if there were no administered prices to go along with administered wages? Consequently, reliance must be placed on individual judgments rather than any universally accepted analysis; and judgments have differed.

The split jury

The jury which has sat most constantly on this case has been composed of economists; and almost any conceivable verdict can be obtained by picking almost any conceivable economist.[1] To illustrate:

To *Lindblom* [2] the union is a "monopoly" and also a "body politic." As a body politic, under the urging of political pressures, it uses its monopoly

---

[1] For a summary of the recent literature see G. H. Hildebrand, "The Economic Effects of Unionism," in *A Decade of Industrial Relations Research,* Harper & Bros., 1958.

[2] Charles E. Lindblom, *Unions and Capitalism,* Yale University Press, 1949.

power to force wages higher and higher. This leads to "unemployment or inflation" and, with government guarantee of full employment, to inflation. As a result, "unionism and the private enterprise system are incompatible."

To *Chamberlain* [3] the unions introduce a "monopoly element" into the labor market and, whether or not they try to maximize the wage bill, they do try to get "more" and this leads to "wage-push inflation." "Unions today do have too much economic power."

To *The Economist* [4] the real cost of trade unions is not so much the loss in productivity per man-hour they cause but rather that they turn full production into full inflation; and to avoid the latter, the former must also be forgone. This is one of the great economic tragedies of our age and our type of society.

To *Hicks* [5] the "Labour Standard" has replaced the Gold Standard. Governments will adjust their policies to maintain full employment at whatever wage levels the unions choose to set; and price levels follow along. But the unions, or at least British unions, may not be so unreasonable that this "Labour Standard" is much more "dangerous" than other monetary systems.

To *Lerner* [6] the problem is not "wage-cost inflation" alone but "seller's inflation." For there is also "profit inflation" as well as "wage inflation," and it is very difficult and even impossible to untangle the two. Wherever there are administered prices and administered wages, and they seem to be nearly everywhere, "seller's inflation" is a possibility, and it must be dealt with as a unitary phenomenon.

To *Slichter* [7] the unions are only one of several causes of inflation, and the others include the reduced availability of new sources of labor and the policy of government; but they are a significant cause. He concludes that, between 1933 and 1953, unions pushed up the general wage level "at least 25 cents per hour and probably more." This is one-fifth of the total increase that occurred during that period.

To *Reynolds* [8] "collective bargaining does not have as much impact on the money-wage level as has sometimes been suggested. My judgment would be that between 1945 and 1955 the money-wage level rose little, if any, more than it would have risen under nonunion conditions."

---

[3] Edward H. Chamberlain, "The Economic Analysis of Labor Union Power," in *Labor Unions and Public Policy*, American Enterprise Association, 1958.

[4] August 2, 1958.

[5] J. R. Hicks, "Economic Foundations of Wage Policy," *Economic Journal*, September 1955.

[6] A. P. Lerner, "Inflationary Depression and the Regulation of Administered Prices," United States Joint Economic Committee, *The Relationship of Prices to Economic Stability and Growth*, March 21, 1958.

[7] Sumner H. Slichter, "Big Unions and Inflation," *American Economic Review Proceedings*, May 1954.

[8] Lloyd G. Reynolds in *New Concepts in Wage Determination*, McGraw-Hill, 1957.

To *Morton*[9] unions are a minor factor affecting inflation and may retard it as well as augment it: retard it in a boom period; increase it in certain industries, where government regulation relates prices to costs, like public utilities and railroads.

To *Friedman*[10] unions have both a "rigidity effect" and "upward-pressing effect." The former holds down wage levels in a period of expansion; the latter forces them up in a period of stability. The two largely offset each other; but, of the two, the rigidity effect may be the more important under recent circumstances.

To *Boulding*[11] it is a certainty "that the main effect of unionism is to hold down wages and to prevent them from rising faster than they otherwise would . . . Unions are the opiate of the people under capitalism. That is why you have got to have them."

From the destroyer of "private enterprise" to the "opiate of the people," from the source of disastrous inflation to a bulwark of price stability, from a powerful monopoly to a minor or even negative force—the judgments vary. Economics is not yet a science; but economists are certainly free thinkers.

As a very part-time economist, I should like to suggest that all of them are right and all of them are wrong. All of them are right to the extent that they suggest that some kinds of unions could have the suggested effects under some kinds of circumstances. All of them are wrong, to the extent they suggest (and some of them do not) that their conclusions are the universal rule. The only universal rule is that there are all kinds of unions operating under all kinds of circumstances and they can have all kinds of effects. But it should also be added that kinds and circumstances and effects can be related—at least to a certain degree. Truth is more likely to emerge from studying the impacts of the unions, than "the impact of the union."

Types, circumstances and impacts

Types

When talking about unions, it is helpful to specify the kind of union one is talking about. In terms of their approaches to price stability, unions can be broadly divided into the following general types:

Agent of the State—The "agent of the state" union, as in Russia or China, is the willing tool of the national administration. It serves its

[9] Walter A. Morton, "Trade Unionism, Full Employment and Inflation," *American Economic Review,* March 1950.

[10] Milton Friedman in *Impact of the Union,* Harcourt Brace & Company, 1951.

[11] Kenneth E. Boulding, *idem,* p. 245.

policies. It has no policies of its own. It is a weapon of social discipline, and the only variation of which it is capable is in the degree of its effectiveness.

Partner in Social Control — Some unions serve as "partners in social control." They may be formal partners, as they have been in Holland, assuming joint public responsibility for the economic welfare of the nation; or they may be informal partners, as they have been in Germany, almost equally committed with the government to reasonably full employment and reasonable price stability at the same time. In Britain and in the Scandinavian countries, the unions have served as such informal partners when Labor or Social Democratic parties were in power. Here again there can be degrees of effectiveness as "social partner."

Sectional Bargainer — The union, as "sectional bargainer," is concerned not with the national impacts of its actions but with the consequences for its members and for its industry or segment of an industry. Its responsibility is relatively narrowly defined. The United States and Canada are representative of this type of unionism. The "sectional bargainer" union may be found in two major phases—(a) a state of excitement and (b) a state of normality. A state of excitement is most likely to exist in a new union, a union subject to the challenge of a rival union or a union undergoing internal political upheaval; and bargaining is likely to be much more aggressive in a state of excitement than in a state of normality.

Class Bargainer — The union, as "class bargainer," endeavors to get a "fair share," which usually means a larger share, of the national income for labor as a whole. It is usually matched by other "class bargainers," as in France, who seek "fair shares" for agricultural producers, the commercial classes, the civil servants, and so forth; and the total of these "shares" is almost certain to add up to more than the national output of goods and services. The "class bargainer" union usually has or develops a class ideology.

Enemy of the System — The "enemy of the system" union is devoted to the destruction of the surrounding economic and political structure. Among its techniques are the sabotage of production and the encouragement of excessive consumption aspirations. Such unions have been really effective only when a society is in the process of disintegration.

These above types suggest more uniformity and stability than is the actuality. Some societies have mixtures at any one moment of time—as in France with Communist, Socialist and Catholic unions. In some societies, the union movement shifts from one "type" or policy to another. The "agent of the state" union will remain an "agent of the state" so long as the state needs an agent. But the "social partner" union may be a partner only when the nation faces an emergency or when a government it favors is in power and then turn to a "sectional" or "class" approach under other circumstances. The "enemy of the system" union may in non-revolutionary periods follow a "class bargainer" policy instead of open full-scale opposition, or even be a particularly belligerent "sectional bargainer."

Each of these types has its own most natural habitat—the "agent of the state" union in an authoritarian society; the "social partner" union in a "social democratic" context; the "sectional bargainer" in a free enterprise system; the "class bargainer" in a semi-class or semi-feudal society; and the "enemy of the system" union in the latter type of society in the course of its decay. A society does not just conjure up the kind of unionism it would like to have after looking at the different models theoretically available; some kinds fit some societies and not others.

But we are concerned here not with the ultimate cause of a certain type of unionism, but with its impact on inflation. In general, unions—if they may all truly be called unions—will make a contribution to economic stability in the following descending order:

Agent of the state
Partner in social control
Sectional bargainer
Class bargainer
Enemy of the system

The merest glance at this list indicates that a society usually cannot pick its type of unionism on the basis alone of its impact on stability; and that its effect on the price level cannot be the only proper test of the desirability of a union movement.

Theoretically, however, it might be expected that unions, from the top of the list to the bottom, would vary from strong supporters of stability to effective agents of instability.

Circumstances and impacts

Unions, of whatever type, operate within an environment, and their potential impacts on the general level of money wages may be almost as much related to the environment as to their type.[12] Among the environmental situations with which we shall treat are those relating to the policies of other institutions (government and employers), to employment conditions, and to labor market conditions.

---

[12] We are discussing here only the impact on the general level of money wages and not the impact on prices. That depends also on changes in the level of productivity and in labor's share of income. Also we are discussing the economic impact of the unions within a given environment and not their political or economic impact in their efforts to change the surrounding environment.

The standard for comparison will be "what would otherwise have happened" had there been no union; and this nobody really knows. The standard will not be the absolute increase in money wages; for unions may sometimes do most when they seem to do the least, and do least when they seem to do the most. For example, in a depression a union may hold up wages which would otherwise go down and we can say they "raised the level"; while in a boom period they may belatedly negotiate a substantial wage increase which would have come earlier under non-union conditions through the operation of market forces, and we can say they "reduced the level."

We shall consider first the policies of other institutions. Guaranteed full employment places the unions in an advantageous position, and two types of unions—"enemy of the system" and "class bargainer"—are in a particularly good position to take advantage of it. Administered prices by employers create a special opportunity for the "sectional bargainer" union, for administered wages can be passed on through administered prices and turn up in administered inflation.[13] With pattern bargaining, high settlements in an area of "administered prices" are likely to be imitated in other areas and thus spread the high "key" settlement. When the government is fearful of strikes and enters the collective bargaining arena to settle disputes, this again creates a favorable environmental situation for each of the three types of unions just mentioned. However, were the government to undertake a critical public review of wage settlements, this would have the opposite effect, and the "sectional bargainer" and particularly the "social partner" unions would be sensitive to such review. Government wage controls create an unfavorable condition for union impact on the general level of money wages and especially for the "social partner" union; the "agent of the state" union is, of course, always subject to wage controls.

In terms of employment conditions, unions probably have the greatest upward impact on money wages in a depression, when their attachment to past levels and the lags inherent in collectively bargained wages work toward stability. Next, in the downswing, particularly the early phases, they may not only be able to hold wage levels but actually increase them, contrary to "normal" tendencies. In a period of stable full employment, union pressure may well keep wages rising at some "standard" rate, say five per cent a year, when under other circumstances they would have risen more slowly. In an upswing, particularly its later stages, and in "overly full" employment, however, unions with their term agreements and formal approaches may cause a lag behind the adjustments which would otherwise

[13] Also administered prices can create profit margins which lure the unions to make higher wage demands.

occur. A general rule might be: the smaller the wage adjustment, the greater the true impact of the union; and the greater the wage increase, the lesser the real impact.

Labor market conditions may also relate to union impact. In a period of rapid accessions to the labor force—women, migrants from rural areas, young people—the unions can protect wages from the depressing effects. But when a labor force has become immobile, due to pensions or seniority rules or excessively specialized training or for other reasons, the union may reduce the upward impact on wages of this immobility. In the absence of unions, employers would tend to respond to individual scarcity situations with selective adjustments; and the impacts of these would spread. Unions, with their more formal wage relationships, tend to dampen this tendency and force employers to make other adjustments than the bidding up of individual classes of skills. This may possibly serve to lower, somewhat, the general level of money wages.

Putting together the variety of types of unions and the variety of environmental settings results in a variety of potential effects. Unions raise the general level of money wages greatly; or perhaps only a little. Unions reduce the general level of money wages substantially; or perhaps only a little. Or perhaps they have no effect at all. It all depends. And it all depends on type and circumstance, as the summary table suggests (see Table 1).

TABLE 1. *Factors Relating to Union Impact on General Level of Money Wages*

	Type of Union	*Policies of Other Institutions*	*Employment Conditions*	*Labor Market Conditions*
Raise level ↑	"Enemy of the system"	"Guaranteed" full employment	Depression	
				New recruits
	"Class bargainer"		Downswing	
		Administered prices		
(As compared with what would otherwise prevail)	"Sectional bargainer"	Government settlements to avoid strikes	Stable full employment	
	a. State of excitement			
	b. State of normality		Upswing	
	"Partners in social control"	Government review of wage settlements	"Overly full" employment	Immobile labor force
Reduce level ↓	"Agent of the state"	Government wage control		

The variety of experience

Experience is different from experiment. There have been no conscious experiments, and in the nature of the case there cannot be, through which a determination could be made with accuracy of the impact of the union on the general level of money wages. There is only experience; and the knowable reality from this experience is little more than conjecture. To speak with full assurance in this area is to speak from prejudice or from ignorance or both. Yet some things can be said.

Possible tests

There are at least four ways in which one might try to test the impact of the union.

1. How have union wages risen as compared to non-union? One might find here the true impact of the union not only on inter-industry and inter-occupational differentials but also on the general level of money-wages.

But union and non-union wages are not in water-tight compartments and what happens to one set of wages may affect the other. If it were found that union wages went up only as fast as non-union wages, this might mean the unions had no impact; however, it might only mean that non-union wages were playing "follow-the leader" and thus that the unions were having an even greater effect on the general level of money wages. Also, if union wages were found to be going up faster, this might imply the unions did have an impact; but it might only reflect the fact that the wages of unionized manual workers, under the impact of broadly available educational opportunities and the breakdown of class lines, were rising faster than those of non-unionized white collar workers who had come into relatively greater supply—the important comparison might be manual and non-manual, not union and non-union.

2. How has recent history, when strong unions existed, compared with earlier history when there were fewer unions? Here again it might be discovered how the introduction of unionism has affected the course of the general level of money wages.

But the statistics, on any really comparable basis, do not go very far back. And if they did, it would still be true that more has happened in the course of intervening events than the rise of a union movement. Even adjusting for the amount of unemployment, there is still the question of what effect the expectation of generally lower rates of unemployment would have had on the behavior of employers in any event. Also, since employers, whenever they can, tend to share their profits one way or another with their workers, what would have been the effect of administered prices even without administered wages? And what has been the consequence of the drying up of the old sources of cheap labor on the general level of money wages?

3. *How has labor's share of national income behaved?* If there is evidence that the unions have really "squeezed" profits below their "normal" levels, then it might be said the unions were pushing wages up against profits and thus against prices.

But labor's share is one of the mysteries of economic analysis. And it is also affected by other developments than union pressure alone. There may be implications to be drawn from the analysis but little or no proof.

4. *How has experience varied from one country to another?* If one country has had a different course of money-wage levels from another, this different course might be related to the presence or absence of unions, or the different types of unionism; and we might find our answer.

But each country varies from the other in more ways than the presence or absence of unions, or the nature of union policy. Also, each type of union policy, as we have noted, is so related to its surrounding environment that it is difficult to say what is the real cause of a different behavior of money wages—the type of union or the type of economy.

With all their imperfections, these are four possible tests and their application to the actual course of events should give us some indications of how much and under what circumstances unions have had an impact on the general level of money wages.

Actual tests

The application of actual or presumed facts to our problem is fraught with a number of perils, some of which have been mentioned earlier. However, their application may indicate a reasonable range of answers to our questions.

The United States — (1) The various studies which have been made of the course of union and non-union wages offer no clear conclusions. Their results depend, to a substantial extent, on the dates taken for the studies and the definitions used. It may be fair to conclude, nevertheless, that, except for periods of active new unionism (as 1936-1937) and for situations with a closed shop (building trades), there is little evidence of a definite upward push by unions on wages.[14]

(2) The history of wage movements in the United States provides some additional evidence. Real compensation per man-hour dropped less from 1931 to 1932 (less than 2 per cent) when unions had strong influence in a

---

[14] For summaries and comment on the literature see L. G. Reynolds, "The Impact of Collective Bargaining on the Wage Structure in the United States," and Clark Kerr, "Wage Relationships—The Comparative Impact of Market and Power Forces," in John T. Dunlop (ed.) *The Theory of Wage Determination,* Macmillan, 1957.

few industries than from 1893 to 1894 (3 per cent) or 1920 to 1921 (3 per cent).[15] Compensation in the 1931 to 1932 period held steadier, as compared with consumer prices, than in the two earlier periods, possibly, in part, because of union influence.[16]

Money wages held much steadier in 1944 to 1945 than in 1917 to 1918. In 1944 to 1945, wage controls were in effect by government as against 1917 to 1918, when there was great freedom in wage adjustments. But it should also be noted that the unions in 1944 to 1945 accepted and even cooperated in the imposition of wage controls, and also that the contractual mechanisms which had grown up since 1917 to 1918 helped make it possible to exercise control over the great mass of wage rates that comprise our national wage structure.

In 1936 to 1937, with new and rival unionism, money wages and real wages jumped much more rapidly than one would normally expect in a period marked with as much unemployment as then existed.

Taking two longer periods, 1900 to 1910 and 1947 to 1957, both eras of quite sustained growth, it is noticeable that money wages rose faster than productivity in both periods. From 1900 to 1910, wages rose by one-third and productivity by one-fourth; from 1947 to 1957, by one-half and by one-third. It would appear that there may be an inflationary tendency, with wages rising faster than productivity, in a period of sustained growth under both largely non-union and largely union conditions. However, the excess gains of wages over productivity were somewhat greater in the second period and this may be due, in part, to unionism. Wages rose roughly one-third faster than productivity in the earlier period and one-half faster in the later period.

At a productivity rate of increase of 2.5 per cent a year and assuming that price rises reflect the comparative changes in wages and productivity (in other words, that there is no change in labor's share of national income), the price impact of the greater comparative wage increase would be about one-half of one per cent a year.[17] But it should be remembered that in the period 1947 to 1957, as compared with 1900 to 1910, there was much less of a labor reservoir of foreign immigrants, rural migrants and women, that administered prices were more widely prevalent, that government had created the expectation of continuing full employment and

[15] For the basic statistics for this and the immediately succeeding comments, see Table 1 in the paper by Albert Rees in this volume.

[16] For other evidence on the increasing rigidity of wages in business contractions, see D. Creamer, "Behavior of Wage Rates During Business Cycles," *The Relationship of Prices to Economic Stability and Growth, op. cit.*

[17] 2.5 plus one-third equals 3.33; 2.5 plus one-half equals 3.75; the difference between 3.33 and 3.75 is 0.42.

thus less risk for the employer who raised wage rates, and that there was the Korean War. Consequently, unionism, by itself, cannot be held responsible for the full one-half of one per cent a year.

Several years ago Garbarino concluded, on the basis of a study of the period 1899 to 1929, that, under non-union conditions, money wages and productivity kept pace with each other with unemployment rates of around 5 to 6 per cent.[18] Most recent experience with unemployment rates above 5 per cent has shown money-wage rates rising faster than long-term productivity rates. In 1958, with unemployment at nearly 7 per cent, hourly rates in manufacturing went up about 3.5 per cent over 1957, as against the 2.5 per cent which might be considered "normal" (the long-term rate of increase in productivity), but then productivity seems to have risen faster than normal also. However it should be noted that wage rates rose only about two-thirds as fast in the second half of 1958 as in the second half of 1957.

(3) Labor's share of national income has tended to be quite constant in the long run after adjusting for changes in the proportion of wage earners and in the inter-industry mix. But there have been occasions when the profit share has been "squeezed" and the wage share increased and, perhaps, partly due to union pressure on wages. These have been periods of depression (1931 to 1934 and 1938), periods when prices were held by price controls or the slower movement of administered prices in an inflationary period (1944 to 1947) and, most interestingly, a period of sustained full employment without substantial inflation, as in 1954-1957.[19]

Perhaps it could then be said that wages were really "pushing" on profits and thus on prices under these three circumstances. When there is no change in the profit share, it is harder to say who or what is "pushing" or "pulling"; and, when the profit share is rising, it would seem to indicate a "pull" rather than a "push." "Wage inflation," or wage pressure on the price level without inflation, would seem most likely to have occurred when labor's share had risen above "normal."

Great Britain — (1) A recent study in Great Britain, by Phillips,[20] relating wage increases to volume of unemployment, as Garbarino has done

---

[18] J. W. Garbarino, "Unionism and the General Wage Level," *American Economic Review,* December 1950. For comment on the relationship of changes in employment and changes in wages, 1947-57, see O. Eckstein, "Inflation, the Wage-Price Spiral and Economic Growth," the *Relationship of Prices to Economic Stability and Growth, op. cit.*

[19] For a review of the literature see Clark Kerr, "Labor's Income Share and the Labor Movement," in George W. Taylor and Frank C. Pierson (editors) *New Concepts in Wage Determination, op. cit.;* and for statistics more recent than included in this review see *Survey of Current Business,* February 1958. See also R. and N. Ruggles, "Prices, Costs, Demand and Output in the United States," *The Relationship of Prices to Economic Stability and Growth, op. cit.*

[20] A. W. Phillips, "Money Wages and Unemployment in the United Kingdom," *Economica,* November 1958.

for the United States, shows some interesting parallels and variations. Working with three periods, 1861 to 1913, 1913 to 1948, and 1948 to 1957, the first marked by relatively weak and the latter two by relatively strong unionization, Phillips found a very close correspondence between the related behavior of money wages and unemployment. The 1913 to 1948 period particularly followed the expectations based on the 1861 to 1913 period with only one major exception. Money wages went up faster in the years 1935 to 1937, a time of active union revival after the depression and also of rising food prices, than the general relation of money wage changes to the volume of unemployment would suggest. Taking the years 1948 to 1957, the "wage restraint" period of Trades Union Congress policy showed a lower than "normal" wage advance, but the years immediately following the end of the policy were noted for an unusually rapid increase, although they were also years of a rapid rise in import prices. As compared with the United States, lower levels of unemployment were found to be associated with the same wage behavior. For example, wages and productivity have seemed to march hand in hand with 2.5 per cent unemployment in Great Britain rather than 5 per cent in the United States.

(2) British experience also shows the importance of the divergence between actual rates and nominal rates—the rates paid in fact and those provided for by collective agreements and other formal documents. This divergence, or "wage drift," varies from one situation to another, but it was particularly great during periods of wage restraint, World War II and 1948 to 1950.[21] Actual rates drifted away from control through local action of employers and unions.

(3) The history of labor's share in Great Britain suggests no different general conclusions than does the history for the United States. Wages have squeezed profits when product markets were "hard" but not when they were "soft." [22]

Western Europe — A review of postwar experience in selected Western European countries, including for the sake of comparisons the United Kingdom and the United States, is instructive (see Table 2). France, with its "class bargainer" approach and the type of economy associated with it, has witnessed the greatest increase in the general level of money wages in manufacturing. Italy, however, with a somewhat similar approach, has had a relatively small increase. This emphasizes the point that other things are happening to an economy aside from union action. In Italy, over this period, unemployment has averaged 9 per cent, while it has been at quite

---

[21] See H. A. Turner, "Wages, Industry Rates, Workplace Rates and the Wage-Drift," *Manchester School,* May 1956. See also B. C. Roberts, "Trade Union Behavior and Wage Determination in Great Britain," in *Theory of Wage Determination, op. cit.*

[22] See E. H. Phelps-Brown and P. E. Hart, "The Share of Wages in National Income," *Economic Journal,* June 1952.

TABLE 2. *Indices of Hourly Money Earnings in Manufacturing in Selected Countries, 1946-57*

(1950 = 100)

	1946	*1947*	*1948*	*1949*	*1950*	*1951*	*1952*	*1953*	*1954*	*1955*	*1956*	*1957*
France	37	53	81	91	100	128	148	152	162	174	187	202
Italy	—	71	94	99	100	110	115	118	122	129	138	—
Norway	79	87	92	94	100	114	127	133	140	148	159	169
Sweden	74	85	93	96	100	121	144	150	156	168	183	—
United Kingdom	79	87	93	96	100	110	118	125	132	143	155	165
Germany	70	73	82	94	100	113	122	127	130	139	152	166
Holland	81	87	92	92	100	108	110	113	132	136	150	—
United States	74	84	92	95	100	108	114	120	123	130	135	141

Sources: International Labor Review, Statistical Supplements; and United Nations *Statistical Yearbooks.*

low (but unmeasured) levels in France. Norway, Sweden, and the United Kingdom have all undertaken "responsible" wage policies during part of the postwar period, and when responsibility was most in practice, up to 1950 and the Korean War, wage increases may have been slowed down a bit; but their records are not much different from that of the United States, where no such policy was in effect. In fact it was in Sweden during this early postwar period that the term "wage drift" was invented.[23]

Holland and Germany have had stronger policies of wage restraint in the postwar period, for the sake of the restoration of their economies, but wages have gone up only somewhat less than in Norway and the United Kingdom, and more than in Italy. In Germany, wage restraint was particularly in force from 1949 (after currency reform) to 1955 with some apparent effect, but this was also a period of great absorption of refugees into the economy. In Germany, with wage restraint by the unions, a "wage drift" began to show up in pronounced form by 1954 particularly in the metal-working industries of North Rhine-Westphalia. And it might be noted that a "wage drift" above contract rates becomes increasingly embarrassing to unions and undermines a wage restraint policy.

Finally, the United States, without wage restraint and with a sectional bargaining approach, has demonstrated a comparatively high degree of wage stability, as Table 2 shows.

Russia — Russian statistics on a comparable basis are not readily available. However, some comparisons can be made. From 1948 to 1952 money wages are said to have risen 8 per cent in Russia as against 24 per

[23] For an early use of the term see Rudolph Meidner, "The Dilemma of Wages Policy Under Full Employment" in *Wages Policy Under Full Employment,* Macmillan, 1952.

cent in the United States; [24] and from 1953 to 1956 the figures are 7 per cent and 12.5 per cent.[25] Also, it should be noted, productivity, as an offsetting force, has been rising faster in Russia (though it is at a much lower absolute level) than in the United States. But even in Russia, with an "agent of the state" union movement and authoritarian control, money wages have been rising; and price rates have been particularly resistant to controls.

Observations

The record, inadequate as it is, does permit some conclusions.

1. The "class bargainer" (or "enemy of the state") union movement, in the type of economy in which it develops, may well add to inflationary wage pressures.

2. The "agent of the state" union movement, in the type of system where it finds its natural habitat, is compatible with a comparatively slow rate of increase in the general level of money wages.

3. The "partner in social control" union movement may join in keeping wage increases somewhat below their normal levels for relatively short periods of time. But the "wage drift" and the internal pressures which develop under a wage-restraint policy make it unlikely that this effect will be long lasting. The results of wage restraint have been modest at best, although useful under the circumstances where they have been applied.

4. The "sectional bargainer" union movement presents a more mixed situation. When in a state of excitement, as around 1937 in both the United States and Great Britain, it may push wages up beyond "normal." In a depression, it may well hold them somewhat higher than they otherwise would be. At the plateau of a period of prosperity or in the early downswing, it may continue rates of wage increases experienced in the recent and more favorable past into the new situation. But in the upswing or a period of demand inflation, it may, as Rees has argued for the basic steel industry in the United States from 1945 to 1948, actually retard wage increases.[26]

Generally, the "sectional bargainer" union movement will probably lead to a steadier advance of the general wage level, neither as fast nor as slow as might otherwise occur. Also, through pattern bargaining, wage increases may be spread more uniformly and more broadly throughout the economy than under non-union conditions. Thus the total long-term effect is likely

---

[24] J. Chapman, "Real Wages in the Soviet Union, 1928-1952," *Review of Economics and Statistics,* May 1954.

[25] United Nations, *World Economic Survey,* 1957.

[26] Albert Rees, "Postwar Wage Determination in the Basic Steel Industry," *American Economic Review,* June 1951.

to be moderately inflationary; for the postwar period in the United States a net impact (after allowance for the influence of other factors) on the price level of somewhat less than one-half of one per cent as compared with "normal" or non-union conditions.

The real question might be why, as compared with the havoc it might wreak as seen by Lindblom, it has had so little effect? The answer must lie, in part, in the general reasonableness of the unions and their leaders in the context of the type of society in which they evolve; and thus in the nature of this kind of union as an institution.

In fact, two reversals of common statements come closer to illuminating the truth. Instead of asking why unions have so much inflationary effect, it might be more pertinent to ask why, as "monopolies," they have so little. Instead of accusing unions of an effective upward pressure on wage levels in a period of expansion and inflation, it would be more pertinent to make the accusation about them in periods of depression and deflation. The wrong question is asked; and the wrong accusation made.

5. The volume of unemployment is closely related to changes in the general level of money wages. In general, the level of employment must be considered the most important single factor. Its influence is over and beyond that of the trade union.

6. A period of expansion in a capitalist economy is normally a period of some inflation. Expansion and inflation are common travelling companions, whether a union movement travels with them or not.

7. Government wage controls can have an effect in holding down wage levels, perhaps more in the short run than in the long run, except in an authoritarian economy like the Russian.

8. Administered prices most certainly can make it easier to pass on administered wages without affecting profits.

The type of union and the character of the environment together determine the impact of the union on the general level of money wages. To view either one alone is to view but part of the scene. Taken together, in Western capitalism, the combination has probably become a somewhat more inflationary one than in earlier times. The union has often become more insensitive to the pressure of unemployment because of seniority rules protecting its older members and unemployment compensation for its newer members; but offsetting this has been the general growth in reasonableness and a sense of responsibility. The major changes are in the environment which is more permissive—full or more nearly full employment, the spread of administered prices and the drying up of pools of readily available labor.

If the unions secure greater wage increases than in the past, it is not so much because they want "more, more and more," which they do, but rather because it is easier to get "more, more and more." The environment is more conducive, rather than the unions more insatiable. The source of the trouble, to the extent there is trouble, is more that there is less pressure on the wage fixers than that the wage fixers are less sensitive to it; is more that there is less power in the environment and less that there is more power in the unions.

If remedies are to be sought, they would seem to lie, first, in strengthening the pressure of the environment toward stability and, second, in making unions more sensitive to that pressure.

Remedies

In considering remedies, in the context of the American economy, it may be well to contemplate these four points:

(1) Some inflation may be a normal cost of growth;

(2) The United States has had a comparatively good record on inflation in the postwar years;

(3) Some mild inflationary pressures are inherent in the kind of unionism which evolves out of American society;

(4) Certain "solutions" are not compatible with the character of this society—"agent of the state" unionism, or even "social partner" unionism, or permanent unemployment in excess (and possibly substantially in excess) of 6 per cent, or, probably, permanent wage (and price) controls by government.

Within the context of our society, however, several things may be possible:

1. To begin with, it would not be wise to guarantee full employment, particularly sector by sector, regardless of wage and price behavior. There should be some costs to irresponsible actions.

2. Next, administered prices are not fully socially accepted and their more unreasonable excesses should be discouraged by all reasonably available means, including anti-trust action and freer trade.

3. Industries of great pattern-setting importance or otherwise crucial to the economy should be made subject to *ex post* and *ad hoc* impartial fact-finding review of their wage bargains (and price policies) to acquaint the public with their consequences. This is one way to mobilize public opinion to bring pressure for stability on the private wage and price fixers.

4. The government should not enter industrial disputes with a "peace-at-any-price" approach except in a true national emergency.

5. All available action should be taken to increase the total supply of labor, for example, by providing part-time jobs for housewives and older persons, and to improve the mobility and adaptability of the labor force.

6. Unions should be open to all qualified workers. At the same time, rival unionism and great internal union instability should be avoided since

the conflicts arising from them usually find their solution, in part, in wage increases.

These are reasonable means and only reasonable results should be expected from them. We are living in an age marked by uneven but rapid economic growth, by a commitment to more-or-less full employment, by an exhaustion of earlier available sources of new accessions to the industrial labor force, by the great advancement of group initiative and group control over the economy, by the substantial freedom of individuals and groups from the imposed power of the state, and by mild inflation. Remedies for the last phenomenon must be seen in the light of the other phenomena which surround it. All things are not possible in all situations; and one thing which is not possible in this situation is full price stability and the wage levels which are consistent with it. The most successful case of wage control in an industralized nation in the postwar period is also the most repugnant.

5. Wage behavior and inflation:

An international view

Lloyd G. Reynolds

This paper will review the problem of wage-induced inflation in the light of experience in Western industrial countries. We shall say nothing about experience in low-income, primary producing economies or in the countries of the Soviet bloc. It is worth noting, however, that the problem is not absent even in centrally planned economies. Throughout the nineteen thirties and forties, the rapidly expanding urban industries of Russia struggled with a chronic manpower shortage. There was little effective restriction of labor mobility, turnover rates were high, and each plant manager scrambled for labor as best he could. One way of getting more labor was to pay more than the official wage scales. Overpayment was common, and the State Bank seems to have been willing to provide extra payroll funds when failure to do so would have meant an interruption of

---

Author of numerous books and professional articles on economics and administration, Lloyd G. Reynolds is Sterling Professor of Economics at Yale University. In 1941-43 Dr. Reynolds was regional price director for O.P.A.; in 1943-45, co-chairman of the appeals committee of The National War Labor Board; and in 1945-47, consultant to the United States Bureau of the Budget. He has also served as president of The Industrial Relations Research Association, as vice-president of The American Economic Association, and as one of the editorial board of *The American Economic Review*. Currently he is a director of The National Bureau of Economic Research.

production. The actual monetary circulation rose considerably faster than the planned circulation, increasing the pressure in retail markets and contributing to the great rise of prices over these two decades. Only in the nineteen fifties was the volume of wage payments brought under reasonably effective central control.

The movement of wages and prices over the past decade in certain of the Western industrial nations is shown in Table 1. If one excludes France

TABLE 1. *Percentage Increase in Selected Economic Indicators in Selected Countries, 1948-1957*

	Money Wages	*Wholesale Prices*	*Cost of Living*	*Real Wages*	*Real GNP Per Capita*
Australia	109	102	102	4	1
Canada	76	17	26	39	31[3]
France	149	66	77	40	60
German F. R.	105	17[1]	14	78	75[2]
Italy	54[3]	−1	28	20[3]	70
Netherlands	61[4]	43	48	15[4]	26[4]
Norway	84	71	53	20	35
Sweden	97[4]	53	47	39[4]	25[4]
U. K.	77	55[5]	51	18	16
U. S.	54	13	17	31	25[3]

1 1948 estimate based on July-December only.
2 From 1950 only.
3 1957 estimated.
4 Through 1956 only.
5 Through 1955 only.

Sources: Money wages, wholesale prices, cost of living, and population from *UN Statistical Yearbooks*, 1955, 1957, and *Monthly Bulletin of Statistics*, September 1958. GNP at market prices from *OEEC Bulletin*, July 1958, except Australia, which is from *IMF Financial Statistics*, January 1956 and January 1959.

(with its chronic inflation problem) and Australia (where the economy was disrupted by the violent upsurge of world wool prices during the Korean War), the consumer price index rose in most countries by from 20 to 50 per cent. Britain, Norway, Sweden, and Holland all experienced roughly a 50 per cent increase, due partly to delayed release of suppressed inflation held over from World War II. At the low end, the United States experienced only a 17 per cent increase and West Germany only 14 per cent.

Considering the overhang of suppressed inflation from World War II, the physical reconstruction effort of the late 'forties, the fresh price upsurge set off by the Korean War, and the very high level of investment and output in most countries during the 'fifties, this rate of price increase is not surprising. It should be noted also that most of the increase occurred during the first half of the period. During the years of peacetime prosperity 1952-57, the cost-of-living index rose by something between 5 and 15 per cent in most of the countries studied, or a rate of between 1 and 3 per cent per annum. This rate of increase may well be considered undesirable, but it is by no means abnormal. Table 2 shows the annual rate of price increase associated with periods of economic expansion in selected countries since 1870 or so. It is clear that output expansion has typically been associated with a rising price level, and that there is nothing novel about the 1950's in this respect.

TABLE 2. *Industrial Production and Prices During Periods of Rising Output, by Country*

(*Average annual percentage change*)

Country and period	*Production*	*Wholesale Prices*	*Consumer Prices*
Germany			
1880–1891	6.8	0.2	...
1892–1899	9.0	0.6	...
1901–1907	6.1	3.2	2.4
1907–1913	6.4	1.5	2.0
1924–1929	9.8	...	4.1
1932–1938	20.4	1.6	0.8
1952–1957	11.6	0.4	0.9
France			
1879–1883	6.7	−1.5	...
1886–1890	6.0	1.3	...
1895–1900	4.6	3.3	...
1902–1907	4.3	3.2	...
1908–1913	6.2	3.0	3.0
1923–1929	8.5	7.6	13.4
1932–1937	4.0	7.6	4.4
1952–1957	8.5	0.6	0.8
Sweden			
1870–1876	12.3	1.1	...
1879–1885	9.1	−1.5	...
1888–1898	18.6	−0.4	...
1901–1907	5.0	2.0	1.7
1909–1913	7.2	3.1	1.3
1923–1929	9.8	−2.2	−0.7
1932–1937	14.1	5.1	0.6
1952–1957	3.8	0.4	3.1
United Kingdom			
1870–1874	3.9	1.6	1.1
1879–1883	7.9	...	0.4
1886–1890	5.2	0.9	...
1893–1899	4.1	...	−0.6
1904–1907	4.0	4.4	1.1
1908–1913	6.2	3.3	1.9
1923–1929	2.7	−2.4	−0.8
1932–1937	8.5	5.3	1.4
1952–1957	4.3	...	3.7

TABLE 2—*Continued*

Country and period	*Production*	*Wholesale Prices*	*Consumer Prices*
United States			
1876–1882	12.0	−0.3	...
1885–1892	10.0	−1.5	...
1896–1903	11.0	4.0	2.2
1904–1907	9.9	3.1	3.2
1908–1913	9.8	2.2	2.4
1924–1929	7.0	−0.6	...
1932–1937	20.0	6.6	1.0
1952–1957	5.0	2.2	1.5

Source: United Nations, *World Economic Survey*, 1957, pp. 19-20.

Money wages rose faster than prices in every country in 1948-57, as would be expected in a progressive economy where rising productivity serves as a partial offset to wage gains. Real wages thus rose substantially in every country except Australia. Excluding Australia on the low side and West Germany on the high side, real wages in most countries rose by between 20 and 40 per cent, or roughly 2 to 4 per cent per year. The greater part of this increase came in the latter half of the period, after postwar reconstruction had been substantially completed and the dislocation of the Korean War had subsided.

There is little relation between the rate of increase in money wages and real wages. Some countries with relatively small money-wage increases show large increases in real wages, and vice versa. There is a much closer relation between the last two columns of Table 1—increase in real-wage level and increase in real per capita output of the economy. (There is of course no reason why the two figures should move *precisely* together. The GNP figure is calculated per head of population, and includes government outlay and capital formation as well as personal consumption. The real wage figure is per hour of time worked, and for most countries covers only manufacturing industry. One would expect a rough relation between the two, however, and this is what we actually find.) Real wages rose most rapidly in West Germany because of the phenomenal increase of production in that country. They rose only moderately in Britain, where the production increase over the decade was also quite moderate, and in Australia per capita output and real wages increased scarcely at all. The productivity basis of real-wage gains stands out quite clearly from the data.

A country-by-country review of experience over the past decade would be tedious and difficult to digest. It seems better to work through the problem of cost inflation in an analytical way, bringing in data from individual countries where they serve a particular purpose. We shall do this under the following headings:

(1) The mechanism of cost inflation.

(2) Statistical indicators of cost inflation.

(3) Structural determinants of cost inflation: the labor market, industrial structure, worker attitudes, union behavior, and the collective bargaining system.

(4) What to do about it?

The mechanism of cost inflation

In Europe, as in the United States, prices and wages have been rising hand over hand for the past twenty years. The statistical measurements, however, provide no direct clue to the underlying sources of inflation. Is it an excess of money demand which has been pulling up prices and wages? Is it unreasonable wage increases which have forced up both prices and the monetary circulation? Or what? This familiar conundrum must be faced at the outset.

Three types of inflation

A rise in the price level may come about in at least three ways:

(1) *An increase in total money demand to the point where it exceeds the productive capacity of the economy at current prices.* Consumers, investors, and government together are trying to buy more goods than the economy can provide. Prices must rise and real demand must be cut back (or, alternatively, a system of physical rationing must be imposed) until demand once more fits within the limits of capacity. This is the traditional case of demand inflation, which appears most clearly during periods of war and defense mobilization.

(2) An important variant of this case occurs *when aggregate demand, while not excessive in terms of* TOTAL *output capacity, exceeds the capacity of one or more key industries which thus become bottlenecks in the expansion.* The structure of money demand does not correspond with the structure of capacity. Thus while there is still under-utilization in many industries, the bottleneck industries find themselves booked to capacity or beyond. Their prices and profits rise, wage increases are readily granted; and this tends to induce price and wage increases elsewhere in the economy.

It is this situation, rather than a general excess of demand, which commonly characterizes the latter phase of a peacetime boom. Consider, for example, the experience of Western Europe and North America during the middle 'fifties. The inflationary forces released by the Korean War were largely spent by 1952. The years 1953 through 1957 were in most countries years of high peacetime prosperity. Except perhaps in France and the Netherlands, there was little indication of anything which could be called aggregate excess demand. There was, however, heavy pressure on a number of raw materials and durable goods industries, leading generally to shortages, order backlogs, increased costs and rising prices. The upward tendency of coal, steel, and machinery prices in selected countries is shown in Table 3. These prices typically rose considerably more than the general wholesale price level, indicating that excess demand was concentrated in the durable goods sector.

In demand inflations of types (1) and (2), costs are clearly not the aggressor, but this does not mean that their behavior is unimportant. On the contrary, the responsiveness or flexibility of costs in the face of price increases will have an important influence on the duration and height of the price movement. A long lag of wages behind prices will have a

TABLE 3. *Wholesale Prices of Coal, Steel, Machinery, and All Commodities, Selected Countries, 1957*

(1953 = 100)

Country	*Coal*	*Steel*	*Machinery*	*All Commodities*
Canada	109	—	—	103
Federal Republic of Germany	112	105	106	105
France	103	114	—	108
United Kingdom	140	122	115	—
United States	116	119	121	107

Source: First three columns from United Nations, *World Economic Survey*, 1957, p. 33. All commodities index from sources cited in Table 1.

dampening or "braking" effect. Conversely, automatic escalator clauses or other measures to speed up wage adjustments will add momentum to the inflation. A long wage lag which cuts workers' purchasing power may well be regarded as inequitable and unfeasible, but there is little doubt of its stabilizing character.

(3) *"Cost inflation" exists when there is no excess of aggregate demand or sectoral demand, and when pressure on prices is being exerted solely from the cost side.* This can happen in a variety of ways. In a country which depends heavily on foreign trade, a rise in import or export prices can set off a cycle of increases in living costs and wage rates. This is a serious problem in underdeveloped countries, but is found also in more advanced economies such as Norway, where imports form close to half of net national product. In Norway a period of near stability in prices during the late 'forties was violently disrupted by sharp increases in raw materials and other import prices after the outbreak of the Korean War. This pushed up the level of finished-goods prices, which stimulated substantial wage demands, which further increased the prices of domestic products. This spiral continued, because of the time lags involved, until well after

the world boom in raw-material prices had subsided. By 1953 the cost-of-living index had advanced 36 per cent, and average hourly earnings in manufacturing 44 per cent over the 1949 level.[1] The raw-materials price movements set off by the Korean War led to similar spirals in other Western European countries and, on a smaller scale, in the United States.

Another type of cost pressure is exemplified by the abandonment of wartime price restraints and consumption subsidies in many countries during the late 'forties and early 'fifties. This raises the cost-of-living index, which stimulates wage demands, which lead to further price increases, and so on. Retail food prices in the United Kingdom, for example, rose about 50 per cent between 1950 and 1956 although prices paid to farmers in Britain rose only about 20 per cent. The main reason was that food subsidies were reduced and state trading was abandoned, so that food imports entered Britain at world prices rather than at specially negotiated prices. This had a substantial inflationary effect. In most countries rents also rose much more than other living-cost items during the early 'fifties as controls were reduced and rents returned to free market levels.

Finally, cost inflation may originate in an effort by some important bloc in the economy to improve its position relative to other groups. If farmers, trade unionists, manufacturers, or retailers attempt to better their position by manipulating prices or wages, the price level may be pushed upward with no ready check. If the economy is operating at full employment, moreover, such a movement may easily become cumulative. Increased money demands by one group will soon be matched by increased demands by others. All may end up in about the same relative position as regards real income, but at a higher price level. Frustrated in the attempt to appropriate more real income, one or more groups may increase their money demands again and set off a new turn of the spiral. To speak of "turns" or "rounds" is of course to speak metaphorically, for when such a process is in motion the interaction of prices is complex and continuous, and one can no longer distinguish cause and effect in a temporal sense.

The feasibility of cost inflation

Economics is a tradition-bound subject, and economists have been slower than practical men to recognize the possibility that the price level may be forced up from the cost side. This springs partly from the habit of theorizing about a competitive economy in which price and wage

[1] This was of course not the only factor involved in the Norwegian situation, but was the dominant factor during this period. See Mark W. Leiserson, *Wages and Economic Control in Norway, 1945-57* (Cambridge: Harvard University Press, 1959), Chap. 5 and 6.

manipulation is impossible, partly from traditional models of inflation in which the impetus comes always from increased spending.

It has even been denied that there can be such a thing as "cost-push inflation" independent of monetary developments.[2] The reasoning proceeds as follows: Suppose that unions enforce wage demands greater than those warranted by productivity increases, and suppose that processors and distributors cover these cost increases by appropriate price mark-ups. Where will the money come from to support the higher price level? If the monetary authorities hold the monetary circulation unchanged, demand will be inadequate to buy the previous output at the new price level. Production and employment will fall, and this will either compel price and cost reductions or at any rate act as a brake on further increases. Suppose on the other hand that the monetary authorities, fearful of bringing on a recession, permit whatever increase in money supply may be necessary to support the higher price level. Then the new price level is feasible, and can be raised step by step for as long as the permissive monetary policy continues. But does this not mean merely that the monetary authorities have been bullied into creating an excess of money demand? If so, do we not end up with the conclusion that all inflation is after all demand inflation? It would then follow that inflation remains a monetary problem to be dealt with by the usual instruments of monetary policy.

There are two main difficulties in this argument. First, it is not true that there is a close relation in the short run between aggregate money supply and aggregate spending. Changes in monetary velocity or liquidity have been revealed as of great practical importance during the postwar period. In some European countries, to be sure, the postwar inflation has been financed mainly by expansion of the money supply. France and Italy are the outstanding examples. But in others, including Denmark, Sweden, the Netherlands, and the United Kingdom, price increases have been financed mainly by a reduction of liquidity, with the money supply rising little or even contracting.

In the Netherlands, for example, the increase in money supply averaged only 1.6 per cent per year over the period 1948-56. Considering that the increase in physical output averaged 5.4 per cent per year, this was a very modest rate of monetary expansion and would suggest a *decline* in the price level. Actually, the price level rose at an average rate of 3.8 per cent per year. How could this happen? The explanation is that monetary liquidity declined consistently and in some years quite sharply throughout the period, except during 1952 and 1953. Over the nine years as a whole, increased velocity added the equivalent of 5.7 per cent per year to

---

[2] See for example Walter A. Morton, "Trade Unionism, Full Employment, and Inflation," *American Economic Review*, March 1950, pp. 13-39.

money supply, or more than three times the rate of increase in actual monetary units.[3]

This element of "play" in the system means that the monetary brakes on cost inflation are not nearly so tight as they otherwise would be. It can still be argued that, if velocity is increasing more rapidly than monetary requirements based on a stable price level, the monetary authorities can always offset this by producing an appropriate decline in money supply. This increases the trickiness of monetary policy, however, particularly since the rate of increase in velocity is variable and difficult to predict.

Waiving this difficulty, however, there is a more fundamental question about the monetary line of argument. What good does it do to re-label price increases arising from cost pressure as "demand inflation"? How does this change the actual situation? It is formally correct that a certain price level is feasible only if adequate monetary demand is available, and in this sense any inflation *must* be a demand inflation. But this does not change the nature of the phenomenon. It does not alter the fact that producer groups can and may demand monetary returns incompatible with stable prices, and that this creates a special kind of problem for the monetary authorities, differing materially from the traditional problem of restraining excessive aggregate demand. Indeed, it may turn out that monetary policy is incapable by itself of coping with cost pressures. We shall return to this issue at a later stage.

How much is "too much"?

While cost pressure may emanate from any producer group, we are mainly concerned in this paper with pressure arising from excessive wage increases. Here we face the initial difficulty that a rising money-wage level based on productivity increases is normal in a progressive economy. Money-wage increases are disruptive only if they rise above some "tolerable," "warranted" or "non-inflationary" rate. There is an initial problem, then, of defining what one means by a non-inflationary behavior of wages.

There are at least two possible approaches to this problem, which we may term the *productivity* approach and the *income* approach. The former, which typically involves comparison of the rate of increase in hourly wage payments and in output per man-hour, has serious limitations for the present purpose, and we must examine briefly why this is so. The year-to-year increase of output in a growing economy arises from three sources:

(a) An increase in man-hours of labor utilized in production. This factor is eliminated when total national output is divided by man-hours

[3] Robert Triffin, "Credit, Money, Production, Prices and Balance of Payments in O.E.E.C. Countries, 1948-56," (Paris: unpublished OEEC memorandum, February 1958), p. 49.

worked, and the increase in output *per man-hour* is attributable to the two remaining factors.

(b) An increase in physical capital used in production. The fact that in the United States the supply of capital has risen considerably faster than the supply of labor since 1900, so that capital per worker has increased about 1 per cent per year, is partly responsible for the rapid rise of man-hour output.

(c) A residual not explained either by the increase of labor or of capital and which, since we cannot explain it, we sweep under the rug by ascribing it to "technical progress." About half the increase in the national output of the United States since 1900 falls in this residual category.[4]

The proposition that wage rates or earnings per man-hour should rise at the same rate as output per man-hour is in no way self-evident. On the contrary, it involves complex assumptions about the operation of a market economy with changing factor supplies, and about equity in income distribution, which cannot be detailed here. Moreover, this or any similar proposition is a statement about the *normal or desirable distribution of real income between capital and labor*—a classic issue in economics, but one rather remote from the problem of inflation. A practical difficulty is that our measures of man-hour output are very incomplete. The figure most commonly cited—man-hour output in manufacturing—covers only about one-quarter of the economy, and has almost certainly risen more rapidly over the last century than man-hour output in general.

For these reasons the income approach seems to have a more direct and useful bearing on the matter of inflation. Rising national output over the course of time creates what the Swedish economist Erik Lundberg has termed "wage space"—room for an increase in money incomes without any upward adjustment of the price level. As a first approximation, one can define a non-inflationary situation as one in which wage income per capita is rising at the same rate as real national output per capita. (A more refined statement would have to specify the behavior of other types of money income, and also the behavior of savings and investment.) For the United States, Kuznets has estimated this at about 16.4 per cent per decade over the period 1894-1954, but the rate of increase since 1940 has been considerably higher than in earlier years.[5]

This figure in some ways overstates, in other ways understates, the feasible rate of increase in basic wage schedules. On the side of overstatement we may note:

---

[4] See Solomon Fabricant, *Basic Facts on Productivity Change* (New York: National Bureau of Economic Research, 1958), Occasional Paper 63.

[5] Simon Kuznets, "Quantitative Aspects of the Economic Growth of Nations," *Economic Development and Cultural Change,* V, No. 1 (October 1956), p. 10.

1. Part of the increase in national output comes about through the transfer of workers from low-productivity to high-productivity industries, notably from agriculture to manufacturing, over the course of economic development. This increase in output is presumably offset by increased earnings of the transferred workers in their new occupations. To use it also as a basis for a general increase in wage schedules would involve double counting. Increases in output from this source should be deducted, therefore, in calculating the feasible rate of wage increase.

2. It is the rate of increase in *earnings* which should correspond to the rate of increase in output. Earnings, however, may rise considerably faster than basic wage rates, particularly during a period of sustained high employment. The reasons include promotion and upgrading of individual workers, overrating of jobs to permit higher wage offers for recruiting purposes, loosening of time standards on piece work so that earnings pull farther and farther above base rates, and straight overpayment of the union scale. This tendency for earnings to diverge farther and farther above official wage schedules, which Swedish economists have termed "wage drift," has been noticeable in most industrial countries during the 'forties and 'fifties.

3. Workers' incomes have also tended recently to rise faster than basic wage rates because of the rapid growth of fringe benefits. These payments form a rising proportion of workers' total compensation, and direct wage payments a declining proportion.

Two important considerations may be advanced in the opposite direction:

1. Why should all types of income in the economy move upward in lock step? Perhaps wage earners' incomes can rise faster than per capita output if other people's incomes are rising less rapidly. Perhaps workers may be able to get "more than their share" of a rising national income at the expense of other groups. There is doubtless something to this line of argument. If one defines "labor" narrowly to include only wage earners, then wages may gain somewhat at the expense of salaries over the long run. Another "squeezable" group includes recipients of rents, fixed interest payments, annuities, and pensions. But these groups receive only a minor part of national income, and their squeezability is limited and tends to get used up over the course of time. One cannot, therefore, rely on income redistribution to allow workers' incomes to rise *much* faster than per capita national output is rising.

2. Another consideration of some importance is the behavior of labor-force participation rates and weekly or annual hours of work. If these two variables are increasing, then hourly wage schedules should rise less rapidly than the desired rate of increase in wage income per capita, and vice versa. In the United States, the overall labor-force participation rate has been remarkably stable since 1900, while the trend of hours has been steadily

downward. This would indicate that hourly wage rates should rise faster than per capita wage income.

Taking all these things into account, it is possible in principle to define a non-inflationary rate of increase in basic wage schedules. Quite elaborate calculations would be necessary, however, to get even a rough idea of what this rate may be in a particular country at a particular time. It is commonly asserted that in the United States at present the noninflationary rate of increase in wage schedules lies somewhere between 2 and 3 per cent per year. This is probably correct, but has not yet been confirmed by rigorous investigation.

The concept of a feasible, or reasonable, or non-inflationary rate of increase in the money wage level is obviously useful. But it is also a dangerous concept, because it is apt to be interpreted as meaning that every wage rate in the economy should rise by a certain percentage every year. This never happens, and it would be unfortunate if it did happen. Wages should rise faster than average in expanding companies, industries, and regions, and less than average in stationary or declining areas and industries, in order to assist reallocation of the labor force to the growth points of the economy. Apart from this, the wage structure always contains inequities and anomalies which can be corrected only if there is flexibility for different wages to advance at different speeds. It may also be undesirable for the *average* wage level to advance at the same rate from year to year. Subnormal wage increases are natural in recession years, while in boom years the rate of increase may be unusually high. The feasible rate of wage increase over the long run should not be construed as a yardstick which can be applied inflexibly to particular wage decisions.

A possible mechanism of wage inflation

Does the actual rate of money-wage increase tend to rise above the rate compatible with price stability, particularly at high levels of output and employment? Factual evidence is difficult to come by, but one can think of reasons why this might happen.

One plausible line of reasoning takes off from the fact that, in a dynamic economy, industries differ widely in their rate of productivity increase. Calculations for eleven countries over the period 1950-56 show that the standard deviation of individual industry rates of increase in man-hour output was typically between 80 and 100 per cent of the mean rate of increase for manufacturing as a whole.[6] The main reason seems to be inter-industry differences in the rate of growth of total output. Young, expanding industries with a rapid rate of growth in demand and production

[6] United Nations, *World Economic Report,* 1957, pp. 36-37.

are able to achieve much larger gains in man-hour output than mature industries with little output expansion. Thus in Canada all manufacturing industries showed an annual increase of 2.4 per cent in man-hour output over the years 1950-56; but the top quarter of industries in terms of output growth showed an average annual increase of 6.8 per cent in man-hour output. The corresponding figures for Sweden are 2.8 per cent for all manufacturing, 6.4 per cent for the quarter of most rapidly expanding industries; for the Netherlands, 2.6 per cent and 4.8 per cent. Less striking differentials in the same direction appear in all the other countries studied.

A related type of evidence has to do with whether rising wage *rates* are accompanied by rising or falling wage *costs*. Over the period 1950-56 covered by the U. N. study, money wages were rising at a substantial rate. Yet in most countries unit wage costs fell in the metals, machinery, petroleum, and coal products industries. Unit wage costs held about even in chemicals, rubber, glass, paper, and wood products industries. Unit wage costs rose in most countries in textiles and clothing, leather and leather products, tobacco products, and food processing. In the mature consumers' goods industries in this last group, the rate of output growth and productivity increase was not sufficient to offset rising wage rates.

Wage rates in all industries advance at a uniform rate—specifically, at the non-inflationary rate defined above. Industries with a low rate of productivity increase will then find their unit wage costs rising, and these cost increases will have to be covered by price increases. At the extreme, in service industries such as barbering where most cost is labor cost and there is little room for productivity gains, product prices will rise *pari passu* with the general wage level. Industries with high rates of productivity increase, on the other hand, will find their unit labor costs falling and can afford price reductions. Given the pervasive influence of oligopoly and the business antipathy to price cutting, however, it seems unlikely that reductions will actually be made on a scale sufficient to offset the price increases in other industries.[7] Thus even under these conditions of "ideal" wage behavior, there is a certain inflationary bias which might cause a gradual increase in price levels.

In actuality, however, it is unlikely that wages will behave in this way. Wages will probably advance, or try to advance, at a higher than average rate in the industries where man-hour output is advancing most rapidly. We have already noted that these tend to be the industries in which total output and employment are also rising most rapidly. It may thus be neces-

[7] Where, then, will the savings from productivity increases go? Perhaps partly into profit, most of which will be reinvested in further expansion. But partly also into improved product quality—a price cut of sorts, but one which does not show up in cost-of-living indexes; and partly into a generous policy on wage rates and other factor prices.

sary to raise wages for recruitment purposes, particularly if the economy is near full employment. Further, with output expanding and prices diverging above the declining trend of unit costs, these industries will be in a position to afford a generous wage policy. There is considerable evidence that profitable companies and industries tend to share their prosperity with employees, even in the absence of union pressure.[8] If a union is present, it will reinforce management's good intentions and may press for even larger increases than would occur otherwise.

The pace of wage advance in the lead sectors of the economy will then be transmitted to other sectors through both institutional and market channels. To the extent that other industries are unionized, and to the extent that there is inter-union rivalry on the wage front, there will be pressure on employers generally to match the "pattern" established in the high-productivity industries. But one does not have to rely on collective bargaining to attain this result. Under high-employment conditions, each employer must keep reasonably well in step with the general pace of wage advance in order to replace or expand his labor force. The market sets limits, albeit rather rough ones, to the feasible size of wage differentials; and as the top of the wage structure rises, the bottom tends to be pulled up after it.

While it seems plausible that things may work in this way, it is hard to check the argument by reference to statistics. If the transmission of wage impulses is rapid and complete, one may find that after a certain period of time all industries have gone up by roughly the same amount. (Indeed, the U. N. report cited previously did find this for the period 1950-56. In most countries the percentage increase in wages for the top quarter of most rapidly growing manufacturing industries was almost identical with that for all manufacturing.) This in no way disproves the hypothesis that the expanding and profitable industries may have been forcing the pace of wage advance. But neither does it demonstrate that this has happened, or give any quantitative indication of the degree of acceleration. Detailed analysis of the *timing* of wage adjustments, industry by industry, might be more revealing, but little evidence of this sort has been collected.

Statistical indicators of cost inflation

To this point we have tried to distinguish cost inflation from other types of inflationary process, to define the rate of money-wage increase which is feasible without producing upward pressure on prices, and to describe a

[8] This was suggested some years ago by Sumner Slichter, and has been confirmed by subsequent studies. See S. H. Slichter, "Notes on the Structure of Wages," *Review of Economics and Statistics,* Vol. 32, 1950, pp. 80-91.

mechanism which might cause actual wage increases to exceed the feasible rate—a mechanism which is not dependent on, though it might be strengthened by, the presence of unionism and collective bargaining. But all this is at a theoretical level. What we really want to know is whether cost inflation is a serious problem in actuality. Given an economy in which wages, prices, profits, and other monetary quantities are rising simultaneously, how does one tell where the inflationary impetus is coming from? Specifically, is there any way of telling whether a "wage push" is or is not present?

Some of the measurements commonly used are not very helpful in this respect. It proves little, for example, to compare the movement of wage incomes and physical output. The conceptual difficulties already noted limit the validity of any simple comparison. More fundamentally, however, a more rapid increase of wage incomes than of physical output would be found in *both* demand-pull and cost-push situations. It thus cannot provide a criterion for distinguishing between them.

It is not much use either to work with leads and lags, to try to determine whether wages rose "before" prices or after them. This would work only if the economy had been for some years in a stable state, with little movement of price indexes and with employment and output expanding steadily along a long-term growth path. If after such a period of stability one found an upsurge of certain prices followed by abnormal wage increases, or vice versa, one might try to analyze causation in a temporal sense. But such a stable economy is an economist's construct, not something which one can hope to find in actuality. What one does find is continual fluctuation of individual prices and wages, and wave-like movements of output and employment, the whole never coming to anything like a condition of rest. Whether one event occurred "before" another, whether wages have risen "more than" prices or vice versa, thus turns entirely on the choice of a base period, on where one chooses to cut into the historical sequence of events. It is always possible to show that one economic quantity has moved "disproportionately" to another by choosing the right base, but such arguments obviously have no scientific usefulness.

There are, however, at least three types of quantitative analysis which may throw *significant* light on the nature of an inflationary process:

(1) *The behavior of profit margins per unit of output or sales.* If product prices are being pulled up in advance of unit wage costs, then profit margins should be widening, and this is in fact a common characteristic of demand inflations. If, on the other hand, an increase in unit wage costs is the active force, one might expect profit margins to be stationary or even falling.

This apparently simple criterion is not without difficulties. First, it is a micro-economic criterion which needs to be applied at the industry or even the company level. Changes in factor shares of income produced for the economy as a whole are not very useful because of their aggregative character, because they are usually annual and thus rather blunt for the present purpose, and because of well-known difficulties of concepts and measurements. Second, while a decline in profit margins can be taken as indicating some type of cost inflation, this need not necessarily be wage-cost inflation. Speculative increases in raw-material prices, for example, such as occurred in the early stages of the Korean War, may for a time get ahead of increases in finished-goods prices, and profit margins in some sectors may shrink on this account.

(2) *The output level of the economy relative to full capacity, and the direction in which output is moving.* If output is pressing against capacity, and rising gradually as the expansion of capacity permits, an observed increase in price levels may reasonably be ascribed to excess demand. If, on the other hand, one sees prices rising at a time when output is either falling or well below the capacity of the economy, one may suspect some degree of cost inflation.

Here again we need more refined measurements than have been used to date. The level of full-time unemployment, which is often used as an indication of the gap between output and capacity, is a very crude measure indeed. The size of the labor force is somewhat responsive, and hours of work are very responsive, to fluctuations in the demand for labor. An observed fluctuation of full-time unemployment between 2 per cent and 8 per cent of the labor force may mean a much larger fluctuation in the gap between output and capacity. Moreover, the economy's capacity is bounded over any short period by the stock of capital equipment as well as by labor supply. One may reach full use of equipment, at least in certain bottleneck industries, before labor supply is exhausted.

It must be remembered, too, that there is considerable lag in the movement of finished-goods prices, particularly at the retail level. Retail price indexes typically lag cyclical downturns and upturns in output by six months or so. The fact that prices continue upward for a time after output has turned downward is not necessarily evidence of cost inflation. It becomes so only if the divergent movement of prices and output continues beyond some "normal" or "reasonable" period of time.

(3) *The detailed character of wage movements.* During the postwar years Sweden, Norway, and a number of other European countries have observed a phenomenon generally termed "wage drift"—a more rapid increase in actual earnings than in the basic wage rates specified by union-management agreements. This comes about through voluntary overpayment of union scales by employers, individual upgrading, merit increases, increased use of incentive systems, loosening of piecework standards, increased overtime, and other decisions at the plant level. Behind it lies a

high demand for labor, stemming from excess demand in product markets, which both enables and forces employers to follow a liberal wage policy.

In a year of large "wage drift," one might conclude that unions have underpriced their labor and that the effective wage level is being pulled upward from the demand side. If on the other hand one finds large basic wage increases accompanied by little or no wage drifting, one might surmise that excess demand is not present. In a very decentralized bargaining system such as that of the United States, with many industries only partially unionized, one might even find at times a "negative wage drift" involving (a) raggedness in the movement of contract rates in different sectors, with the high-productivity-increase sectors moving up faster than others; (b) raggedness within individual industries, with nonunion companies tending to lag behind union companies; (c) a tendency for earnings to advance less rapidly than basic rates. This would suggest a cost-push situation in the sense that some contractual rates are being pushed up more rapidly than is warranted by demand levels in the economy as a whole.

One could perhaps make a case that price and wage movements, industry by industry, should be more nearly uniform under conditions of excessive aggregate demand than under cost-push conditions. If so, something could be learned from the dispersion of wage and price movements during a particular period. Once more, however, one encounters the perhaps insuperable difficulty that the results will depend entirely on the time period chosen.

What this comes down to is that aggregative data are virtually useless in trying to separate demand and cost inflation. The useful lines of work involve micro-economic data, laborious tabulations and analyses, and sophisticated judgment in interpreting the results. To do this even for one country for a short period is a formidable task. At an early stage of this paper I thought that it might be possible to make such an analysis for at least a few countries, and to say that cost inflation was or was not important during certain periods; but it quickly became apparent that this was a subject for a treatise, not an essay.

Structural determinants of cost inflation

The fact that wage-push inflation is a hypothetical possibility need not mean that it will actually occur. It may occur in some economies at some times, but not in other times and places. What determines the susceptibility of an economy to wage inflation? The following structural characteristics appear to be particularly important: the flexibility of the labor force and the efficiency of labor markets; competitive relations and pricing practices in product markets; worker attitudes and expectations in the matter of wages; and certain characteristics of union organization and collective bargaining arrangements.

Labor mobility and labor markets

The important considerations here are the willingness and ability of workers to shift freely among employers, industries, and geographical areas in response to economic inducements; and the existence of clearing-house arrangements to facilitate the transfer and placement of labor. High propensity to move and effective clearing-house arrangements make for a flexible labor force, for moderately sloped rather than steeply sloped labor-supply curves.

This is important in two respects. First, the greater the flexibility of the labor force, the higher is the level of employment attainable before the economy encounters a general shortage of labor and enters an inflationary phase. In an economy with a very flexible labor force it may be feasible to define "full employment" as corresponding to 2 per cent of the labor force unemployed. In an economy with a sluggish labor force and poor labor markets, it may not be feasible to reduce unemployment below 5 per cent without inducing price inflation.

Second, we noted earlier that a demand inflation may occur because an economy, while still operating below capacity in most sectors, encounters production bottlenecks in a few key industries. We ordinarily think of these bottlenecks as arising from capacity utilization of plant and equipment. But the impediment to production may also be a shortage of labor in particular industries and localities, even though labor supply is generally adequate. This may induce substantial wage increases at the bottleneck points, which are then transmitted through market and institutional channels to other types of employment. The greater the flexibility of the labor force, the less likely is it that such labor bottlenecks will occur; and where they do occur, it will not require such large wage increases to overcome them as would be necessary otherwise.

In both respects, then, a flexible labor force raises the production ceiling of the economy. It permits rising demand to carry production and employment to a higher level before demand becomes excessive and inflation sets in.

Competitive and pricing arrangements

The customary argument here is that monopoly, "cooperative" oligopoly, and cartel arrangements are favorable to cost inflation, while competitive pricing acts as a restraining force. This hypothesis may well be correct, though not for the reason most commonly offered. There is little indication that monopolistic sellers are *directly* responsible for inflation by seeking to expand profit margins more rapidly than other factor costs. On the contrary, profit mark-ups seem to be governed by conventional rules which remain stable for long periods of time. The UN analysis of inflation in the Western European economies over the period 1952-57 found that profit margins had not risen more on the average in "administered price" industries than in industries where competitive pricing prevailed.

For all countries as a group, gross margins between prices and direct costs did not show any greater tendency to widen in the industries that are commonly considered to have administered prices than they did in other industries; in fact, during the latter part of the period (1950-56) there was, if anything, a balance in the other direction. In only one of the 'administered price' industries did margins widen in more countries than they narrowed; this was petroleum and coal products, and in the particular period under review the widening margins may have been due to changing technology and product mix. Nor does it appear that there was any widespread tendency for margins to widen in the industries where prices increased most. Industries where widening margins were associated with increasing prices or narrowing margins with decreasing prices were no more common than industries showing the reverse relationship.[9]

It may be, however, that employers in an administered-price industry concede wage increases more readily than they would under free market pricing. The administrative ease of converting higher costs into higher prices, and the certainty that this can be done fully and rapidly, may lower employer resistance to wage increases, whereas uncertainty about the product market would have led employers to put up a harder fight. The argument is not that administered-price industries raise wages faster than other (competitive) industries in the same economy over a given period. This is by and large not true, and cannot be true because of the labor market linkages explained earlier. The argument is rather that administered-price industries raise wages more rapidly than those same industries would have done if organized on a competitive basis. If these industries happen also to be those in which productivity is advancing most rapidly, they may generate a rate of wage increase which is inappropriate for the economy as a whole and yet which the entire economy must follow.

This is an "iffy" argument which is obviously difficult to test, and no satisfactory tests have yet been devised. If the hypothesis is correct, one could say that administered pricing arrangements contribute *indirectly* to cost inflation by providing a more permissive atmosphere for wage increases.

Worker expectations

It clearly makes a difference whether workers expect substantial wage increases to occur every year, or whether they expect wage increases to be moderate and intermittent. Worker expectations generate union policies, political pressures, and individual demands on employers which may have considerable effect on the course of wages.

---

[9] United Nations, *World Economic Survey*, 1957, p. 34.

Little is known about worker attitudes on this point and how they are generated. Experience over the recent past must have some influence. If wages have been advancing rapidly for a number of years, it is natural for workers to project this trend into the future; and if living costs have also advanced considerably, they will be all the more insistent on substantial wage gains. One of the most difficult features of the present situation in many countries is the history of unbroken wage and price increases over the past twenty years. There will soon be few workers living who can remember a wage cut or even a year in which wages did not rise. This has generated a momentum in money-wage movements which is much harder to check today than it would have been a decade ago.

A related matter is worker expectations about union objectives and accomplishments. At one extreme, workers may regard their union dues as a business investment and judge the union's effectiveness by the monetary gains which it wins. At the other pole, workers may regard unionism as a political and social movement, and may attach primary importance to worker participation in management, nationalization of industry, or redistribution of income through government. Wage bargaining is never unimportant, but it plays a more central role in some union movements than in others. In the years since World War II, for example, it has been less significant in Germany than in Britain, and less significant in Britain than in the United States.

The structure of unionism and collective bargaining

The linkage between wage inflation and collective bargaining is a good deal looser than is often assumed in popular discussion. Unionism is not a prerequisite for the appearance of wage inflation, nor does the presence of unionism guarantee that wage inflation will follow. Unionism does make a difference, however, and the characteristics of collective bargaining in a particular country can be of substantial importance. Most significant among these characteristics are probably the following:

1. *The incidence of union organization.* It makes a difference whether unionism is strongest in the sectors where conditions are most favorable to money wage increases, or whether the contrary is true. In the United States, strong textile unionism and weak automobile unionism would produce a rather different wage atmosphere than exists at present.

2. *The locus of control over union policy.* Aggressive membership participation in union government and insecurity of tenure among union leaders may be applauded on democratic grounds, but it probably also makes for larger wage demands than would occur otherwise. Top union officials have better economic information, a longer-range outlook, and greater concern with employment and other side-effects of wage increases

than do union members. To the extent that the leaders can proceed without direct membership control, they are likely to be more moderate and realistic in wage demands and wage settlements. The strongly entrenched leadership of British trade unions, for example, has contributed to a less frenetic wage policy than prevails in the United States.

3. *Inter-union relations and the scope of collective agreements.* The labor movements of industrialized countries exhibit wide differences in this respect. In some countries, including the United States, local unions typically carry on the bargaining with general advice and assistance from national headquarters, and the single-company agreement is the general rule. In others, including Britain, the collective agreement is typically negotiated by national officers and is coextensive with the industry. A few countries, including Holland and Sweden, have experimented with still more centralized systems in which a central trade union federation strikes a master bargain with a national confederation of employers, and this provides a general framework for more detailed bargaining in individual industries.

The differences among these collective bargaining systems are not as great in practice as they can be made to appear on paper. In American industries where employers compete in regional or national markets, the national unions try to ensure substantial uniformity in the terms of local settlements and the situation often approaches that of industry-wide bargaining. Conversely, in countries such as Sweden, Norway, and Holland, wage decisions are less centralized than they appear to be. The national master agreement sets certain guide-lines, but these are later applied and modified through separate negotiations in each industry. Similarly, the terms agreed on at the industry level may be modified a good deal in their application to individual plants and groups of workers. The master agreement typically ensures a certain minimum increase for every unionized worker; but there is a great deal of bargaining up from this minimum, and the actual realized increases vary considerably from one plant and industry to another.

There has been considerable discussion of the relation between centralization of collective bargaining and the aggressiveness of union wage policies. Perhaps the commonest hypothesis is that greater centralization is likely to produce more moderate wage demands, demands which are adjusted to national economic necessities and are held within the bounds permitted by productivity increases. The rationale for this is that leaders of the top union federation are strongly insulated against grassroots opinion and pressure, that they have comprehensive economic information and a broad outlook on the national economy, and that they are in a position to check what might otherwise become a competitive scramble for wage advantage among individual unions.

This is an interesting and persuasive hypothesis, but one cannot say that it has yet been verified by experience. Individual instances can be cited. During the late 'forties the labor movements in Britain, Norway, Sweden, and Holland, cooperated with their national governments in a policy of wage restraint, amounting at times to a virtual prohibition of negotiated wage increases. Money wages rose very little in these countries from 1947 to 1950, and real wages scarcely at all. In Holland the policy of wage restraint continued through the early 'fifties and was sufficiently severe that real wages were actually lower in 1953 than in 1947, and labor's share of national income produced declined appreciably.

One must remember, however, that the circumstances of this period were very unusual. The countries concerned were recovering from the physical destruction and economic dislocation of a six-year war, and were struggling to rebuild their productive capacity and restore their export markets. It was thus easier than it normally would be to enlist cooperation of all economic groups in a national effort. Incomes of non-wage-earning groups were restricted by price controls and heavy profits taxation, which put government in a stronger position to ask restraint of wage earners. The governments in office were labor governments resting largely on trade union support, and union leaders were consequently reluctant to embarrass them by opposing their economic policies.

After the peak of the Korean crisis, restraints on wages and other money incomes were loosened in most countries. Price controls and subsidies were increasingly abandoned, and the economies moved toward normal peacetime operation. From this point on, it is difficult to make a case that centralized collective bargaining had a braking effect on the rate of wage increase. From 1952 to 1957 money wages rose somewhat more in Britain, Holland, and Scandinavia than in Canada and the United States with their decentralized bargaining systems. This may have been partly a catching-up from the previous period of wage restraint, and partly also a reflection of unusually high levels of demand and employment. The West European economies have probably operated somewhat closer to capacity during the 'fifties than those of Canada and the United States, which might well account for faster increases in the wage-price level. In any event, collective-bargaining procedures and union policies in these countries do not seem to have had any clear-cut effect in producing a different behavior of the money-wage level than that found in Canada or the United States.

4. *Contract renewals and wage reopenings.* In the United States we tend to take it for granted that collective agreements must expire and a new wage bargain be negotiated every twelve months, but this is in no way inevitable. British union agreements are of indefinite duration, though annual wage demands have become more common during the nineteen fifties than they used to be. Moreover, since there is no contract expiration

date after which a strike must occur, there is no deadline on the negotiations, which therefore proceed at a more leisurely pace than in the United States. A lag of a year between initial demand and final settlement is not uncommon. This slower tempo of wage movements lengthens the wage lag during a demand inflation and probably also reduces the likelihood of cost-push inflation.

What to do about it?

Before discussing remedial measures it should be re-emphasized that we are not sure that there is a serious problem of secular inflation, or at any rate that the problem is more serious today than in earlier decades. It was noted earlier that the rate of price increase in most countries since 1952 is not at all out of line with the rates in earlier periods of peacetime economic expansion. Price-level increases are also to some extent illusory in that quality changes are not adequately represented. One of my colleagues argues that it is quite doubtful whether there has been any genuine increase in consumer prices in the United States since 1949.

The argument is as follows: give a sample of consumers a 1949 Sears, Roebuck catalog and a 1959 catalog. Give them also $1,000 each, and permit them to order from either catalog. If they choose the 1959 catalog, as my friend surmises most of them would do, this must mean that quality increases have outweighed price increases and that the price level has not risen in any significant sense.

The question under discussion here, then, should be stated as follows: *if* there is a problem of secular inflation, and *if* this arises in some measure from cost pressure of the wage-push variety (neither of these things being certain), what remedial measures might be taken? To the extent that the problem exists, it is clearly not amenable to a single once-for-all solution, any more than one could hope to "solve" cyclical instability or any other deep-rooted structural problem by a single reform. It is sounder strategy to think of "weathering down" or encircling the problem by a variety of flanking maneuvers.

The one-shot remedies most frequently proposed for wage inflation do not stand up very well under close examination. Some of the commonest proposals are:

(1) *Weakening the power of unionism by enforced decentralization*—for example, by confining collective bargaining to a single company and representatives of that company's employees only. This would be a radical departure from our past policies in labor relations, since it would mean dismemberment of national unions. The proposal is doubtless impracticable from a political standpoint, but even if practicable would be undesirable. In order to eliminate a possible (and in my judgment not really serious) adverse effect on the behavior of the money-wage level, we would

have sacrificed the numerous positive benefits of strong union organization. Any decision on such a fundamental matter should clearly be based on a comprehensive evaluation of all the effects of unionism—good and bad, wage and non-wage, economic and non-economic. My judgment is that an evaluation of this sort yields a positive score for national unionism; but it is impossible to explain and justify this judgment in the space available here.

(2) *Centralizing collective bargaining in order to "rationalize" wage decisions.* This recommendation runs directly counter to the one just discussed. The argument is that, if bargaining could be centralized along Swedish lines, the top federation leaders would be willing and able to follow a "responsible" wage policy, i.e. one which does not raise the money wage level at an inflationary rate.

This proposal is also impracticable in the sense that a democratic government can do little to bring about greater centralization of wage decisions. The present centralization of decision-making in the Swedish labor federation was not planned by anyone, but resulted from gradual internal evolution over several decades. The same has been true in other countries. In none of the Western democracies has the scope of wage bargains been shaped in any large measure by public policy.

Moreover, the power of top federation leaders to control and moderate the pace of wage advance should not be exaggerated. They are leaders, not dictators, and political leadership involves survival by judicious responsiveness to pressure. Too tight a control on wages from the center would threaten the very structure of the union movement by drying up local initiative and membership support. A large measure of wage negotiation at the industry and company levels persists beneath the forms of centralization, and these supplementary bargains always work upward from the national norms established at the center. It is quite common to find Swedish federation leaders prescribing a 3 per cent wage increase in a particular year and to see an actual increase of 5 or 6 per cent at the end of the wage movement.

(3) *Government intervention in specific price and wage decisions.* This category embraces a considerable variety of sub-proposals. One of these may be termed the "coaxing" approach, under which the government would intervene informally in, say, the 1959 basic steel negotiations and persuade the parties to accept a modest wage increase and no price increase. Another suggestion is that the government should be given legal power to review, or even to veto, proposed wage and price increases. Still another suggestion is that the government should announce each year a ceiling figure for wage increases—some percentage rate of increase which is judged to be noninflationary in view of the expected growth of national output—and that proposed increases above this level must be justified to a government agency.

Proposals of this type appear to be either ineffective or harmful. "Coaxing" can scarcely have much effect unless accompanied by some type of sanction. Government review and alteration of wage and price decisions runs counter to the rationale of a private economy and could clearly hamper efficient use of economic resources. Announcement of a "target" figure for wage increases in a particular year implies that all wages can or should advance at the same pace over time, which is not the case in a dynamic economy. The announced maximum would almost certainly be taken as a guaranteed minimum increase throughout the economy, and bargaining would proceed upward from there.

(4) *Controlling wage inflation through monetary policy.* This is the commonest of all proposals in this area, and is often assumed to provide a conclusive answer. It is held that price increases resulting from a wage-push simply demonstrate that the monetary authorities are not doing their job and that increases can be avoided by a tougher line of policy. If an effort is made to push up wages faster than the warranted rate, the monetary authorities should withhold the additional working capital needed to cover the wage increases. This will compel a reduction of output and employment, stiffen employer resistance to wage increases, and bring the inflationary process to an end. After this has been done several times, the unions may "get wise" and refrain from demanding excessive increases in the future.

Space does not permit a thorough evaluation of this line of argument, but we may note several deficiencies in it. There are obvious technical difficulties: first, of ascertaining that a cost push is in process and judging its approximate size; and second, of adjusting money supply to just the right extent in face of the notorious instability of velocity noted earlier in this paper. More serious, the policy involves a break in the growth trend of the economy and loss of output over a considerable period. (Even in the mild United States recessions of 1949-50, 1953-54, and 1957-58 it was 18 to 24 months before the previous output peak was regained, and still longer before the economy was back on its long-term growth path.) To the extent that such recessions involve a reduction in capital investment, the subsequent rate of increase in national output is also reduced, and the long-term growth path is lower than it might have been. It is quite possible that the depressing effect of a recession on output growth may be greater than the depressing effect on money-wage increases, in which case the tight-money policy would turn out to have been inflationary rather than the reverse.

The dampening effect on money-wage increases, moreover, is by no means certain. Unemployment *per se* cannot be counted on as very effective in an economy of bargained wage rates. The reduction of sales and profits during a recession, with the consequent increase in employers' incentive to resist wage demands, is a more powerful force. But it might require a substantial cut in output extending over a considerable period to really break the momentum of an upward wage movement. The United States recession of 1957-58 was not large enough to do this, and brought only a slight drop in wage increases in 1958 compared with 1957.

This line of policy thus appears to be almost a counsel of despair. Deliberate creation of unemployment is justifiable only after every alternative has been exhausted, and then only if the costs of reduced output and slower economic growth are considered less important than the costs of a rising price level.

What, then, are some of the other approaches which one might take to the problem? The most hopeful lines of approach fall under three headings:

(1) *Raising the rate of growth in national output.* It is curious that economists tend to take this as a datum and to regard the money-wage level as the variable which must be adjusted. It is usually argued that if the rate of output growth is 3 per cent, and if workers and union leaders demand wage increases of 5 per cent, the problem is to persuade them to desist and settle for 3 per cent anyway. Suppose that one turned the problem around, took the 5 per cent annual wage increase as a datum, and asked how we might be able to raise the rate of output growth to this level. The rate of increase in output is certainly not invariant. The indications are that it has increased materially over the past two or three decades. Perhaps it could be further increased by heavier investment in scientific and technological research, by policies designed to encourage business investment in plant and equipment, and by other methods.

Putting the problem in these terms leads to different policy conclusions from the alternative approach. It leads to an emphasis on a high growth rate for the economy, a high level of investment, and continuous capacity operation. It leads, in short, toward a positive monetary policy oriented toward economic expansion rather than a restrictive policy designed to punish excessive wage demands through periodic unemployment. This positive policy should not mean open courting of inflation, and it admittedly contains some danger of encouraging excessive wage increases. One must hope, however, to achieve an acceleration of productivity growth which will more than offset any intensification of wage demands. Nor will wage demands necessarily be intensified if some of the other measures suggested below are taken.

The importance of looking at the output side of the picture as well as the wage side is underlined by the events of 1956-57 in the United States. The Consumer Price Index rose by 5 per cent between 1955 and 1957, and this was attributed by many to excessive wage increases. Actually, the increase in money wages during 1956 and 1957 was very closely in line with the rate of increase in preceding years. The rate of output growth during 1956 and 1957 was abnormally low, however, with the necessary result of a rising price level. The significant question to ask about these years is not "Why did wages rise so much?" but rather "Why did output increase so little?"

(2) *Increasing public understanding of economic affairs.* This is an obvious and even trite suggestion, but one whose long-run importance should not be discounted. After a century of economics teaching in the United States, popular discussion of wage issues is still studded with obvious fallacies concerning the interrelations of wages, profits, income distribution, prices, and output. The level of economic literacy in collective bargaining is noticeably lower in the United States than in Britain or Scandinavia. To say that this situation cannot be improved is to abandon hope of rationality in economic affairs. Informed self-discipline by economic groups is the alternative to state compulsion, and better economic data and economic analysis are an essential basis for this. Education in the economics of wages cannot come in any great measure from the parties at interest, whose motives are suspect and whose "informational" material typically reflects self-interested pleading. The lead must be taken by disinterested economists in universities and research agencies, who until now have failed to make any marked impact on the general public. Popular, literate, economically informed writing for a mass audience needs to be made as respectable in this country as it already is abroad. Credit should go also to the small band of economists who are trying with some success to improve the economic content of history and social studies courses in the high schools.

(3) *Institutional reform.* I pointed out earlier that the susceptibility of an economy to wage inflation depends on a variety of structural characteristics. These are often deep-rooted and incapable of rapid change through government action. Over a period of decades, however, economic institutions do change and the rate of change can often be accelerated by conscious forethought. It is important, therefore, to be clear about the *direction* of movement which would be desirable.

Desirable directions of movement in the United States at this time would include:

a. Improvement of labor markets and rationalizing of labor mobility both within localities and between localities. This is desirable for many reasons. In the present context, it would have the consequence of flattening labor supply curves, reducing the chances of labor supply bottlenecks at growth points of the economy, and consequently reducing the size of wage increases needed to reallocate the labor force in new directions.

b. Strengthening of competitive forces in product markets and discouragement of open or tacit price agreement. Henry Simons, that eloquent advocate of a liberal economy, was wrong in asserting that a unionized industry is "doomed to full cartelization." Witness textiles, clothing, shoes, food processing, and many other branches of industry in which unionization has coexisted with vigorous price competition. A national union does not produce a cartel, but it will ride the coat-tails of a cartel or an oligopoly group which has come into existence for other reasons. It may well demand wage increases larger than could be obtained under competitive conditions, and large enough to have inflationary consequences. Vigorous enforcement of competition in product markets thus strikes indirectly at a possible source of undue wage pressure.

c. Strengthening employer solidarity in collective bargaining. This may seem logically to run counter to the previous proposals, but pragmatically it need not do so. There is no reason why employers cannot present a united front to the union in collective bargaining while continuing to compete actively on other fronts. In retailing, service industries, and some small-scale manufacturing industries, growth of national unions with no corresponding organization on the employer side has produced for the time being an imbalance of bargaining power in favor of the union. Even the large and powerful automobile companies find themselves at a disadvantage when the union can pick them off one at a time. Initiative in rectifying such imbalances of bargaining power must come from employers themselves, but it could at least be made clear—by fresh legislation if necessary—that joint bargaining by employers does not contravene the antitrust laws. The alternative approach of breaking down the national unions to company-size units is neither feasible nor desirable for reasons already given.

d. Building lags into wage adjustments. The hurried, nervous procession of annual wage "rounds" which we have experienced since World War II may be unavoidable in an economy undergoing continuous inflation; but it should not be necessary in a country committed to a reasonable measure of price stability. We can doubtless not go all the way to the British pattern of agreements without a terminal date; but three-year and even five-year agreements are certainly to be encouraged. There would have to be provision for annual reopening of the wage issue; but this does not *compel* a major wage push to the same extent as actual expiration of an annual agreement. Salary schedules for civil servants, college teachers, and other white-collar people, are typically raised only every two or three years, and since this is customary it is generally accepted by those concerned. There seems no reason why manual workers, whose conditions are becoming more like those of white-collar people in most respects, should not also adjust to a more leisurely pattern of advance in wage schedules.

6. Policy problems:

Choices and proposals

John T. Dunlop

In the United States during the period 1953-58 gross hourly earnings for production workers increased 4.1 per cent a year in manufacturing; the Consumer Price Index rose 1.6 per cent a year; wholesale prices (other than farm products and foods) rose 2.1 per cent a year, and output per man-hour in the private economy increased almost 3 per cent a year. Total compensation including fringe payments probably increased 4.5 per cent a year in this period. The prospects of a long-term or secular average rise in prices of 1.5 to 2.0 per cent a year is one way of stating the central policy problem. The purpose of this paper is to state and to appraise, from one man's point of view, the major policy alternatives and choices for the scrutiny of debate and discussion.

John T. Dunlop, Professor of Economics at Harvard, has served in various governmental capacities, including: Staff Member, National War Labor Board (1943-45); Consultant, Office of Economic Stabilization and Office of War Mobilization and Reconversion (1945-47); Member, Atomic Energy Labor Relations Panel (1948-1953); Public Member, Wage Stabilization Board (1950-1952); Member, Emergency Board, Conductors Case (1955). He served as Impartial Chairman, National Joint Board for Settlement of Jurisdictional Disputes in the Building and Construction Industry (1948-1957).

Professor Dunlop is author of *Wage Determination Under Trade Unions; Collective Bargaining: Principles and Cases; The Theory of Wage Determination,* (Editor); *Industrial Relations Systems;* and other books and articles.

The policy issues raised by the experience since 1953 are often distinguished from the classic inflations related to World War II and its aftermath and to the sudden distortion of expectations and world raw-materials prices associated with Korea. While all periods of inflation may be treated as a whole at some level of generality, and while the events of 1939-52 no doubt decisively shaped many features of the ensuing years, a relatively new species of inflation—the long-run, secular, creepy kind—is of current concern.

Types of policy prescriptions

A year ago in England I also found intense interest and discussion over long-term inflation.[1] Average earnings had increased 7.5 per cent and prices had risen almost 4 per cent a year on the average in the preceding five years. The British discussions suggested four different lines of diagnosis by the local economic doctors. Each view of the source of the malady and each explanation of the inflationary symptoms carried its own policy prescription. In considering the experience and discussion in the United States since 1953, with minor variations, the same four groups of diagnoses and prescriptions may be distinguished.

(1) According to the first group of economic doctors, the central difficulty is an excess of demand. The unwarranted expansion in credit and in the velocity of circulation under a variety of monetary authorities stimulates a rise in wage rates and prices. The disease is of the circulatory system, an excessive secretion of the monetary gland. Secondary complications soon set in with this well-known ailment, and the British patient suffers an acute loss of sterling, while in the case of the United States there is even concern over seepage from Fort Knox.

"On my conception, up to recently the rise of wages has usually been the *result,* not the *cause,* of the general inflation." [2]

". . . the 1955-57 inflation was in fact basically similar to inflations of the past . . . the role of costs in this inflationary episode has been greatly exaggerated." [3]

The cure prescribed is a tight monetary and fiscal policy to eliminate excess demand. Some of the doctors, regarded as less sound by those who pride themselves as being most sound, are worried that the amount of this medicine required to cure may be almost as bad for the patient as the

---

[1] See for instance, the symposium on wages policy, *Scottish Journal of Political Economy,* June, 1958; Council on Prices, Productivity and Income, *First Report,* February, 1958; *Second Report,* August, 1958.

[2] Lionel Robbins, "Thoughts on the Crises," *Lloyds Bank Review,* April, 1958, p. 23.

[3] Richard T. Selden, "Cost-Push versus Demand-Pull Inflation, 1955-57," *Journal of Political Economy,* February, 1959, pp. 1-2.

illness itself. The medicine may damage output and real investment essential to the long-term growth and recovery of the patient.

(2) The central difficulty, says another group of diagnosticians, lies deeper in the economic body. "The removal of excess demand does not necessarily restore equilibrium . . ." [4] or economic health. The real problem is that money rewards rise faster than productivity. The malady is wage costitis. The old-fashioned remedy was a complete rest—idleness for five to ten per cent of the work force. But most modern physicians regard this cure as too drastic; the patients these days simply will not take such medicine. Modern doctors are a little uncertain what to prescribe for wage costitis. There is the sugar pill of advice to unions and managements to take sweet moderation three times daily before negotiations. A number of other research workers have been discovering the bargaining mechanism, a part of the economic anatomy hitherto left to a little-regarded fringe of the profession. Some have associated the disease of inflation with uncoordinated or sectional bargaining, and they propose an operation, of Swedish or Dutch origins, to graft on centralized bargaining. Others have associated the malady with enlarged bargaining units, and they propose that the anti-trust knife cut out industry-wide bargaining and sever the nerves that connect local unions and national unions. It is understandable that with such conflicting advice the patient has stoutly resisted submitting his bargaining mechanism to any operation.

(3) The central difficulty, says another group of economic doctors, is psychological. The malady is of the economic mind or will. The patient wants too much of too many good things; the combination is beyond its means. The patient refuses to face reality and stern choices. It wants a continuing high degree of employment, full utilization of capacity to meet demands from home and abroad, increased leisure and shorter working weeks, the full continuation of the era of human relations and labor peace which has been adopted in an increasing number of enterprises since the end of World War II, the absence of all direct government controls over production, prices and wages, no more stringent or detailed fiscal or monetary controls, and only an occasional dose of monetary aspirin when critically ill. In the British case the patient wishes to continue to play the role of banker for a large part of the world on small reserves, and the inflation morality of a banker must be more correct than others. In the case of the United States, the patient cannot bring himself to abandon the flesh pots and face the stern discipline of economic competition with the East. The widespread view that a high degree of all desirable goodies can be simultaneously achieved is a neurosis. There is nothing structurally

[4] F. A. Burchardt, "Cost Inflation," *Bulletin of the Oxford University Institute of Statistics,* November, 1957, p. 327.

wrong with the patient; it wants too much of too many conflicting objectives. It fails to understand the elementary concept of opportunity costs. The stern prescription is simply to choose a more limited group of objectives and to arrange a clearer scale of priorities: to take more unemployment, or more labor strife, or more specific fiscal and monetary controls or more direct controls over wages, prices and production, or reshape one's responsibilities abroad to accommodate to the resources.

(4) The central difficulty lies in temporary or permanent structural defects in the economy, says another group of economic doctors. In the British economy, increasing levels of investment in machinery and equipment have shown relatively small results in productivity and output per worker. Coal mining and railroads are older industries, and a great deal of capital is required to overcome the difficulties of a misspent youth or the natural failings of old age. It is doubtful if a high rate of increase in productivity can ever be restored in these industries, but they are indispensable to the economic body. A less pessimistic view would hold that the capital has been flowing in Great Britain into an infrastructure of power, transportation and services which have not shown full results in these five years, but the increasing investment has been for a brighter long-run future. In the case of the United States the temporary or more permanent structural defects include such items as the failure of agriculture to provide lower prices, the shifting composition of output toward government activities and the service industries in which productivity increases appear to be lower or unmeasurable, the inflation-generating role of oligopolies and the rise of strong unions in such sectors. In the view of this school of doctors the malady is a temporary or more permanent defect in organic structure, and any cure is always slow and painful.

The preceding brief survey of major points of view respecting secular inflation emphasizes that analysis and policy prescription are usually closely linked.

The community's priorities and preferences

In his inaugural lecture as professor of political economy in Cambridge University, Professor J. E. Meade said:

> I personally find little difficulty in reaching the conclusion that inflation as well as deflation is an evil which deserves a very real effort to avoid. But let us be very clear that there are worse evils than inflation. The stagnation of the 1930's is a much worse evil than the inflation of the 1950's. We must give very careful thought to the question whether a serious attempt to prevent a continuation of the inflation of money prices would lead to a cessation of growth of economic output and to a rise in the general level of unemployment.[5]

[5] *The Control of Inflation,* Cambridge, England, Cambridge University Press, 1958, p. 11.

What are the relative preferences of the community for price stability and for other objectives which may have to be given up in order to achieve price stability? What are the social opportunity costs of stability? What is the price of a lesser degree of price inflation? All economists should be cautioned against imposing their own preferences upon the community. What the community ought to prefer by some standard and the priorities it does in fact establish are not to be confused. What is the distribution of priorities among different segments of the community? Price stability can only be achieved at a price or at the cost of other values forsaken. Before anyone gives price stability the top policy priority, it is essential to explore some of the costs of stability.[6]

The price of stability

(1) How high a price is the community willing to pay for price stability in terms of more labor strife? A lesser rate of wage increase—and a lesser rate of price increase—probably requires more strikes. If managements are to secure settlements on the average below a figure of 4 or 5 per cent per year, or 8 to 10 cents an hour in manufacturing, there will probably be more strikes over the money package at contract renewal times. But is there much disposition on the part of managements to take a strike over another 2 or 3 cents when profits are high, when relations have become friendly, when a strike may cause an intensive search for alternative sources of supply and substitutes on the part of customers, and when the friendly cooperation of the union and work force is vital to the introduction of new machinery and other means of raising productivity? It is not the preachments on the part of national employers' associations against "inflationary" wage increases that counts, nor the urging on another firm to take the lead ("Let's you and the union fight"), nor the smooth and catchy speech of business leaders printed in attractive form and distributed to stockholders, the press and educators. It is what the firm actually does at five minutes before midnight when it must balance going a little higher on wage rates against taking a strike with the related complaints of customers and potential loss of accounts. It is on such occasions that the price of stability is tested.

(2) How high a price is the community willing to pay for stability in terms of unemployment? It is possible to enhance wage and price stability by creating a higher average level of unemployment. In the six-year period 1953-58 unemployment averaged 4.7 per cent of the civilian labor force, 4.3 per cent for the period 1953-57. In 1958 the figure averaged 6.8 per

[6] See, John T. Dunlop, *The Secular Outlook, Wages and Prices,* Institute of Industrial Relations, University of California, 1957, pp. 14-17.

cent. These figures are considerably above unemployment rates in Great Britain and most of Western Europe. Is the American community prepared to increase these figures to achieve more stability? Or is the community's desire for goods, its fear of unemployment and its concern with comparative production records of the Soviet bloc such that it would be unwilling to trade more unemployment for additional price stability? It is easy to want both higher levels of employment and more price stability. But in the hard choices the community makes in the market and through its elected representatives it reveals the price it is willing to pay for stability in terms of unemployment. It is well to remember that the American community already tolerates a higher level of unemployment (as a percentage of the civilian labor force) than most northern and western European countries.

(3) How high a price is the community willing to pay for price stability in terms of a wider range, more detailed and more flexible government controls? The community comes to see that any system of controls over inflation has its limitations and can be pushed only so far, and that each control device has some drawbacks. While direct controls are likely to be most effective, at least for short periods, in stopping upward movements, the community most distrusts these devices. Every schoolboy can tell of the evils of bureaucracy and the effects of direct controls on distorting the most effective allocation of resources. But general monetary and fiscal controls also have their limitations. Small businesses, home builders, farmers, state and municipal governments and other types of borrowers may be relatively disadvantaged by stringent monetary controls. A larger proportion of capital may go to established borrowers or to those who can finance from within than may prove desirable to the community. A more flexible and detailed system of fiscal controls with more sensitive and variable tax rates and allowances has not been devised on an acceptable basis. Such fiscal controls would seem to require modification in accepted views of the process of exercising effective taxing powers. In the willingness to accept further controls—direct, monetary or fiscal—is to be seen the price the community is willing to pay for stability.

We need to be quite explicit about our own individual priorities or preferences for price stability relative to other objectives and also to be quite clear about our estimates of the preferences of the various groups and the aggregate which comprise the American community. We can avoid much needless debate by being clear on these matters at the outset. What price is each of us prepared to pay for increased stability in terms of more labor strife, more unemployment or more detailed and stringent government controls? While estimates of the community preferences will vary widely among us, I submit there is not much evidence to indicate the community is now willing to barter for more stability.

I trust we are involved in no sentimental condemnation of inflation without also measuring the opportunity costs or the price of the measures required to induce greater price stability. Some degree of price stability is an affirmative value, and some degree of inflation is an evil. This is not an issue, but rather the policy choice is how much are we willing to pay, what are we willing to give up for more stability, and what do we get for more inflation. This is a tough issue and we need a tough-minded approach to these hard choices.

I respect the relative priorities which each person selects with internal consistency among the four sets of objectives noted above: (1) stability or inflation, (2) labor peace or industrial strife, (3) employment or unemployment, and (4) government controls or free markets.

Personal preferences

There is probably no standard by which to adjudge one consistent combination of preferences superior to another. There is one preference of mine, however, which should be made explicit, namely, that the American community has been paying too high a price for the degree of stability achieved in terms of unemployment, loss of production and loss of relative position with the Soviet bloc. In my preference scales, we can no longer afford, even at the cost of more inflation, the average level of unemployment of the past five years.

Barbara Ward has said, ". . . the technique of checking production in order to stop inflation—the most drastic and dangerous 'cure' conceivable in the face of Russia's rising production—does not cure at all. Inflation goes on. New thinking is thus in order." [7]

Professor Sumner Slichter has stated the relation between inflation and economic growth in these words:

> The way to accelerate the growth of the economy is to stimulate the demand for goods. When demand presses hard upon productive capacity, that capacity is used and industry takes steps to increase its capacity. Pressure of demand upon capacity tends to produce creeping inflation, but this pressure is necessary to attain the maximum rate of growth.[8]

In my scale of preferences the United States requires a much higher rate of growth and capital formation in the next five years than we have had in the last five, and it is imperative to our national interests that we use our labor force to a higher degree. This will further complicate the inflation problem, and I am glad for the present discussion, for the concern with inflation has no doubt been a major factor retarding public policies

[7] "Now the Challenge of An Economic Sputnik," *The New York Times Magazine*, February 8, 1959, p. 66.

[8] "The American Economy—Current Trends, Problems and Prospects, January and Early February, 1959," Prepared for Nihon Keizai Shimbun of Tokyo.

designed to create a higher rate of utilization of resources and to create new capacity. Whether you accept these personal priorities or not, we should be able to agree upon the policy alternatives involved in restricting price (and wage) inflation. When we come to express choices among the alternatives, we shall need to make explicit our relative priorities for stability, labor peace, full employment, a rapid rate of growth and freedom from additional government controls.

There will be those who will resist making these choices, feeling that "new thinking," to use Barbara Ward's phrase, is in order. The policy decisions are to be sought less in choices within the existing framework than in changes in the private and public institutions which make the decisions on wages and prices in the economy. The section which immediately follows considers some proposals for changing the institutional framework. These particular ideas seem to me to offer no alternative, simply because they are not likely to produce the results on wage and price formation which their sponsors claim. But they have received widespread attention.

The wage bargaining institutions

Internal union reform

There is an oft repeated view that strong upward pressure from wages is attributable in part to an alleged lack of "democratic procedures" within labor organizations, and that reform of internal union government will make a significant contribution to the control of inflation. A variety of internal union reform legislation, including provision for government-conducted strike votes, has been seriously argued for on these grounds. The premise is that the leadership has been pushing for wage increases, even to the point of strikes, which the rank-and-file would otherwise forgo. Internal union reform issues should stand on their own merits in my view, unrelated to the inflation discussion; union reform in general is not before us. But even Professor Arthur F. Burns, who apparently agrees to the separation of these questions, seems to regard internal labor reform legislation as having an indirect impact on prices. In a chapter on "Policies for Coping with Inflation," he says:

> The least we can do with regard to trade unions is to subject their finances, as well as the election of their officials, to standards defined by law. Such legislation would of itself have no effect on what happens at the bargaining table; but it should help to remind the leaders of our trade unions that unless they practice greater restraint and foresight, the government may need to take drastic steps to curb their power to push up costs and prices.[9]

---

[9] *Prosperity Without Inflation,* New York, Fordham University Press 1957, p. 84. A similar statement by Professor Burns appears in *United States Monetary Policy: Its Contribution to Prosperity Without Inflation,* The American Assembly, Columbia University, New York, 1958, p. 215.

The attempt to support proposals for internal reform of unions by resort to the inflation argument reflects a serious misunderstanding of the actual relationships between union officers and members. A leadership more responsive to the immediate preferences of workers would no doubt on balance result in larger wage increases and more strikes. This view is supported by the experience with bargaining under union rivalry and weak leadership and by the fact that the bargaining process necessarily requires that in most settlements workers accept the recommendations of the leadership. The experience with right-to-work legislation is further evidence. It appears that some degree of weakening in the status of the union leadership often leads to more militancy and the processing of more questionable grievances.[10] The line of argument is misinformed which holds that union power pushing up wages is derived from the role of leaders and that legislation reducing the power of union leaders or providing for more detailed participation by union members in decisions of the union will curb wage increases. It reflects a lack of understanding of union government and bargaining procedures. The historical experience of our unions with the referendum and the factors which led to the rise of the national executive demonstrates that our present union government was not capriciously achieved.[11] It is time that the case for needed internal labor reform be separated from the inflation problem. Indeed, it is likely that we shall have to pay for internal labor reform in the form of some further wage increases as officers are made more timid or insecure and their powers to deal with dissidents are limited.[12]

Area of bargaining

The view is often expressed these days, by serious students of economics who are without experience in labor-management relations, that the power of unions to raise wages should be curbed by legislation designed to circumscribe the area of bargaining or to limit the methods of conflict or pressure. These proposals include the further application of the antitrust laws to unions and wage setting, the further restriction of boycotts and secondary action and further limitations on strikes and picketing.

Concretely, prohibition of violence and coercion, especially of picketing, protection of those willing to work, prohibition of closed shop agreements and

---

[10] Frederic Meyers, *Right to Work in Practice,* New York, The Fund for the Republic, 1959.

[11] Lloyd Ulman, *The Rise of the National Trade Union,* Cambridge, Harvard University Press, 1955, pp. 203-301.

[12] Limitations on the powers of the international union to place locals under trusteeship are likely to reduce the intervention of the international in local negotiations when the local is striking for increases regarded as excessive by the international. The case of the International Union of Operating Engineers and its Philadelphia local is instructive on this point.

application of the Sherman Act to trade unions, or, to put it briefly, a mild stiffening of the Taft-Hartley Act, may be sufficient to bring about the desired results.[13]

This is not the forum in which to discuss public policy on the legal framework of labor-management relations. But the issues cannot be avoided insofar as such proposals are urged to make a serious contribution toward holding down secular price increases, such as took place in the period 1953-58. I believe serious economists who support these views have an obligation to develop the details of such proposals and to submit them to scrutiny if they are to continue to urge such policies. It is my considered judgment that such policies are impractical, unadministrable and would not produce the intended results on secular inflation. I have deliberately not used the argument that such proposals are politically unpopular, for popularity is fickle.

More specifically, the proposals to break up industry-wide bargaining usually refer to nation-wide settlements, such as steel, automobiles, coal and railroads. But the argument in support of the break-up of negotiating districts by legislation depends on market-wide wage setting, local, regional, or national. The proposal to break up wage negotiations that are product-market wide would involve a vast paper reconstruction of bargaining mechanisms which could not succeed basically because it fails to recognize that wage interdependencies in the labor market, and the scope of uniformity of wage rates or changes in wage rates, derive basically from product-market interdependencies among enterprises. Market-wide wage setting is involved in many local or regionally oriented industries—garment, construction, hotels, printing, trucking, etc. In theoretical terms union bargaining power may be greater in some of these sectors than in national market-wide bargaining. Market-wide wage setting—either in a single wage conference or by wage leaders setting a pattern generally followed within a wage contour—arises not because legislation has conferred status or power on unions but because of product market inter-relations. Legislation did not create market-wide wage setting and legislation cannot take it away.

We need in this field, as in others, more appreciation of what can be accomplished by law and what is beyond the method of legal enactment. We need to discern when legislation results only in the dead letter, the loophole, evasion, administrative blackmail, the technical quagmire, perpetual litigation, and the lawyer at the elbow of every decision-maker. This is no condemnation of particular proposed legislation, but in some

---

[13] Gottfried Haberler, "Wage Policy, Employment, and Economic Stability" in *The Impact of the Labor Union,* David McCord Wright, ed., New York, Harcourt, Brace and Company, Inc., 1951, p. 61. Also see, E. H. Chamberlin, *Labor Unions and Public Policy,* Washington, D. C., American Enterprise Association, 1958, pp. 29, 45.

areas of labor-management legislation, such as some areas of picketing and secondary boycotts, we have already reached saturated confusion.

Instead of splitting up areas of uniform wage setting, a more likely development is the transformation of wage leadership—under which most enterprises in the wage contour follow the wage adjustments of the leaders —into more formal arrangements for market-wide bargaining. In the basic steel industry the single wage leadership of the United States Steel Corporation has been gradually replaced in the past decade by a formal negotiating committee representing a number of the major producers. In the automobile industry the negotiations of 1958 saw a much closer relationship among the big three producers than in previous years, although joint negotiations have not yet emerged. The airlines industry in 1958 saw an agreement among carriers to share gains attributable to a strike with the struck company, in limited circumstances. The growth of more formal bargaining arrangements on a multi-company basis may be expected in meat packing, aluminum and other industries in which wage leadership and pattern followers has prevailed.

Managements increasingly believe that their bargaining position may be enhanced and settlements can be made at lower figures if they negotiate as a group, particularly in wage contours where they have previously followed a pattern-making settlement. This is the likely direction of development in bargaining institutions rather than any artificial or paper fractionalizing of bargaining. It is difficult to predict the magnitude of impact of such developments on the size of contract settlements, but it is possible that contract changes may be more modest and that the larger scope of bargaining may more explicitly consider the consequences of settlements on the larger community.

Preachments

One of the most persistent ways in which government spokesmen have sought to influence the results of bargaining institutions is through gratuitous advice and general preachments to the parties. The following excerpts from the *Economic Report of the President* are illustrative:

> Of particular importance in a prosperous economy is the responsibility of leaders of business and labor to reach agreements on wages and other labor benefits that are consistent with productivity prospects and with the maintenance of a stable dollar.[14]

> Leaders of labor unions, in view of the great power lodged in their hands, have a particularly critical role to play. Their economic actions must reflect awareness that stability of prices is an essential condition of sustainable economic growth and that the only road to greater material well-being for the Nation

[14] Transmitted to the Congress, January 23, 1957, p. 12.

lies in the fullest possible realization of our productivity potential . . . Self-discipline and restraint are essential if agreements consistent with a reasonable stability of prices are to be reached within the framework of the free competitive institutions on which we rely heavily for the improvement of our national welfare . . . [15]

Preachments from this sort of text do not give much promise of driving out the devil of inflation. Professor Arthur F. Burns has well said:

Official appeals for restraint in wage and price adjustments may be salutary, but experience suggests that it would be unwise under ordinary circumstances to expect a broad response to exhortation.[16]

A command to halt wage and price increases spoken by the President has no more effect on the tides of inflation than the words of King Canute confronting the rising waters of the English Channel.

Despite this hard-headed judgment, it seems to me that the full potential of the leadership of the federal government has never been used persistently and imaginatively to shape decisions by private parties on wages and prices or to influence the climate of ideas within which such decisions are made. Over long periods, it is no doubt substantially true, that as Keynes concluded in the *General Theory,* ". . . it is ideas, not vested interests, which are dangerous for good or evil." If the federal government expects to influence the ideas of the parties to collective bargaining, it must leave the level of repetitive platitudes and generalities and meet with labor and management representatives regularly to discuss and debate in free exchange and with detailed statistics the economic setting and outlook in which wage and price decisions are made. More specifically, the following suggestion might be tried.

After the Economic Report of the President has been transmitted to the Congress and there have been hearings before the Joint Congressional Committee each year, the Secretary of Labor might convene each year in the early spring a three-day conference with leading representatives of labor and management. The Chairman of the Council of Economic Advisers, the Secretary of the Treasury and other government officials should present their detail analysis of the short-term and the long-term economic outlook. Representatives of management and labor should be given the opportunity to discuss these views of the Administration and to present materials and judgments of their own. In addition to formal sessions there might well be informal off-the-record periods of free give-and-take.

The purpose of these annual discussions should be to develop a consensus of opinion, insofar as possible, or to narrow the range of views concerning the major problems confronting the economy as a whole and

---

[15] Transmitted to the Congress, January 20, 1959, pp. 5-6.
[16] *Loc. Cit.*, p. 75.

the expectations of the short-term and longer-term business outlook by principal sectors. These discussions would not be negotiations nor should they be designed to prejudice any particular contract negotiations. But the government would help to sketch the economic problems and climate; the interchange would benefit all three groups. The fundamental point is that imaginative government leadership should press beyond annual cautions and preachments to more direct exchange of ideas and information in a society of free men and free collective bargaining, and particularly in a society in which the level of general education and the detail and the quality of statistical and economic information has been growing rapidly in the past generation.

Strategic sectors of secular inflation

In recent years there have been many studies of the mechanics of inflation. In the main these models have been concerned with the short-run relations between costs and prices, or among consumption, investment and income.[17] These aggregate models have been built with varying assumptions concerning the decision making of households, enterprises and governments and with varying lengths of lags in reactions within a system. They have included various wage functions.

In passing, I should like to state briefly my own views about appropriate wage functions in such models of inflation. Wage determination most fruitfully should be divided into two parts—the determination of the *wage rate* schedule and the determination of the *wage drift,* defined as the change in hourly earnings arising from other than changes in scheduled wage rates. Changes in the wage drift are a function of levels of output, unemployment, rates of technical change and of premium hours. Changes in scheduled wage rates are primarily a function of profits and consumers prices. Even such general statements have implications for policy; for instance, high profits can be expected to attract wage-rate increases. It is as much in the nature of a labor organization to seek a part of high profits as it is for a cat to stalk birds.

The threshold to inflation

Generalized propositions and models of inflation suggest that policy might well be oriented toward raising the critical level of employment (or unemployment) at which wage and price increases accelerate as the system

[17] See, James S. Duesenberry, *Business Cycles and Economic Growth,* New York, McGraw-Hill, 1958.

moves from low levels to high levels of business activity. What can be done to raise the threshold to inflation? What can be done to lower the degree of inflationary response to high levels of activity?

In 1954, under the auspices of the International Economic Association, a number of economists met at Seelisberg, Switzerland, and in the course of their discussion of wages they considered the factors determining the inflation potential of a system. The propositions developed in that international discussion provide a useful starting point for policy, and they may be briefly summarized as follows:[18]

1. The less unbalance there is in the structure of production and the more evenly spread the expansion of demand, the higher the level of employment without inflation.

2. The greater the increase in productivity and the more evenly spread the increases in productivity among sectors, the higher the level of employment without inflation.

3. The more favorable the terms of trade, the higher the level of employment may rise without inflationary pressures.

4. The more compressible profit margins, the higher wages may be pushed without price increases.

5. The more adaptable or flexible the wage structure, the higher the level of employment that may be reached without inflationary developments. In a flexible wage structure, wage increases in one sector need not result in wage increases in other sectors.

6. A policy of wage restraint adopted by trade unions or by government policy will normally raise the critical level of employment at which wages and prices rise.

7. The response of the labor force to an increase in demand for labor—the greater the mobility and the lower the terms on which additional people and hours of part-time work can be drawn into the labor market—the higher the critical level of employment at which wages and prices rise.

8. The methods of wage payment, including the prevalence of incentive methods of pay, will help to determine whether wages rise early or late during an expansion in employment.

9. The more specific the direction and the impact of fiscal and monetary policies, the higher the level of employment that can be achieved without inflationary developments.

Such statements have merit as a starting point for general policy discussions since they suggest the diverse fields in which contributions may be made by structural adaptations to raise the inflation threshold of the

[18] *The Theory of Wage Determination,* John T. Dunlop, ed., London, St. Martin's Press, 1957, p. 417.

system. At comparable levels of output, employment, labor peace and direct government controls, the inflationary potential of the system may be reduced in a variety of ways noted in the above propositions.

A more constructive policy discussion may begin with an analysis of the strategic sectors of the economy which have been particularly prone to inflation, or which have not made potential contributions to price decreases, or which diffuse wage and price increases widely throughout the system. In this view of the structure of the economy, and of the mechanics of long-term inflation, all sectors of the economy are not equally important. Some are more significant than others in generating and diffusing inflation. If secular inflation is to be curbed, without the cost of large unused resources, institutional changes are required in such strategic sectors. The basic view is that secular inflation is to be tackled in policy terms at these strategic sectors of the economy, although not necessarily by governmental action and certainly not necessarily by legislation.

Input-output relations

In seeking to identify such strategic sectors of the economy, the concept of input-output tables has been utilized.[19] If one assigns the inputs of materials and services into each industry to the sectors from which they are derived, and in turn if one assigns the outputs of each industry and traces them through the system to their points of use, it is clear that the output of some sectors is widely diffused while the output of other sectors may flow outside a given sector in only very small quantities and to only a few other sectors. Some outputs are more largely directed to households than to intermediate stages. Common sense suggests that coal mining, basic steel, power generation and construction can be expected to have more diffused effects throughout the economic system than the amusement industries, education, restaurants or tobacco manufacturing. Common sense also suggests that agriculture has more direct effects on households than on intermediate stages.

The input-output tables enable us to show the structural impact of any one sector upon the system more generally by computing two measures of significance. The first might be called the household effect or its importance to the expenditures of households including indirect effects. Thus, the significance of steel to households would sum the effects through automobiles, household appliances, razor blades, canned foods, toys, etc. The combined relative significance of steel in the Consumer Price Index on this

---

[19] See, W. Duane Evans and Marvin Hoffenberg, "The Interindustry Relations Study for 1947," *Review of Economics and Statistics,* May 1952, pp. 97-142.

basis is only a few percentage points.[20] The second measure of significance would indicate the ratio of intermediate deliveries of a sector to its total gross output and might be called the diffusion effect. The significance of steel on this basis would be very much greater since the interest is its widespread diffusion as a raw material and semi-finished good throughout the economy.[21]

A sector which has a high diffusion rating may be expected to spread cost and price increases widely through the system unless such increases are otherwise offset. The rate of increase in productivity in these strategic sectors with a high diffusion rating is vital to the spreading or dampening of inflation.

The fifteen industries which show the highest diffusion rating out of the forty-five industry table in order of greatest diffusion are as follows: [22]

Scrap and miscellaneous industries
Fabricated structural metal products
Business services
Nonferrous metals
Iron and steel
Lumber and wood products
Paper and allied products
Coal, gas and electric power
Motors and generators
Stone, clay and glass products
Metal-working machinery
Other fabricated metal products
New construction and maintenance
Other electrical machinery
Chemicals

The five industries which show the lowest measure of diffusion are as follows, starting with the very lowest: Medical, educational and non-profit organizations; eating and drinking places, amusements, apparel and rental.

The relative effects of different industries on the Consumer Price Index are shown in the following tabulation. The first column shows the fifteen industries with the largest total requirements in the goods and services which enter into the Consumer Price Index. The second column shows the

---

[20] Jules Backman, "Importance of Steel Prices in Consumer Price Index," United States Steel Corporation, *Steel and Inflation, Fact vs. Fiction*, New York, 1958, pp. 75-81.

[21] Almost 95 per cent of gross output consisted of inter-industry deliveries.

[22] I am indebted to Professor Alfred H. Conrad of Harvard University for the computations of the ratio of inter-industry deliveries to total gross output from the 1947 table.

fifteen industries with the largest total requirements multiplied by wages per dollar of output.

(1)	(2)
Food and kindred products	Agriculture and fisheries
Agriculture and fisheries	Food and kindred products
Non-distributed	Non-distributed
Personal and repair services	Chemicals
Apparel	Other machinery
Products of petroleum and coal	Nonferrous metals
Rentals	Other fabricated metal products
Chemicals	Other electrical machinery
Motor vehicles	Apparel
Textile mill products	Miscellaneous manufacturing
Coal, gas, electrical power	Other transportation
Eating and drinking places	Products of petroleum and coal
Railroad transportation	Iron and steel
Medical, educ. and nonprofit	Coal, gas, electrical power
Trade	Medical, educ. and nonprofit

Impact of any sector

The contribution which any sector makes to cost-price movements of the system as a whole can be regarded as comprised of the following components:

(1) The direct effect of a wage-rate change on other wages in the system. These are the impacts through the labor market, the collective bargaining mechanism, the influence of key bargains and wage leadership. Special interest centers on those wage bargains which tend to spread in an interdependent wage structure.

(2) The direct effects of wage-rate increases on total costs. This impact of a wage-rate increase depends on two factors—the ratio of labor costs to total costs and the rate of increase in labor productivity. When labor productivity is increasing rapidly and wage costs are a very small fraction of total costs, the cost impact of a wage-rate increase in one sector on the system is mitigated. It is recognized, of course, that in some types of markets the gains in productivity might have yielded lower prices rather than higher wage rates.

(3) The impact of other cost components on total costs, and,

(4) The impact of demand for the output of the sector on prices given the market characteristics of the products of the sector, that is, the number of sellers, availability of substitutes, entry conditions, product standardization and other well-known features of a market structure.

We should expect the most serious contribution to inflation to arise in sectors (a) which diffuse output widely throughout the system, (b) where demand is inelastic with respect to price, (c) where labor costs are a relatively high proportion of total costs and where productivity is increasing much less than the average, and (d) where wage-rate increases have a tendency to spread widely throughout the wage structure of the economy. Ideally, we should analyze each sector of the economy from the vantage point of these tests.

Only a few of the most strategic sectors are selected here for brief comments. But this discussion illustrates the type of approach, when implemented with a comprehensive inquiry, that is advocated as policy oriented toward secular inflation.

1. *Agriculture* — It may seem strange to select agriculture as a strategic sector for this purpose even though the products of agriculture spread moderately throughout the system and constitute a significant proportion of the expenditures of households. Prices received by farmers did not even increase in the period 1953-58; they actually declined by 1.2 per cent compared to an increase of 8.3 per cent in the wholesale price of all commodities; 22.1 per cent in the wholesale price of producer finished goods and 7.9 per cent in the Consumer Price Index. But farm output per man-hour increased 25.2 per cent in these five years, materially above the rate of increase in manufacturing. Moreover, public policies alone were responsible for maintaining agricultural prices at their levels. Professor Slichter has said:

> Certainly the program of supporting the prices of farm products is one of the most ridiculous ventures ever undertaken by any government anywhere—truly Alice-in-Wonderland economics. The Federal government is undertaking to prevent the great technological revolution in agriculture from depressing the relative prices of a few favored crops—and the American people are docilely permitting themselves to be taxed to support this madness. No one has ever explained why wheat growers, cotton growers, tobacco growers, corn growers, or peanut growers are entitled to have the country taxed to buy their output. It makes no more sense than would an undertaking by the government to buy up other surpluses, such as empty seats in railroad trains, street cars, or moving picture houses, or to buy the surplus output of buggies, harness, old-fashioned coal furnaces, moustache cups, and a vast variety of goods that the public no longer wants except in very limited quantities.[23]

Had different public policies been followed with respect to agricultural price supports, it is not unreasonable to estimate that the price of the food component in the Consumer Price Index would not have increased at all, or might well have declined, reducing the rise in the aggregate index by one fourth. The estimate is important only to indicate that the magnitude of impact of this sector is substantial. Moreover, the prospects of price movements in the next five years are also likely to be significantly influenced

[23] "The American Economy—Current Trends, Problems, and Prospects, January and Early February, 1959," Prepared for Nihon Keizai Shimbun of Toyko.

by agricultural policies. This sector is certainly one not requiring the intervention of government for the first time. Rather is the task to secure government policies which encourage a redistribution of resources within agriculture. A proper agricultural policy will in addition make a significant contribution to price stability.

2. *State and Local Government Services* — The purchase of goods and services by state and local governments increased from $24.9 billions in 1953 to $39.6 billions in 1958. The national accounts data indicate that, in 1958 prices, the cost of these purchases increased from $29.5 billions to $39.6 billions, which reveals an increase in an implicit price index of 18.5 per cent in this five-year period.[24] Such price increases clearly ramify widely throughout the system.

These price increases for local government purchases are derived in part from the fact that municipal wages and salaries for many years lagged behind those in other sectors; in more recent years the compensation of teachers, firemen, policemen, and other employees has been increased more substantially. The period of relatively high employment levels, the growth in the scale of government operations, the spread of more modern personnel practices into municipal and state governments and the expansion of union organization into these governmental units have all been factors at work. Moreover, in service-type industries it is difficult to calculate the productivity offsets, if any, to increases in the prices of services purchased. These higher prices of government services have been diffused in this period not only by increases in property and income tax rates adding to the costs of intermediate producers, but also by the expansion in excise taxes to final consumers which directly affect the Consumer Price Index.

Any view of the future suggests that the prices of services purchased by state and municipal governments are likely to continue to rise as wages and salaries in this sector adjust to the levels already achieved in other private and public sectors and as the competition for skilled technical and professional manpower increases generally in the next decade. The trends in financing local and state governments increasingly by sales and excise taxes suggest further direct impacts upon prices to final producers. Here is a sector which is likely to contribute to secular inflation for a long time. Improvements in quality of government services do take place, contrary to much popular opinion, but there is apparently no simple way to distinguish a price increase from a quality increase at a constant price. Some of the secular inflation may really be an improvement in quality.

3. *Basic Steel* — The most strategic industrial sector for purposes of policy considerations of secular inflation has been the basic steel industry.

---

[24] *Survey of Current Business,* National Income Number, July, 1958, Table 8, Implicit Price Deflators for Gross National Product by Major Segments, 1929-57.

A vast literature and controversy have grown up around recent price and wage movements in this industry. The unions blame the price policies of the industry.[25] The industry regards itself much more a "victim rather than a cause of inflation"[26] and stresses the role of wage-rate increases which rose more than the increase in productivity. The academic profession is divided, some taking one side or the other and others taking the attitude of "a plague on both your houses." We are likely to see this controversy become even more intense.

The essential statistical facts are fairly simple, although the choice of periods in which to make comparisons has often been adapted by the parties to suit the argument; the following comparisons are made for three different periods:

	Percentage Increase		
	1953-1958	*1947-1958*	*1939-1958*
Average Hourly Earnings, Basic Steel	33.8	100.8	244.9
Average Hourly Earnings, Automobile	18.7	72.4	177.6
Average Hourly Earnings, Durable Goods	21.9	76.5	226.6
Average Hourly Earnings, All Manufacturing	20.3	72.2	236.5
Consumer Prices	7.9	29.2	107.7
Wholesale Prices, All Commodities	8.3	23.7	137.9
Wholesale Prices, Producer Finished Goods	22.1	62.0	n.a.
Wholesale Prices, Steel Mill Products	34.6	108.6	174.4
	Percentage Increase Per Year		
	1953-1957	*1947-1959*	*1939-1957*
Output per man-hour, Private domestic economy[27]			
Unweighted	2.8	4.0	4.1
Weighted	2.8	3.5	3.1
		1947-1955	*1939-1955*
Output per man-hour Steel[28]		2.8	2.7

In the period 1953-58 steel wages rose very significantly faster than automobiles[29] and the average of all manufacturing and durable goods industries. Steel wages were rising materially faster than the rise in productivity in steel or the private domestic economy. Steel prices have risen

[25] Industrial Union Department, AFL-CIO, *Labor, Big Business and Inflation,* September, 1958, pp. 18-23.

[26] United States Steel Corporation, *Steel and Inflation, Fact vs. Fiction,* 1958, p. 91; Roger M. Blough, *Inflation as a Way of Life,* November 9, 1956, p. 12.

[27] Solomon Fabricant, *Basic Facts on Productivity Change,* New York, National Bureau of Economic Research, Occasional Paper 63, 1959, p. 45.

[28] Bureau of Labor Statistics, *Man-Hours Per Unit of Output in The Basic Steel Industry, 1939-55,* Bulletin 1200, Washington, D. C., September, 1956, p. 6.

[29] This experience is the more interesting in light of the steel industry rejection of the Wage Stabilization Board's recommendations in 1952 which sought to restore a relationship between wage rates of steel and automobiles.

very sharply more than all wholesale prices and even more than producer finished goods which are much influenced by steel. After surveying various industrial sectors, Otto Eckstein concluded: "The chief bottleneck appears to have been in the steel industry. Here prices and wages rose most." [30]

The same general conclusions are appropriate to a lesser degree for the period 1947-58. When one considers the period of the last twenty years as a whole, the steel picture is less distinctive, since during the war period wages and prices did not move up in steel as much as in other sectors, for a variety of reasons. There arises the question whether the period 1953-58 represents a new and a continuing sector problem for the economy or largely the realignment of longer-term relations.

Basic steel is a pivotal sector from the analysis of the spreading effects of inflation because: (1) it rates so high in the diffusion of its output; (2) demand for steel is said to be inelastic for most uses; (3) labor costs are a significant proportion of total costs, and productivity has not increased materially faster than the average of industry; and (4) the steel wage contract is a key bargain, along with automobiles, in the whole heavy goods sector, and steel wage rates exercise influence on other wages in such areas as Chicago and Pittsburgh.

There seems to me little point in getting into the argument between the union and the industry as to whom to blame for the experience of 1953-58 particularly. It is important to understand that the result has followed from each operating within its own framework. In the industry's view it has sought valiantly to resist unwarranted wage increases by five nationwide strikes since the end of World War II. It has had to push up prices in order to meet these higher wage costs, the increasing costs of replacement of equipment not allowed in depreciation for tax purposes, and to secure profits to meet the needs for expansion. The union on the other hand has chosen to emphasize the oligopolistic power of the industry to set prices and to assert that profits warranted higher wage rates, particularly when the industry was operating at peak capacity as it was during the period surrounding the decisive last contract negotiations in 1956. I do not believe that theoretical understanding or policy wisdom is to be found in pursuing the arguments of whether the pot or the kettle is blacker. Product market and labor market power of buyers and sellers are highly interdependent.

My analysis of the decisive mechanism of wage and price movements in basic steel in recent years may be stated briefly, recognizing that other factors may have been operative. The central problem of the industry

---

[30] "Inflation, The Wage-Price Spiral and Economic Growth," *The Relationship of Prices to Economic Stability and Growth,* Compendium of Papers submitted by Panelists Appearing Before the Joint Economic Committee, Washington, D. C., 1958, p. 370.

bearing on inflation has been how to finance expensive new capacity in an industry where increases in productivity have not been significantly different from the average of manufacturing. If the industry is to finance new capacity substantially from within,[31] prices must be increased to provide the profits for expansion. But such profits necessarily stimulate higher wage increases than would otherwise take place. This has been the central dilemma, and the fundamental reason which led the financial interests in the industry in the 1956 negotiations to seek a five-year contract.

The community has a major problem in the steel industry if it continues to demand additional capacity, as is indispensable in the context of both the international obligations and economic growth. The expansion of steel capacity, financed by the industry, generates wage and price increases in this strategic industrial center. From the point of view of short-run public policy, it seems to me there is a particularly strong case for the reexamination of the issue of financing steel capacity by rapid amortization or by other methods used in wartime. From the longer-run point of view, the gradual growth of effective substitutes for steel, a process under way in a number of industries, is likely to prove the most effective deterrent to wage and price increases in this sector. The community will slowly become less dependent on steel, and a relatively smaller proportion of its materials requirements will be provided by steel. The growth of concrete structures in construction and the expansion of aluminum and plastics in manufacturing are examples. I have little confidence in seeking to affect price and wage movements by public policies designed to alter product or labor market structures.

The contrast between basic steel and two other industries which ramify widely throughout the system will underscore the combination of circumstances which has characterized steel in this period. In the postwar period (1947-57) wages and prices in bituminous coal have both increased—wages particularly sharply, although not quite as rapidly as in steel (85 per cent compared to 100 per cent). But prices in coal increased only one-third the percentage rise in steel, and productivity increased more than double that of steel. The substitution of other fuels for coal, the rapid rise in output per man-hour and the absence of the problem of expansion in heavy cost capacity made the difference, particularly in the latter part of the period. The electric power industry is another which ramifies strategically throughout the system, but the effect of wage rate increases on prices has been mitigated by both the small proportion of operating labor costs to total costs and by the rapid growth in size in generating plants and productivity.

---

[31] The argument may be made that steel capacity should have been financed to a greater extent by external borrowing, but new public policy in this direction is not likely.

4. *Construction* — Another strategic sector which diffuses widely through the system is the building and construction industry. In the period 1953-58 construction wages increased 24.6 per cent, and in the period 1947-58 the increase was 83.8 per cent, almost the same as in bituminous coal mining. Construction costs increased but not to the same degree as the rise in producer-finished goods. This sector is particularly significant for growth, for it also strategically influences the cost of investment goods. The industry has a high degree of internal competition, not alone among different enterprises in given specialties, but also among different types of contractors and different methods of construction and materials.

The unions and the contractors in this industry are in the process of establishing a new joint machinery to provide a continuing forum in which all labor-management problems of the industry may be considered (which are not provided for by existing machinery). The objective is to promote the industry and to work systematically on such questions as difficult localities, work practices, training, labor productivity, and a host of other issues affecting costs and efficiency. The response of costs to increased demand in this industry is very significantly determined by such practices and institutional arrangements. The possibility of making this sector of the economy less inflation prone in the long term lies in dealing with such detailed problems.

The inflation potential of the construction industry, as many others, cannot well be dealt with by general monetary policy, which cuts volume of new construction, but rather by a direct approach to the real problems of efficiencies. There are few short cuts to the control of secular inflation. It seems to me that slow and hard work in institutional transformations is the path likely to lead to most constructive results in the long run.

Summary

1. This paper has been concerned with longer-term movements in wages and prices in contrast to the problems associated with war and postwar periods. The interest has been with the period 1953-58 and projections for the future.

2. The relative preferences of the community for production, employment, price stability and labor peace are vital to policy prescriptions. These objectives are not entirely consistent. There is no great overriding preference discernible in the American community to pay a higher price for stability. From my own preferences, the community in recent years has undervalued production, capital formation and employment in part because it has been concerned with inflation. Our international position desperately requires us to push these objectives more strenuously and thereby to make the inflation problem the more serious.

3. Legislation, to revise the internal procedures of labor organizations or the scope of bargaining, should stand apart from the inflation problem. Such measures, without regard to their merits on other grounds, are not likely to result in more stable wage rates and prices. These measures simply will not create the results on the inflation problem which is claimed for them.

4. An annual conference of labor and management representatives to discuss the economic climate of wage negotiations is suggested each year (following the Economic Report of the President) to be convened by the Secretary of Labor. The Administration should exchange with representatives of the parties statistical information and views on the short-term and longer-run economic outlook. These sessions should not be concerned with any particular contract negotiations; they should provide detailed discussion of the economic outlook of the community within which particular negotiations take place. Moreover, the proposal conceives the role of government to provide leadership in ideas, stimulate discussion and to make general proposals rather than simply to legislate or regulate in the area of economic policy.

5. For the purposes of policy formation treating secular inflation, it is important to analyze the structural characteristics of various sectors of the economy. Input-output tables permit the measurement of the impact of any sector upon households through consumers goods, and the diffusion effect of a sector is indicated by the proportion of gross output which flows to other sectors.

6. The most serious contribution to inflation arises in those sectors which diffuse output widely throughout the system, where demand is inelastic with respect to price, where labor costs are a relatively high proportion of total costs and where productivity is increasing much less than the average, and where wage rate increases have a tendency to spread widely throughout the wage structure of the economy.

7. Secular inflation is to be approached in terms of strategic sectors of the economy rather than in terms of further applications of general monetary or fiscal policy. As an illustration of this method, the problems of agriculture, local governments, basic steel and construction were briefly discussed. Institutional changes of various forms in such sectors may be expected to reduce the inflation potential of the system, or raise the threshold to inflation as the system moves at high and increasing levels of output. These strategic sectors may be expected to change over time under the impetus of different types of expansion; and so continuous and detailed reappraisal of the economic structure is required. There are few short cuts to control of secular inflation.

Address to the nation from Arden House:

Productivity and the consumer

JAMES P. MITCHELL

Dr. Wriston, I am glad to have this chance to talk with you and this impressive group of experts at this Assembly, and at the same time, by radio, with a lot of other people who have a big stake in the outcome of your discussion.

This stake is the stake of the consumer, you and me, 170 million of us, going to the store for a shirt or a pair of shoes, going to the market for the week's groceries, buying another chair for the living room, or, maybe, buying a new stove or even a car, paying the dentist's bill, or a tuition fee for school. As consumers a lot of us are concerned with prices and our ability to pay them with the wages we earn.

Reading over the learned and impressive papers prepared for this meeting, I felt that I could contribute most by talking from the consumer's point of view. The consumer isn't heard too often, but his actions, in the market place, add up to a series of demands which all of us in Government, in labor or management, must heed.

At the Fifteenth Assembly, JAMES P. MITCHELL, United States Secretary of Labor, delivered this address, on a nationwide radio broadcast.

First, our economy must continue to grow, and at the same time we must have a reasonably stable level of prices.

Second, we must increase our productivity, to achieve that growth, to permit that price stability.

Third, labor and management must bargain together responsibly and reasonably, so that our products can compete in present markets, and for new markets.

These must become new American imperatives. Most of the postwar period until recently has been described as a seller's market. It has been a time when the American producer had a very receptive market both at home and abroad.

Shortages of goods during the war had helped to build up a great backlog of demand. Washers, refrigerators, radios, and many other appliances were hard to get during the war. Automobiles were not being made. Housing was scarce. People had saved their money during wartime and looked forward to buying. The postwar surge of pent-up demand lasted a long time. And another surge of buying occurred during the Korean War. The American consumer was easy to please. But recently the consumer is looking more carefully before he buys, and grumbling about prices, and this is all to the good.

Internationally, the world markets which American producers could once fill with our products, at our prices, are no longer reserved to us. Plants in Germany, Japan, Britain, France, Italy which were bombed out or didn't exist in 1945 are now producing products to compete with ours. Theirs is a stiff challenge. Look at the brands of typewriters, dishes, woolens, *and* automobiles you see in our shop windows and on the streets. On the other hand, some of our products are in very great demand abroad: we are still selling more overseas than we are buying. But we are going to have to sell harder, against tougher competition, to stay in these markets.

American workers and American industry have a big stake in our ability to sell products in foreign markets. This ability depends upon our keeping costs and prices down. Upon this ability will depend not just present jobs but new jobs we will need in the future.

At home consumers will buy selectively, looking for quality, and they are increasingly conscious of price.

Since we are talking about the consumer's interest, *we* should be more conscious of what prices have done, here, in our own home market. Since World War II, prices have been following a staircase upward. They have leveled off during recent periods, but taken together they have not gone down.

Under these circumstances, some buyers in some markets have shifted to other products or have not bought at all. We have, for example, lost a part of the domestic market for automobiles. Some people could not find a car they wanted at a price they could pay, so they either didn't buy a car or bought a foreign car.

When the consumers don't buy because prices have gone too high, producers don't produce as much, and that means they don't employ as many people. Higher profits or higher wages, resulting in higher costs and prices that consumers won't pay, mean that some people may pay with their jobs. Workers and management have to recognize that consumers may not be willing to follow prices upward indefinitely.

Some people whose incomes have not gone up have been feeling the pinch of high prices. People planning for retirement, people saving to educate their children will feel that pinch even more later. They want and need a stable-price level. We all want and need growth. The question is, how can we get both.

Two approaches are usually suggested. The first is greater production and improved productivity. This is, I believe, a sound approach. A second idea is heard in some places: it calls for Government to move in on wages and prices. This approach is not, I believe, a wise one, for reasons I want to discuss in a moment. But first, let's look at productivity.

Productivity, in its simplest terms, means the amount of a product a worker turns out in an hour—how many bricks, sheets of steel, or shirts, how many columns of figures added.

More productivity means turning out more product in the same working time. Usually this involves better machines, better-trained workers, and improved management. Productivity improvements in factories, mines and on farms have made possible much of our great national prosperity in the past. Out of increased productivity must come further increases in our standard of living.

Increased costs should be covered by increased productivity, for, if they are not, prices rise. Some people think that the benefits of productivity increases should be divided only between labor and management, but there is a third party, the consumer. The consumer should share in increased productivity through better quality goods or lower prices. This is why increases in labor costs for the economy as a whole ought to be so related to productivity improvement that increases in price levels will *not* result.

Applying this general principle to specific bargaining situations is difficult, and I want to say just a word about it. National productivity figures are averages drawn from many different producers: farms, factories, mines, offices. Applying such averages mechanically is like taking the average size of a dozen assorted men and making them all wear the average size suit. The same is true even of industry-wide figures: as labor and management well know, there are great differences in the economic situation of different companies and plants within any one industry.

In arriving at what might be a proper wage increase in a particular industry or enterprise, management and union negotiators have no simple, ready-made formula. They should be extremely cautious in the way they use productivity figures. There are many factors other than productivity which determine whether a wage settlement is fair in a specific industry. There is also a national interest at stake.

Certainly labor and management in the major industries must realize that their wage and price actions are often followed by other industries whose situations may be vastly different, with the result that wages and prices go up all along the line. This has frequently been the case.

Labor and management have a tough assignment in arriving at fair wage settlements which will not cause price increases. Workers and union leaders must be more concerned about real wages, not merely money wages. When making wage demands they should consider what these wages can buy.

Another challenge that lies ahead for labor leaders is to be more constant in conveying to their members what rising costs and prices and the goods they produce can cost *them*. Wage increases that result in price increases can cut the market for the goods they produce, and, ultimately, cost jobs.

The challenge that lies ahead for management is just as difficult. It is not always possible to take the easy way out of passing along all cost increases to the customer. Some must actively seek ways to trim inefficient practices and tighten up to face competition. Others must recognize that lower and more flexible prices can improve sales and create jobs. It may even mean reassessing attitudes toward profit margins. It will certainly mean talking frankly about the effect of wage-cost increases, discussing fully the economic facts with union representatives.

This brings me to the last point I want to make: Labor and management should not depend upon Government action—involvement in collective bargaining—to relieve them of any of their responsibility to bargain reasonably.

This is true for two reasons; first, experience shows that when the Government does step in it keeps on walking into a much wider field than just a wage settlement; second, experience also shows that when a third party is making the final decisions, the other two parties whose interests are at stake act differently than they would were they making the decision themselves. They get reckless. They exaggerate their claims and charges. After all, what have they got to lose?

Ultimately if enough decisions are taken out of the hands of both the workers and the employers, the Government assumes the responsibility for finding just solutions. What may follow is that Government finds itself setting wage scales, fixing prices, profits and the conditions of work, determining hours, hearing grievances, and throwing its weight around in other private matters.

This should be especially significant to a society like ours that is rooted in free institutions. We have to consider and preserve the freedom of negotiation and agreement. This freedom depends upon its responsible exercise. Labor and management have an obligation to work toward settlements fairly and objectively, in full possession of the facts. They must recognize that they are not alone at the bargaining table: the customer, the public, are also there.

The peaceful settlement of negotiations is one measure of labor-management progress, but is meaningful *only* if achieved with full recognition of the public interest in the growth of our economy and in stable prices. Labor and management, especially in the industries at the heart of our economy, are, I think, becoming more responsible and realizing that their actions have consequences far outside their own pay envelopes and profit margins.

Among these consequences are those I have been discussing tonight. Consumers, we consumers, are getting very suspicious of further price increases, and we believe we have the right to demand a greater share in the benefits of increased productivity. And, as workers, we recognize two things—first, that jobs may be lost in some industries if prices get so high that consumers may not buy the goods they produce, and, second, that rising prices shrink the value of our own paychecks.

Address to Fifteenth American Assembly:

Labor costs and prices

SUMNER H. SLICHTER

I

I start with the elementary proposition, too often overlooked, that the principal purpose of an economy is to produce and distribute goods. Its purpose is not to produce a stable price level—though it does a better job of distributing goods when the price level is stable. But keeping the price level stable may interfere with producing the maximum quantity of goods. Hence, there may be a conflict between the best possible job of production and the best possible job of distribution.

The economy has developed the kind of institutions that tend to produce a slow rise in the price level. One of these is technological research which stimulates demand partly by developing new investment opportunities and partly by developing new consumer goods thereby keeping down the rate of saving. Another price-raising institution is the trade union. Even before the days of trade unions, there was a strong tendency for technological

SUMNER H. SLICHTER, Professor of Economics at Harvard, has a long and distinguished record in education and public affairs as scholar, author, teacher, consultant, and director.

change to produce higher money wages rather than lower prices, but the trade union greatly increases the tendency of wages to rise both in response to increases in demand, and even in the absence of increases in demand.[1]

Although the economy has developed a strong tendency to produce a slowly rising price level, the problem of inflation has turned out to be less serious than important government officials and businessmen would have the country believe. Ill-informed talk about inflation has aroused unjustified fears and has given Americans an inferiority complex on the subject of inflation that the facts do not warrant. Few Americans are aware that the rate of price increase is diminishing. The Consumer Price Index rose 73 per cent in this country in the decade 1939 to 1948 and only 20 per cent in the period 1948 to 1958. In the five years ending in 1953 the Consumer Price Index rose by 11.3 per cent; in the five years ending in 1958, by only 7.8 per cent. Few Americans are aware that the country has done a far better job of limiting the rise in the price level than have most other industrial countries. Few Americans know that the index of consumer prices has risen in the United States during the last ten years less than one-third as much as in the United Kingdom, only one-fourth as much as in France, one-seventh as much as in Austria, one-third as much as in Norway, less than half as much as in Sweden, the Netherlands, or Denmark, and over one-third less than in Italy or Canada.

The predictions that creeping inflation would produce dire consequences have turned out to be untrue, or the predicted results have turned out to be avoidable or not serious. For example, the country has been told again and again that the expectation of inflation would produce an accelerated rise in prices that would ultimately end in a crash; that inflation would cause the United States to be priced out of world markets; that inflation will impair the quality of business decisions; that inflation will seriously injure recipients of fixed-dollar incomes and owners of fixed-dollar assets.

Events have shown the error in the theory that creeping inflation will soon break into a gallop. Among 16 industrial countries in Europe and North America the rise in the Consumer Price Index between 1953 and 1957 was less than the rise between 1948 and 1953 in all cases except two. The two exceptions were Belgium and Switzerland, where the rise in the Consumer Price Index in both periods was small. In the United States the rise in the consumer price level in the second period was less than half the rise in the first period. Even in countries such as Austria, France,

[1] Many supply prices, especially the supply price of labor, are sensitive to shifts in demand. Let the demand curve for labor shift to the right and the supply curve will shift to the left—not because the unemployed hold out for more, but because the employed demand more. It is a mistake to assume that the unemployed have much effect upon wage rates. These rates are influenced by the employed who may or may not be influenced by fear of becoming unemployed.

Norway, Sweden, and Great Britain, where the rise between 1948 and 1953 was very rapid, the rate of increase did not accelerate—it dropped substantially in the subsequent five years.

Rise in the Consumer Price Index in Sixteen Industrial Countries in Europe and North America in Two Recent Periods

	1948-53	*1953-57*
Austria	100.0	12.0
Belgium	5.3	7.0
Canada	19.0	6.0
Denmark	23.5	16.0
Finland	56.3	20.0
France	66.7	6.0
Great Britain	29.9	16.0
Ireland	26.6	12.0
Italy	16.3	10.0
Netherlands	28.2	8.0
Norway	35.1	12.0
Spain	26.6	23.0
Sweden	29.9	13.0
Switzerland	4.2	5.0
United States	11.1	5.0
West Germany	7.5	6.0

The most important reason for the rate of increases in prices to drop is the simple and obvious fact that it takes money to buy goods. If people wish to buy in anticipation of higher prices, either they must draw on their idle cash balances or they must draw on their credit. Their ability to draw on their cash balances is limited and their ability to draw on their credit depends upon the reserve position of the banks. Consequently, whether or not creeping inflation becomes a gallop rests in the last analysis with the monetary authorities. Unless they see fit to provide the necessary reserves to finance galloping inflation, inflation will never become a gallop.

Creeping inflation is not likely to cause the United States to be priced out of world markets. The superiority of the United States is great, particularly in manufacturing, as is shown by the fact that in 1958 our exports of finished manufactured goods were 2.4 times the value of our imports of finished manufactures.

No one can be sure what the future will bring, but, as I have pointed out, prices in most other industrial countries have risen faster than in the United States. Unfortunately, some foreign countries are hampered in competing with the United States by various special circumstances. In Britain, the largest manufacturer outside the United States in the free world, taxes are exceedingly burdensome and efficiency in much of industry is held down by wasteful union rules and, in the metal trades, by an unruly shop stewards' movement which in many plants has prevented management from exercising proper control of operations.

But American business must expect foreign competition in some fields to become stiffer—particularly in products requiring considerable handwork. The stiffer competition will be good for the United States—a useful spur to efficiency, a stimulus to the development of much-needed plans for training craftsmen, a modest deterrent to increases in prices. The need for stronger foreign competition in American markets is shown by the howls of anguish which arise whenever a few imports enter the country. Our exports of iron and steel products in 1958 were more than twice as large as our imports; our exports of machinery were seven times as large as our imports; our exports of cotton manufactures were nearly twice as large as our imports. Nevertheless, all of these industries have expressed alarm over the influx of imports—as if they had the right to sell to American consumers unchecked by foreign competition.

Creeping inflation is not likely to cause a flight from the dollar. The gold losses of the last year show in the main that the international monetary system is working as it should work and that the United States is playing its proper role of banker to the world.

The people who predict a general withdrawal of balances from the United States neglect to say where the money is to go or what the money will be looking for. Short-term funds can earn a higher rate of return in money markets other than New York, but the great trade of the United States creates a demand for dollar balances. New York also offers the attraction of a free and stable rate of exchange. If the owners of funds are looking for attractive long-term investment opportunities, they can find such opportunities in limited quantities in Canada and some parts of Western Europe, but the United States offers a combination of good return and political security that has strong appeal to conservative investors. Investors who put their funds in the Near East and parts of Africa and the Far East had better plan to recover their original investment rather promptly because there is real danger that the investments will be confiscated.

There is no evidence that creeping inflation or the expectation of it has undermined the quality of business decision making, that managements have been careless in making decisions on the ground that the rise in prices would bail them out. The outcome of competition depends upon conditions in specific markets, not on the general course of the price level. Hence, business enterprises have had to study specific market conditions as much as ever before. There have been important cases of overinvestment (petro chemicals and aluminum, for example,) but these cases are attributable to the desire of various producers to get a strong position in markets that were being made attractive by technological change. The greatest mistake in business decision making in recent years was the persistent efforts of the

Big Three automobile manufacturers to sell longer, lower, and wider cars after the public had begun to revolt against the acrobatics required to get in and out of these cars, the inconvenience of parking them, and the high cost of operating them. But the blunder of the Big Three was not due to creeping inflation; it was due to the difficulty of changing the trend of thinking in big organizations.

Creeping inflation tends to diminish the purchasing power of pensions of the conventional type. Fortunately, this problem can be dealt with in various ways. One way is to base the pension on earnings during the last ten years of service. These earnings are usually higher than the employee's lifetime average and tend to rise with the price level. Another method is to liberalize the pension plan from time to time as hundreds of companies have done and as has been done with the federal old age and survivors' plan. In the latter plan the average monthly old-age pension was increased 168 per cent between 1946 and July, 1958. In the same period the Consumer Price Index rose less than 49 per cent. Finally, the problem may be met in large measure by the use of variable annuities.

Creeping inflation diminishes the purchasing power of savings accounts and life insurance. In a world of perfect markets in which people bought and sold with foresight, expectations concerning increases in the price level would lead to increases in the rate of interest. A compensating rise in interest rates has not yet occurred, but in the course of time it will probably occur. Certainly the government officials have been far from frank with the people. While attempting to scare them with unrealistic predictions about the consequences of inflation, government officials have neglected to urge people to stand out for a decent rate of return. A proper rate of interest will compensate owners of savings accounts and life insurance policies for the decreased purchasing power of their investments.

II

The causes of the rise in prices in the last ten years are numerous, and I do not intend to discuss all of them. There was a rise of $324 billion, or nearly 75 per cent, in the total net public and private debt between 1948 and 1958. And yet in spite of this enormous growth in debt, the economy was less liquid in 1958 than in 1948. Between 1948 and 1958, the gross national product in current dollars increased 69 per cent; in dollars of constant purchasing power, 35 per cent; and the money supply (demand deposits and currency outside of banks) 28 per cent. The annual rate of turnover of demand deposits in 337 or 338 reporting centers increased 38 per cent between 1948 and 1958. The rise in the rate of turnover shows that there has been considerable inflation originating in demand even in a period when rising costs were pushing prices up.

The aspect of inflation that I wish to discuss is the influence of trade unions. This influence is broader and considerably different from the role usually attributed to trade unions. A realistic view of the influence of unions leads to changes in conceptions of the economic theory of unions and important modifications in the theory of wages and the theory of employment. Unions are not only a major reason why labor costs have risen in the last ten years about twice as fast as output per man-hour, but they are important generators of income thereby tending to raise the demand for goods as well as the cost of goods.

The traditional view of economic theory has been that the success of a group of employees in enforcing a higher supply price for their labor in the absence of changes in the demand for their services simply means a redistribution of incomes to the advantage of those members of the wage-increasing group who succeed in keeping their jobs. What these persons gain, others lose either in the form of less employment, lower profits, or lower wages.

But the traditional analysis is incomplete—it overlooks the fact that bargained wage increases which occur in the absence of increases in demand, frequently, though not always, raise the total volume of spending in the economy sufficiently to maintain or even increase the total volume of production and employment. Hence, bargained wage increases do not merely transfer and redistribute money income; they often generate gains in money incomes and production. Three types of cases should be distinguished:

> Type One—selling prices are raised as a result of wage increases, and the demand for the product is elastic.
>
> Type Two—selling prices are raised as a result of wage increases, and the demand for the product is inelastic.
>
> Type Three—selling prices are not changed as a result of the wage increases.

Type One—selling prices are raised by the firm, but demand for the commodity is elastic. In this case the effects of the wage increase are deflationary. Expenditures by the firm's customers for its products drop, and some of the money not spent for the products of the firm goes into liquid reserves of the customers. The payroll of the wage-increasing firms drops too, except in a few freak cases in which the demand for labor in the short run is quite independent of changes both of output and of wage rates. As a general rule, the drop in employment associated with a drop in sales would produce some drop in payrolls despite the wage increase, and, in addition, the drop in the total income of the firm would produce some drop in the non-payroll expenditures of the firm. Thus the effect of wage increases when the demand for the product of the firm is elastic is deflationary.

Type Two—selling prices are raised by the firm but demand for the product is inelastic. Under these conditions the wage increase is inflationary. It leads to offsetting increases in prices, and since the demand for the product is inelastic, the price increase will raise the total amount spent for goods of all kinds—the product of the firm raising wages and the products of other firms as well—since the higher price will ordinarily cause some shift in the use of money from speculative uses to transaction uses. The increase in spending resulting from higher prices charged the wage-increasing firm will not, of course, be sufficient to maintain the previous physical volume of production. Observation of this fact frequently leads economic theorists to reach erroneous conclusions concerning the total effect of wage increases. The theorists fail to take account of the expenditures by the firm itself (including its employees) as well as by the firm's customers.

The demand for labor in the short run is almost invariably inelastic. Hence, the wage increases will raise the firm's payrolls. Its non-payroll expenditures will shrink. Ordinarily, however, the shrinkage in the non-payroll expenditures will be less than the expansion of payroll expenditures. The enterprise must be expected to use its resources so that for every use the ratio of marginal cost to marginal advantage is the same as the ratio for every other use. Hence, when outside influences (the union) force the firm to increase its payrolls, the enterprise will meet the cost, not solely by cutting other expenditures, but partly by drawing on liquid resources and partly by greater use of credit. Only in a few extreme cases, where wage increases force the firm out of important markets or impair its credit, will payroll increases reduce the total expenditures of the firm.

The increase in the outlays of the wage-increasing firm has the same effect on the rest of the economy as any autonomous increase in spending. The increase is financed by a draft on liquid resources—a shift of money from inactive (speculative) uses to active (transaction uses) or greater use of bank credit for working capital. The effect of the autonomous increase in spending falls into two parts—the effect on consumption and the effect on investment spending by non-wage increasing firms. The effect on consumption is determined by the marginal propensity to consume in accordance with the familiar Keynesian multiplier. The effect upon investment depends upon the shift in the investment function in the rest of the economy. This function is the result partly of the state of liquidity of business concerns and partly of the appraisals of the business outlook that are constantly being made.

The combined increase in spending by customers of the wage-increasing firm and by the wage-increasing firm and its employees may be expected to increase the total amount of spending in the economy more than sufficiently to sustain or increase production at the new higher price level. It cannot be asserted that this is an inevitable or necessary result, but it can be asserted that it is almost inevitable in those cases in which the demand for the production of the wage-increasing firm is inelastic. The autonomous increase in spending would have to be very small or the multiplier very small for the total volume of spending to rise too little to sustain an increase in physical production.

Type Three—the selling price is not raised by the firm. If one or a minority of several competitors is organized, the firm may find itself compelled to grant a wage increase that its rivals are not granting. Thus the management must choose between raising a price with the prospect that the demand will be found highly elastic because rival firms do not raise their prices, or of holding the line on prices in spite of the wage increase. If the first course is selected, the case becomes one of Type One which has already been discussed. If the second course is selected, the situation becomes one of the Case Three type.

In this third type of case, expenditures of the firm's customers are not changed, but there is usually some increase in the outlays of the firm and its employees. The demand for labor in nearly all cases is inelastic. Hence, payroll expenditures rise. Non-payroll expenditures drop, but not sufficiently to offset the rise in payroll expenditures. The reason is that cuts in non-payroll expenditures can be made only by accepting increasing disadvantages. Hence, the enterprise has an incentive to take various steps to avoid cuts in its non-payroll expenditures. These steps may include drawing on the firm's liquid resources or relying to a greater extent upon bank loans for working capital. Thus, there is an increase in spending similar to the increase in situations of Case Two. Both consumption and investment throughout the economy are stimulated. But the effect on expenditures is less than in situations of Case Two.

III

Whether or not trade unions on balance are instruments of deflation or instruments of inflation depends upon the relative importance of the several types of case.

Cases of Type One in which the demand for the product of the firm is elastic are found when the firm is exposed to special cost influences that do not affect rival firms. An example might be a firm compelled to bargain with a union under conditions that prevent the wage settlements made with the union to have much effect upon the wages paid by rival firms. Merely to describe the situation shows how unusual it is. Most firms are exposed to pretty much the same cost influences as their rivals. Hence, all are more or less affected alike by changes in costs. This means that all rivals make more or less the same adjustments of prices to changes in costs. If that is so, the elasticity that counts is the elasticity of demand for the product of the industry rather than the elasticity of demand for the brands of the several enterprises. The elasticity of demand for the product is much less than the elasticity of demand for the several brands and is much more likely to be less than minus one. Hence, one concludes that cases of Type One are not particularly frequent—at least after unions become strong and pervasive. There are, however, a few industries in which new firms are so easily started that the elasticity of the demand for the product, as distinguished from the several brands, is high. Shoes and men's and women's garments are examples.

It follows that cases of Types Two and Three—the situations in which unions are generators of income—predominate. I do not think that Type Three is particularly numerous. The most common is the Type Two situation in which all competitors negotiate wage settlements more or less simultaneously and make price adjustments more or less in unison. In these situations expenditures for the product are governed by the elasticity of demand for the output of the industry rather than by the elasticity of demand for the output of individual firms. The elasticity is likely to be less than minus one and the wage increases are inflationary.[2] Examples of Type Two are steel, rubber, automobiles, meat packing, paper, oil, farm equipment, much of construction, airplane manufacture, air transportation, trucking.

The conclusion is that trade unions as a rule do more than transfer income from some parts of the economy to others. They affect the size of the total flows of income as well as the relative size of its components. A few of the settlements negotiated by unions are deflationary—they reduce the size of the total income flows. More often the effect is inflationary—the effect is to increase the size of total income flows. As trade unions become stronger and as they become more pervasive, the greater becomes the tendency of their wage settlements to affect the prices charged by all firms in the industry. Consequently, an important difference between a large, well-established and strong trade union movement and a weak, poorly established movement is that the strong, well-established movement can bargain on the basis of the industry elasticity of demand, whereas the weak movement must bargain on the basis of the firm elasticity of demand.

All of this is a way of saying that as the trade union movement gains strength, its economic significance changes. A weak movement may produce only a small preponderance of deflationary effects because a large proportion of its bargains will be of Type One. The strong trade union movement will be inflationary because most of its bargains will be of Type

[2] The amount of investment in most industries is such that the inelastic segment of the demand curve extends a considerable distance above the point at which goods are priced.

Two. At present the trade union movement in the United States is sufficiently extensive and powerful so that most of its bargains are of Type Two. Our trade union movement has become a powerful income generating instrument—a built-in source of demand for goods and a source of inflation.

IV

If trade unions are in most instances income generating organizations, the economy is stronger than we have supposed it to be. The influences making for expansion are stronger than we had supposed them to be. Likewise, the influences tending to sustain personal incomes and personal consumption expenditures in times of recession are stronger than we had realized. What evidence is there that trade unions on balance have become generators of income?

One bit of evidence is the behavior of wages in the face of stationary or slightly declining corporate profit rates during the last ten or eleven years. The profits of all non-financial corporations as a percentage of sales have fallen substantially during the ten-year period. Even the sum of profits plus depreciation allowances as a percentage of sales have remained about the same with a slight tendency to fall.[3] With profit margins nar-

Changes in Compensation of Employees Compared with Changes in Real Output per Man-hour and with Changes in Prices from 1947 to 1958

	Increases in average hrly compensation of workers in private industry	*Change in real product of private industry per man-hour*	*Change in consumer price index*	*Change in non-farm wholesale prices*	*Changes in wholesale prices of finished goods*
1947–48	8.5 per cent	3.6 per cent	7.6 per cent	8.5 per cent	7.9 per cent
1948–49	2.7	2.9	−0.9	−2.0	−2.8
1949–50	5.7	7.1	0.9	3.7	1.8
1950–51	9.3	2.5	8.0	10.4	9.5
1951–52	5.8	2.2	2.3	−2.3	−0.5
1952–53	5.9	4.1	0.8	0.7	−1.0
1953–54	3.5	1.8	0.3	0.4	0.3
1954–55	2.9	4.4	−0.3	2.2	0.2
1955–56	6.0	0.6	1.5	4.4	2.8
1956–57	6.0	2.7	3.4	2.8	3.6
1957–58	3.0	1.0	2.7	0.3	2.3

[3] In the five years ending 1952, the sum of the profits of all non-financial corporations plus depreciation after taxes was 5.83 per cent of sales; in the five years ending 1957 it was 5.58 per cent. Profits of all non-financial corporations after taxes were 4.0 per cent in the five years ending 1952, and 3.2 per cent in the five years ending 1957.

rowing one would not expect wages to be bid up faster than the rise in output per man-hour, and yet in the ten years from 1948 to 1958 hourly compensation of employees exceeded the gain in real product per man-hour in all of private industry in eight years, and for the entire period the rise in compensation per man-hour was nearly twice as large as the gain in real output—63.3 per cent against a gain of 33.3 per cent in real output per man-hour. A second bit of evidence is the fact that in every one of the last 10 years without exception average hourly compensation of all employees in private industry rose more than the Consumer Price Index, and in 9 out of the last 10 years hourly earnings of all workers in private industry rose more than the wholesale prices of finished goods and more than non-farm wholesale prices. A third bit of evidence is the tendency of wages to continue rising in the face of falling demand for labor, as happened in 1949, 1954, and 1958.[4] A fourth bit of evidence is the success of unions in pushing up wages in various industries regardless of market conditions—the success of the coal miners in enforcing large wage increases in the face of falling employment; the success of the steelworkers in raising wages in southern can factories far above the market; the success of the steelworkers in enforcing considerably higher scales in paper container plants of the can companies than are enforced by the paper makers' unions in the same companies; the success of the hosiery workers in driving virtually all union full-fashioned mills out of business.

V

The success of unions in raising wages far faster than the increase in productivity has created a difficult problem of explanation for trade unions. The unions like to claim credit with their members for raising wages and to deny blame with the public for contributing to inflation. Union spokesmen argue that prices have risen for reasons independent of wage increases and that unions have simply made offsetting increases in wages. Union spokesmen argue that wage increases in conjunction with gains in productivity have raised labor costs only about the amount of price increases.

---

[4] Between 1948 and 1949, employment dropped from 59,117,000 to 58,423,000 and the unemployment rate rose from 3.8 per cent to 5.9 per cent. The consumer price level dropped by 9/10 of one per cent, but hourly compensation rose by 2.7 per cent. Another drop in employment occurred between 1953 and 1954 when there was a decrease from 61,945,000 to 60,890,000, and a rise in the unemployment rate from 4.9 per cent to 5.6 per cent. Again the consumer price level dropped, this time by 3/10 of one per cent, but hourly compensation of employees rose by 2.9 per cent.

A third drop in employment appeared between 1957 and 1958. The decrease was from 65,011,000 to 63,966,000, and the unemployment rate rose from 4.3 per cent to 6.8 per cent. Despite this substantial rate of unemployment, hourly compensation of all workers in private industry rose by 3 per cent, and the consumer price level by 2.7 per cent.

Hence, wage increases have been the result of price increases, not their cause. This theory meets certain difficulties. The rise in value product per man-hour between 1948 and 1958 is almost exactly the same as the rise in labor costs per unit of product. Does this fact mean that unions knew the coming change in output per man-hour and the coming changes in prices? Otherwise how would the union negotiators know how much of a wage increase to bargain for? Since output per man-hour rose by various amounts (as little as 6/10 of one per cent in 1955-56 to 7.1 per cent in 1949-50) and since the year-to-year change in the Consumer Price Index varied widely (from minus 9/10 of one per cent in 1948-49 to plus 8.0 per cent in 1950-51), there is no reason to believe that unions can predict these changes.

A simpler explanation that involves no heroic assumptions about ability of unions or anyone else to predict increases in output per man-hour or changes in price attributes the rise in prices to the rise in labor costs, and the rough correspondence between changes in labor costs and changes in the price level to the fact that in a consolidated income statement of the American economy compensation of employees represents two-thirds of all costs—in other words, is twice as important as all other costs combined. When labor costs are twice as important as all other costs combined, a tendency for labor costs to rise about twice as fast as output per man-hour is bound to lead to higher prices.

VI

What should be done about the tendency of unions to generate incomes? This is not the sole cause for inflation, though in the last few years it has probably been the most important single cause. It has been a useful influence in important respects—especially in contributing substantially to sustaining incomes during periods of recession. The tendency of unions to generate incomes is also useful in accelerating recovery in times like the present. Finally, the income-generating capacity of trade unions tends to stimulate the growth of the economy by accentuating the tendency for demand to outrun productive capacity.

In spite of these important contributions of trade unions to economic welfare, an effort should be made to limit wage increases as a general rule to increases in output per man-hour. Relying upon wage increases to produce autonomous increases in spending creates too many special gains for groups in strong bargaining positions. It is better for the economy to get its autonomous increases in spending in ways that benefit all groups —through tax cuts or planned budget deficits.

There is no known and proven way of limiting the generation of income by trade unions sufficiently to prevent them from raising the price level.

It has been suggested that unions be deprived of some of their present extraordinary privileges, such as their use of coercive picketing or the conscription of neutrals in labor disputes. These changes in the law are overdue, but they would have little effect upon the outcome of most bargains. It has been suggested that the unions be broken up so that there would be several in each industry. Unions would lose some of their present ability to support strikes by some members while other members work and pay dues and special assessments. But there would be rivalries among the new unions, and each would feel a strong urge to make a better settlement than any of the others. Hence, there is little reason to expect that breaking up unions would as a general rule diminish their upward pressure on wages.

A series of somewhat unrelated steps might add up to a significant restraint on upward pressure on wages. A great expansion in the use of industrial engineers producing capital-saving inventions would be useful. A larger proportion of capital-saving inventions (the typical product of the industrial engineer) would weaken the tendency of technological change to increase the demand for labor. Labor-saving inventions are inflationary because they increase the demand for labor, and labor-saving inventions will probably continue to predominate. Nevertheless their preponderance can be reduced.

We have just been through a period of strong rivalry among trade unions. Nearly all the workers who present attractive organizing opportunities have been organized. In the next two or three decades rivalries will probably subside somewhat, reducing the upward pressure of unions on wages. The aims of unions can be broadened and made more constructive by the adoption of the Scanlon Plan or variants of it—it marks in my judgment an important step forward in the art of management and it increases the influence of trade unions for good. I like John Dunlop's suggestion of an annual stocktaking of the economic outlook by representatives of labor and management in a government-sponsored conference. Unions are not sensitive to public opinion, but they are not immune to the climate of opinion. Several years might be required before the stocktaking meetings become matter-of-fact. As industry and labor acquire economists whose loyalties are first of all to economics and only secondarily to business and labor, it will be possible to have more or less objective appraisals of the economic outlook. But real professionals, who value the good opinion of their colleagues more than the good opinion of their bosses, will be necessary.

Finally, in the event that the country becomes seriously interested in halting the slow rise in prices, duties and quotas may be gradually removed. This step would have the advantage of retarding the rise in prices and at the same time of stimulating growth and efficiency. It would stiffen the resistance of employers to wage increases, and at the same time it would stimulate the search for cost-saving methods and would encourage the shifting of labor and capital from less productive to more productive uses. But progress in eliminating duties and quotas will be slow. One fact that stands out conspicuously in this discussion of inflation is that ours is a producer-dominated economy—the consumer is the forgotten man. We have the institutional arrangements that makes gains in productivity produce higher wages and higher prices, but no one even speculates about the possibility of altering our institutions so that gains in productivity will produce lower prices. This absence of concern for the consumer is understandable because the consumer does not demand lower prices.

Would the several steps that I have suggested check the tendency for unions to push up wages faster than the rise in output per man-hour? I do not know. Other influences are growing in importance and combine with the trade unions to produce rising prices. For example, we stand only on the threshold of the age of science. Nine-tenths of all the scientists who have ever lived are said to be alive today. Science is likely to stimulate the expansion of credit by discovering investment opportunities faster than the community generates investment-seeking funds. Furthermore, science will create large profits in various parts of the economy and these profits will stimulate stiff wage demands by workers throughout industry. The most profitable firms will choose to concede much of what the unions ask. Hence, wages will continue to outrun output per man-hour.

Let us try to recover common sense and perspective in dealing with our problems. Speaking before the Associated Press recently Secretary Robert B. Anderson said, "This country cannot have an enduring bright economic future with inflation." That narrow and pessimistic view of our economic prospects is unrealistic. No one can be sure whether or not we are going to have inflation. But with science and technology rapidly expending and with the art of business management rapidly developing, it is clear that substantial gains in productivity are ahead. There is a strong likelihood that technological progress in conjunction with our strong trade unions will be a cause of inflation. But regardless of whether we continue to have inflation or not the economic future of America is bright.

Final report of the Fifteenth American Assembly

At the close of their discussions, the participants in the Fifteenth American Assembly, at Arden House, Harriman, New York, April 30 - May 3, 1959, on WAGES, PRICES, PROFITS AND PRODUCTIVITY, reviewed as a group the following statement. Although there was general agreement on the Final Report, it is not the practice of The American Assembly for participants to affix their signatures, and it should not be assumed that every participant necessarily subscribes to every recommendation included in the statement.

* * * *

We have examined four main aspects of wage-price-profits-productivity relationships: the measures and their limitations, factors in the postwar inflation, the compatibility of national economic goals, and policy proposals.

I. The measures and their limitations

Informed public discussion of wages, prices, profits and productivity depends upon a better understanding of the measures used and their limitations. There are many types of measures; which should be used in any specific case depends upon the purposes of the user.

Limitations of existing measures were discussed. Wage data, for example, often relate only to production workers. There should also be data for non-production workers, further data on supplements to wages and salaries ("fringe benefits"), and better data for non-manufacturing industries. The Consumer Price Index (formerly called the "cost-of-living index") overstates the upward movement of prices, since quality improvements, which are difficult to measure, cannot be taken fully into account. There was general agreement that the Consumer Price Index is so often used for wage and salary adjustments today that it needs to be continuously improved. Among other limitations, productivity measures tend to understate increases, because quality improvements are difficult to calculate. Estimates of profit need a better statistical base, and adjustments to reflect changes in accounting procedures. The impact of price changes on depreciation allowances and the relationship between profits and investment should be studied.

At best, available statistical measures are rough, and significance should not be attached to small or short-period changes. Care should be used in selecting the time periods for which comparisons are made.

There was general agreement that more financial support is needed for governmental and private statistical agencies both for collection of data and, even more, for their analysis. It was urged that funds be appropriated for a survey of consumer expenditures to provide new weights for the Consumer Price Index. Funds should be made available for collection and more prompt publication of better data on all resources used in the economy, including labor and capital by type and amount actually used. Also, funds should be made available for needed knowledge of the composition of unemployment, and compensation of nonproduction workers and employees outside of manufacturing.

II. Factors in the postwar inflation

Money wages and retail prices have not risen as much in the United States as in most other industrial countries since 1948. The base year partially explains this difference, but if a more recent base year were chosen, our record would still be good by comparison.

There was considerable discussion of the relative importance of the upward pull of demand on prices as compared to the upward push of costs since the end of the war. It was generally agreed that during the immediate postwar period (1945-48) price movements were dominated by demand factors—the pent-up demand carried over from the war, and the relatively easy money policies. After the outbreak of the Korean War in 1950, demand forces were again dominant for a brief period.

There was general agreement that the 1953-57 period had somewhat different characteristics: monetary restraint was greater, demand forces less buoyant, output growth less rapid, price rises somewhat smaller, and profit margins lower. Wages continued to increase. The investment boom in 1955-57 created a demand-pull for many producers' goods, and the shifts in consumer demand toward services (for example, medical services) contributed to the rising price of services, so that cost and demand factors were both operating. However, the continued advance of prices and wages in the late 1957-58 period could hardly be explained by general excess demand.

There were differences of opinion regarding the relative significance of these factors. Some participants placed primary stress on negotiated wage increases, especially in those industries where wages seem to have been "pushing against an open door," and pointed out that they tend to be transmitted in wage increases throughout the labor market and in price increases throughout the economy. Others called attention to the price policies of firms, particularly in highly concentrated industries, the effects of which are also transmitted throughout the economy. The inter-relationship of market structure, wage policies, price policies and profits is seen clearly in the contrasting experience of the steel and clothing industries, for example. Since these forces often operate concurrently and are frequently interdependent, many participants felt it may be misleading to blame any particular factor or group for increases in labor costs and prices.

III. The compatibility of national economic goals

There was considerable discussion of national economic goals and the extent to which they are compatible. These include a sustained and strong rate of economic growth, full employment, reasonable price stability, national security and industrial peace within the framework of our free institutions. There was general agreement that the achievement of some of these goals may involve the partial sacrifice of others.

Many felt that the average level of unemployment during 1953-58 of 4.7 per cent (approximately three million unemployed) was too high. Reliance on large-scale unemployment to achieve price stability is intolerable in our present society. If the cost of price stability is a high level of unemployment (which may not be the case) many would prefer a mild increase in prices.

There was consensus that the rate of growth in the American economy should be increased, even if this interferes with the full attainment of other economic goals. Many believed that this would mean a 4 or 5 per cent rate instead of the recent lower rate. They shared the view that a lower rate of economic growth imposed by an unduly restrictive monetary policy, the principal aim of which is price stability, impairs our international position, makes financing much-needed public improvements difficult, involves loss of production, increases unemployment, wastes skills, bears unevenly upon certain sectors of the economy, and imperils marginal firms. Some, however, dissented, holding that a higher rate of growth requires price stability, accompanied if necessary by a restrictive monetary policy.

Some thought that preoccupation with inflation impaired the attainment of other economic goals. Many believed that the Consumer Price Index is not likely to increase very much in the next several years. A minority felt that we will have more inflation unless vigorous action is taken to arrest the cost-push as well as to restrain demand. This difference was reflected in the discussion of policy choices.

IV. Policy proposals

1. We should seek maximum sustained economic growth as a primary national objective because it is essential to the improvement of living standards and national security. In the pursuit of economic growth, however, we should seek to maintain a reasonably stable price level and to hold unemployment to the minimum necessary to preserve flexibility in the economy. Although the United States has done reasonably well since 1951 in maintaining price stability, we should develop a higher utilization of the labor force and achieve faster economic growth through increased productivity.

2. It is urgent that management, labor and government take measures to accelerate the rate of increase in productivity. Among the steps that can be taken are these: increasing expenditures on research and development; improving the quality of education; training more scientific, technical and managerial personnel; upgrading the skills of the labor force; eliminating restrictive practices by labor and management; and stimulating the ideas and energies of our work force.

3. Measures should be taken to increase worker mobility and to improve the operation of the labor market. Such measures might include severance and relocation allowances, retraining programs, employment of qualified older workers, transferability of pension rights, the extension of seniority units, provision of part-time jobs, and diversification of economic activity in distressed areas.

4. Although reliance on unemployment is not an acceptable method of controlling inflation, it is recognized that a dynamic economy brings about fluctuations in employment in particular occupations, industries and areas.

5. Radical change in our present wage-setting machinery would not be a fruitful approach to the inflation problem. Foreign experience does not suggest the desirability for the United States of economy-wide bargaining as an alternative to our more decentralized system. Breaking up national unions into smaller units would also not be an effective way of seeking greater wage and price stability.

6. The average increase in output per man-hour in the economy as a whole is a relevant consideration in wage negotiations, but in view of the numerous other factors to be weighed and reconciled, it cannot be the only criterion of a proper adjustment.

7. Appropriate monetary and fiscal policies are necessary to deal with inflation arising from excessive demand. However, sole reliance on these measures is inadequate for dealing with price increases in the face of excess capacity and unemployment.

8. Despite the seriousness of our present international position, direct general government controls of prices and wages are incompatible with the institutions of a free economy.

9. As one means of achieving price stability, the government should work toward a freer market in agricultural products, reflecting advances in productivity. Special measures should be provided to ameliorate economic hardships upon individuals.

10. Price stability should be encouraged by reducing tariffs and other impediments to international trade. Measures to provide temporary relief for areas adversely affected by tariff policy may be appropriate to facilitate readjustments.

11. Effective competition will help bring down prices raised by monopoly power. We favor vigorous enforcement of the anti-trust laws. Acts in restraint of trade in the market for goods and services, now illegal when committed by business firms or by firms and unions jointly, should also be illegal when undertaken by unions alone.

12. Pleas by government officials for restraint and responsibility in wage and price decisions are likely to have little effect on the course of wage and price movements.

Some participants thought that industries of importance as pattern setters should be subject to impartial fact-finding review of their wage bargains and price decisions to acquaint the public with their consequences. However, very few supported a procedure delaying the putting into effect of wage and price increases in key industries pending public investigation.

13. An annual conference of labor, management and government representatives should be convened, shortly after the presentation of the President's Economic Report, to discuss wages, prices, profits and productivity as related to national economic goals. These sessions should not be concerned with any particular contract negotiations. The objective is to reduce the diversity of views about the short-term and long-term economic outlook and to discuss appropriate private and public policies to achieve growth and stability.

Participants in the Fifteenth American Assembly

HUGO A. ANDERSON
First National Bank of Chicago

HARRY ROBERT BARTELL
Harriman Scholar
Columbia University

ATHERTON BEAN
President
International Milling Company
Minneapolis

RALPH H. BERGMANN
United Rubber, Cork, Linoleum and Plastic Workers of America
Akron

RICHARD W. BOLLING
United States Congressman from Missouri

WILLIAM G. BOWEN
Industrial Relations Section
Princeton University

COURTNEY C. BROWN
Dean
Graduate School of Business
Columbia University

THOMAS H. CARROLL
Vice President
The Ford Foundation
New York

EWAN CLAGUE
United States Commissioner of Labor Statistics
Washington, D. C.

JOSEPH S. CLARK
United States Senator from Pennsylvania

JOHN COWLES
President
Minneapolis Star & Tribune
Minnesota

CATHERINE B. CLEARY
Vice President
First Wisconsin Trust Company
Milwaukee

GERHARD COLM
National Planning Association
Washington, D. C.

JOHN T. DUNLOP
Professor of Economics
Harvard University

JULIAN B. FEIBELMAN
Rabbi
Temple Sinai
New Orleans

PHILIP J. FITZGERALD
Dean Witter & Company
San Francisco

WILLIAM C. FOSTER
Vice President
Olin Mathieson Chemical Corporation
Washington, D. C.

HENRY H. FOWLER
Fowler, Leva, Hawes & Symington
Washington, D. C.

JOSEPH FRIEDMAN
Harriman Scholar
Columbia University

EDWIN B. GEORGE
Dun and Bradstreet, Inc.
New York

BEN S. GILMER
President
Southern Bell Telephone & Telegraph Company
Atlanta

W. AVERELL HARRIMAN
New York

LELAND HAZARD
Professor of Industrial Administration and Law
Carnegie Institute of Technology
and
Director-Consultant
Pittsburgh Plate Glass Company

BENJAMIN HIGGINS
Professor of Economics
University of Texas

GEORGE H. HILDEBRAND
Professor of Economics
University of California
Los Angeles

JOHN M. HOUCHIN
Vice President
Phillips Petroleum Company
Bartlesville, Oklahoma

NORRIS O. JOHNSON
Vice President
First National City Bank of New York

J. M. KAPLAN
New York

EVERETT M. KASSALOW
Industrial Union Department
AFL-CIO
Washington, D. C.

LESTER S. KELLOGG
Deere & Company
Moline, Illinois

JOHN W. KENDRICK
Associate Professor of Economics
George Washington University

CLARK KERR
President
University of California
Berkeley

ROBERT L. KIRKPATRICK
Kirkpatrick, Pomeroy, Lockhart & Johnson
Pittsburgh

ALLAN B. KLINE
Western Springs, Illinois

JAMES N. LAND
Senior Vice President
Mellon National Bank & Trust Company
Pittsburgh

T. A. LANE
Major-General, U. S. A.
Commanding General
Fort Leonard Wood

ISADOR LUBIN
Franklin D. Roosevelt Foundation
New York

DANIEL MAY
Chairman
May Hosiery Mills
Nashville

JOHN G. MCLEAN
Vice President
Continental Oil Company
Houston

WILLIAM B. MILLER
Executive Secretary
Town Hall
Los Angeles

CHARLES A. MYERS
Director
Industrial Relations Section
Massachusetts Institute of Technology

ROBERT R. NATHAN
Robert R. Nathan Associates, Inc.
Washington, D. C.

FRED M. NELSON
Chairman
Texas Gulf Sulphur Company
Houston

GUSTAV PECK
Legislative Reference Service
Library of Congress
Washington, D. C.

HOWARD C. PETERSEN
President
Fidelity-Philadelphia Trust Company
Philadelphia

SYLVIA F. PORTER
The New York Post

JOHN POST
Continental Oil Company
Houston

JACOB S. POTOFSKY
President
Amalgamated Clothing Workers of America
New York

ALBERT REES
Associate Professor of Economics
The University of Chicago

Henry S. Reuss
United States Congressman
from Wisconsin

Benjamin C. Roberts
Professor of Economics
London School of Economics

Arthur M. Ross
Director
Institute of Industrial Relations
University of California
Berkeley

Stanley H. Ruttenberg
Director of Research
AFL-CIO
Washington, D. C.

Charles B. Shuman
President
American Farm Bureau Federation
Chicago

Leonard Silk
Economics Editor
Business Week
New York

Sumner H. Slichter
Professor of Economics
Harvard University

S. Abbot Smith
President
Thomas Strahan Company
Chelsea, Massachusetts

Herbert Stein
Committee for Economic Development
Washington, D. C.

Nat Weinberg
United Auto Workers
Detroit

John L. Weller
President
Seatrain Lines, Inc.
New York

The Rev. Hugh C. White, Jr.
Detroit Industrial Mission
Michigan

David J. Winton
Minneapolis

Emmett Wallace
Harriman Scholar
Columbia University

Allen Wallis
Executive Vice Chairman
Cabinet Committee on Price Stability for Economic Growth
The White House

The American Assembly

The American Assembly is a program of conferences which bring together business, labor, farm groups, the professions, political parties, government and the academic community. These meetings develop recommendations on issues of national concern. The American Assembly is a non-partisan public service designed to throw light on problems confronting citizens of the United States.

Dwight D. Eisenhower, as president of Columbia University, established the Assembly in 1950. It is incorporated as an educational institution by the Regents of the University of the State of New York.

Subjects for American Assembly discussion are screened for timeliness and importance by a Faculty Advisory Committee of Columbia University and considered by the Assembly's Board of Trustees. Leading authorities are retained to write background papers presenting the major issues in each problem.

The American Assembly discussions at Arden House, Harriman, New York, are based on this background material. The recommendations of the Assembly participants and the background papers are published in a Final Edition which is distributed to libraries, colleges, government, adult education groups, and organizations of industry, labor and the community for further study and discussion.

National meetings at Arden House have been held on the following subjects:

1951 UNITED STATES—WESTERN EUROPE RELATIONSHIPS

1952 INFLATION *(two Assemblies)*

1953 ECONOMIC SECURITY FOR AMERICANS

1954 THE UNITED STATES STAKE IN THE UNITED NATIONS
THE FEDERAL GOVERNMENT SERVICE

1955 UNITED STATES AGRICULTURE
THE FORTY-EIGHT STATES *(State Government)*

1956 THE REPRESENTATION OF THE UNITED STATES ABROAD
THE UNITED STATES AND THE FAR EAST

1957 INTERNATIONAL STABILITY AND PROGRESS *(Foreign Aid)*
ATOMS FOR POWER

1958 THE UNITED STATES AND AFRICA
UNITED STATES MONETARY POLICY

1959 WAGES, PRICES, PROFITS AND PRODUCTIVITY

Follow-up sessions on Assembly subjects are also held on the regional, state and local level. Institutions which, with Assembly staff cooperation, have sponsored, or are scheduled to sponsor, these meetings are:

Stanford University
University of California (Berkeley)
University of California (Los Angeles)
University of Wyoming
University of Denver
University of New Mexico
University of Oklahoma
Dallas World Affairs Council
The Rice Institute
Tulane University
Southwestern at Memphis
Duke University
University of Florida
Emory University
University of Illinois
Minnesota World Affairs Center
University of Washington
Cleveland Council on World Affairs
University of Missouri
Washington University
Drake University
Indiana University
University of Vermont
Tufts University
Foreign Policy Association of Pittsburgh
Southern Methodist University
University of Texas
Town Hall of Los Angeles
North Central Association
United States Air Force Academy
University of Arkansas
International Relations Council of Kansas City
Vanderbilt University
Michigan State University
The University of Puerto Rico
Lawrence College